# Policing the Elephant

MAP OF THE
MARITIME
AND OVERLAND ROUTES
TO
CALIFORNIA

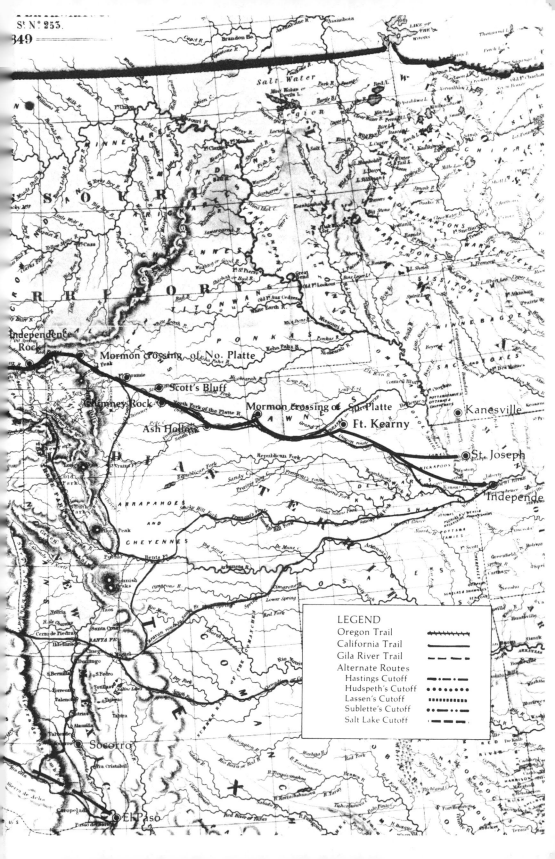

LEGEND
Oregon Trail
California Trail
Gila River Trail
Alternate Routes
  Hastings Cutoff
  Hudspeth's Cutoff
  Lassen's Cutoff
  Sublette's Cutoff
  Salt Lake Cutoff

# Policing the Elephant

*Crime, Punishment, and*
*Social Behavior on the Overland Trail*

## by John Phillip Reid

Huntington Library
San Marino, California

Library of Congress Cataloging-in-Publication Data
    Reid, John Phillip
        Policing the elephant : crime, punishment, and social behavior on
    the Overland Trail / by John Phillip Reid.
        p.  cm.
        Includes bibliographical references and index.
        ISBN 0-87328-159-4 (alk. paper)
        1. Criminal justice, Administration of—West (U.S.)—History—19th
    century.  2. Crime—West (U.S.)—History—19th century.  3. Frontier
    and pioneer life—West (U.S.)  4. Overland journeys to the Pacific.
    I. Title.
    HV9955.W4R45  1997
    364.978—dc20                                                  96-30677
                                                                      CIP

Printed in the United States of America

for Sharon Elizabeth and Hadley Ann
Sydney Reid and Kalyn Elaine

# Contents

## *Illustrations*

# 1 | *Damning the Elephant*
## INTRODUCTION

Emigrants crossing America's overland trails from Missouri or Iowa to Oregon or California kept an eye out for the elephant. "To see the elephant" or "seeing the elephant" were common expressions during the antebellum years. "When a man is disappointed in anything he undertakes," one contemporary explained, "when he has seen enough, when he gets sick and tired of any job he may have set himself about, he has 'seen the elephant.'"[1] More often, "to see the elephant" meant undergoing hardships, to learn the realities of a situation firsthand, or to encounter the unbelievable. After crossing the Missouri River at St. Joseph in 1850, Benjamin Franklin Dowell met a returning emigrant who had traveled seven hundred miles westward before taking the "back track." "He said he had seen the 'Elephant' and eaten his ears, and that he was now going home to Sally his wife, and that he would stay with her in the states as long as he lived."[2] As he approached the Humboldt River in today's Nevada, Mendall Jewett knew it was now too late to turn back. "I am hartly tired of the journey [and] have seen enough of the Elephant," Jewett confided in his journal. "It is a great place to try a mans patience and show him in the worst light that it is possible for a man to assume."[3]

In that one sentence Jewett summed up a major theme of the overland trail story. Emigrant after emigrant echoed what he said. "There is no place in the world," Katherine Dunlap observed,

---

[1]Quoted in *Law for the Elephant*, p. ix.
[2]Entry for 25 May 1850, Dowell, *Journal*. See also entry for 25 May 1850, Dowell, *Letter Journal*.
[3]Entry for 23 June 1850, Jewett, "Journal to California."

"where the qualities of a man will show themselves sooner than crossing the plains, let them be good or bad."[4] Although many praised the "good,"[5] more condemned the "bad." "It seems, this trip, instead of being calculated to bring about warm feelings, among acquaintances, and stronger ties of friendship, has an opposite tendency," a forty-niner observed.[6] Another forty-niner agreed: "here one can learn human nature in all its aspects."[7] "Yes," a third remarked to a fellow emigrant, "if a man has a mean streak about him half an inch long, I'll be bound if it wont come out on the plains."[8]

"This much I have learned since we started across the continent," E. W. Conyers wrote when more than halfway to the Pacific, "[t]hat if there is anything in the world that will bring to the surface a man's bad traits" it was the overland trail. "If there is any meanness in a man, it makes no difference how well he has it covered, the plains is the place that will bring it out."[9] The overland trail "makes a man manefest a quarrelsome disposition a feverish temper and anything but the man he was at home," Jewett had concluded, two years before Conyers, in 1850.[10] "If a man is predisposed to be quarrelsome, obstinate, or selfish, from his natural constitution, these repulsive traits are certain to be developed in a journey over the plains," Edwin Bryant wrote in 1846, in a journal intended for publication. "The trip is a sort of magic mirror, and exposes every man's qualities of heart connected with it, vicious or amiable."[11]

---

[4]Entry for 23 June 1864, Dunlap, "Journal," p. 20.

[5]For example, letter from George L. Curry to St. Louis *Reveille*, 15 May 1846, in Morgan, *Second Overland*, p. 540; Unruh, *Plains*, p. 77.

[6]Letter from H. H. Downer, 28 July 1849, quoted in Lorch, "Gold Rush," p. 361.

[7]Entry for 21 May 1849, Decker, *Diaries*, p. 79.

[8]Entry for 8 June 1849, Delano, *Life*, p. 72.

[9]Entries for 6 July and 23 August 1852, Conyers, "1852 Diary," pp. 460, 490.

[10]Entry for 23 June 1850, Jewett, "Journal to California."

[11]Entry for 1 June 1846, Bryant, *Journal*, p. 68.

Even before they started on the overland journey emigrants knew they were in for trouble. "I suppose there never was another place that there was so much danger of mens quarrelling as the California trip," an emigrant decided while still at the Missouri River.[12] And, of course, once on the trail emigrants found behavior every bit as bad as they had feared. After he had arrived on the desolate Humboldt River an artist, on his way to the gold diggings, wondered whether any "body of men left the states, on any expedition, that had so much quarrelling and fighting . . . as the California expedition in 1849."[13] When members of a District of Columbia train began to quarrel about how much weight their animals could safely haul, the captain took a new look at the men he was leading across the continent. "All the bad traits of the men are now well-developed," he lamented, "their true character is shown, untrammelled, unvarnished. Selfishness, hypocricy, &c. Some, whom at home were thought gentlemen, are now totally unprincipled."[14]

We should stop for a moment and consider just what was said, and what it means. The captain had been very proud of the high quality of the men he had recruited for the company and had boasted of their sterling characters. Now he was calling them "totally unprincipled." Our lesson comes not from the fact of the quarrel itself but from what they were quarreling about. The men had wanted him to jettison surplus beans and were upset that, after he had discovered that "the wagon with weak team had discarded the spare axle hung underneath," he had "sent back & recovered it."[15] When we dwell on the cause of quarreling, rather than on the quarrel itself or on the antisocial behavior resulting from quarrels, we

---

[12]Entry for 7 May 1850, Thompson, "Letters."
[13]Entry for 25 August 1849, Wilkins, *An Artist*, p. 67.
[14]Entry for 24 July 1849, Bruff, Journals, p. 53.
[15]Ibid.

may be surprised to find that usually the cause is not the unreasonableness of the demand. It is, rather, that the demand was made at all. This is why behavior that some emigrants termed "unprincipled," others thought nothing of, having not even noticed that a quarrel had taken place. "Bryant in his journal speaks of having seen much difficulty among the imigrants on the route, & remarks that the worst passions of men show themselves on this trip," Joseph Warren Wood recalled three years after Bryant wrote. "His experience is different from mine for since I have left St Jo I have not heard 2 men quarrel in the least. I never passed so long a time in my life with seeing less quarrelling. All move along in harmony & in most instances the true gentleman displays itself in all, by their perception of the wants of others & readiness to oblige."[16]

Had he been asked, N. H. Stockton might have said that, after only eighteen days on the trail, Wood had not enough experience to know if Bryant was wrong. "The feelings are quite different now to what they were when we left Ft Smith," Stockton wrote when he was about two months into his journey. "Then all was life gayety & cheerfulness. We were then buoyant with hope &c. Now all are cast down worn out & disponding & may often wish themselves back at home."[17] Lucy Rutledge Cooke may not have wanted to be back home, but by the time she reached today's Utah she knew she could no longer travel with her husband's parents. On leaving Council Bluffs to start overland she had been both fond of and very close to her in-laws. When she and her husband, William, reached Salt Lake City, however, they left the emigration rather than continue with his father. After the elder Cooke arrived in California

---

[16]Entry for 22 May 1849, Wood, *Diaries*. For a more extensive summary of what was probably the majority point of view, see Perkins, *Gold Rush Diary*, pp. 61–62.

[17]Entry for 20 July 1850, Stockton, "Journals."

he wrote me a very kind letter said he did it to tell he loves me. this perhaps he thought best from the fact of Wm & I having several disagreements with them on the road so much so that I think it unlikely either party will think as much of the other again. . . . we used sometimes to come to very high words so much as that Wm tried to get a waggon & team for us to travel alone but Pa was unwilling consequently we determined to stop at Salt Lake But coming to California has many disagreeables few very few companies get through without disagreeing & separating it is the most trying to a persons temper, even dear Pa I saw twice in a passion such a thing as I never witnessed before & thought it impossible almost.[18]

Cooke not only saw the elephant. She damned it to hell.

---

[18]Letter of October 1852, Cooke, "Letters," p. 267.

2 | PRESSURES, ANXIETIES, AND
RESTRAINTS

Much of the criticism emigrants leveled against each other must be taken with some grains of salt. Often they mistook the new and unexpected for the menacing and dangerous. They did so quite often because so many things were strange or unfamiliar on the overland trail, even personal appearances. During June 1849 several old acquaintances met somewhere on the trail beyond Fort Laramie. "[M]ustachoes & beards & burnt faces [had] so alter[ed] them" that they did not recognize one another "until their names were mention[e]d when they were surprised at their mutual transformation."[1] Three days later an unidentified physician passed a typical judgment on the consequences of physical change. "If you could see us all seated around our camp fires," he confided to his journal, "all covered with dust, long beards and dirty ragged clothes, and for a moment contrast our present situation with what it was one year ago, and I surely think you would imagine we had greatly and speedily retrograded into almost savage condition." If he could only take his messmates on a tour of the states, he thought, he could make "2 bitts a sight." "I would have them nicely caged and just before I exhibited them, I would call the attention of the audience by proclaiming 'Stand back gentlemen and give the animals a chance I am going to feed them.'"[2]

There were many like this doctor, emigrants who thought that they were commenting on substance when actually they were writ-

---

[1]Entry for 17 June 1849, Gray, *Passage.*
[2]Entry for 20 June 1849, Dr. T., *Journal.*

ing mainly of appearances. The focus on dirty, unshaven faces and degenerative eating habits tells us more of the middle-class status of the observers than about behavior on the trail. Emigrants were forever astonished by their own deterioration. "Changed shirt this evening for the first [time] from St. Joe," a Pennsylvanian wrote.[3] He had been wearing it for twenty-seven days. "Filthy" his friends at home would have said, but a fur trapper he might have passed on the Platte would have thought him unduly fastidious.

We should pinch even more salt. The standards of emigrants were the standards of home. People judged one another by behavior learned in youth, not by the conditions of the overland trail. The captain of one company of overlanders was shocked to discover that "[t]he men have taken to card playing and neglect of duty."[4] "Card playing," an Indiana judge complained after twenty-nine days on the trail, was not only "a general custom," but a game "at all times well seasoned and interspersed with oaths and imprecations."[5]

That was perhaps the second most common complaint—swearing. "I do not think there ever was as many men ever together or on any road so shockingly blesphemiss as the emigrants on this route to California," a forty-niner wrote while traveling down the Humboldt River. "[T]hey hardly use any expression to horse mule or ox except G'd D'n your soul (or heart) to H'll or to damnation. I think I hear it 50 times a day — woe for California, if such is to be the character of its future population."[6] Profanity on Sunday was particularly distressing. "O, the wickedness of the wicked," a preacher wrote of sabbath-breaking on the overland trail. "We have nothing but swearing, fishing, etc."[7]

---

[3]Entry for 22 May 1852, Johnston, "Diary," p. 3.
[4]Entry for 11 September 1849, Lord, *Journal.*
[5]Entry for 2 June 1852, Crane, *Journal.*
[6]Entry for 31 July 1849, Chamberlain, *Diary.*
[7]Stewart, *California Trail,* p. 15.

One did not have to be a clergyman to be shocked by sabbath-breaking. Traveling on Sunday was condemned by emigrants of various religious persuasions.[8] Even worse was not to travel and still to desecrate the day. "We remained in camp all day cooking, washing & making hay," an emigrant wrote on the Humboldt. "Fine example for a christian people to be setting the Indians far in the interior of a heathen land."[9] We should not marvel too much at this comment. Able to carry with him out onto the trail the values learned at home, in his community, and at his church, he was more typical than might be thought. Still, it is difficult to imagine what examples could have been set. His company was amidst the very primitive Paiutes who had never heard of Sunday, let alone of Christianity or of the luxury of a day set aside for religious contemplation.

Most wicked of all were those few emigrants given the greatest blessing imaginable on the overland trail, not only able to remain in camp on a Sunday but to be in a camp where divine services were conducted. There were always, shockingly, emigrants who did not attend. "The meeting was in the centre of the encampment, in the open air," one observer noted on a Sunday while he was still on the banks of the Missouri River. "A considerable number, however, stayed in their tents, playing cards, during the exercises, and others continued their work, within a few yards of the preacher's stand." It was, he feared, "a foretaste of California morals."[10]

We might suspect these emigrants were exaggerating for effect, comparing life on the overland trail with life at home to underline the dangers of the trail. Not so. Generally, the emigrants were reporting what they saw. "There are," a Christian preacher wrote of

---

[8]For example, entry for 22 May 1853, McClure, "Journey," p. 15; entry for 20 May 1849, Decker, *Diaries*, p. 78; *Law for the Elephant*, pp. 20–25.

[9]Entry for 1 September 1850, Dowell, *Letter Journal.*

[10]Entry for 12 May 1850, Langworthy, *Scenery*, p. 15.

his traveling company in 1841, "as wicked people among them as I ever saw in all my life." He had a criterion for judgment. The company was "mostly composed of Universalists and deists."[11]

Still, it does not do to overemphasize the censures emigrants cast on one another. When writing they may have been using the values of home, but in daily life they had to cope with the tribulations of the overland trail. It was the stress of travel—the anxieties, the dangers, the unfamiliar, the relentless demands, the unexpected, the weariness—and not the upbringing or the morality of the emigrants that were the ingredients for the anger, animosity, contempt, and violence which occasionally broke out. "I cannot say that we hav[e] any thing very hard or disagreeable in our journey," an emigrant wrote his family from Fort Laramie in 1850, "but when you consider our situation among strangers, and the continually increasing distance from home and friends, you may immagin[e] that our conversations are not allways of the most agreeable nature."[12] What he meant by "our situation" was never better summarized than by a fellow emigrant of that same year. That man's twelve companions should have been pleased with their progress. They were well in advance of the emigration. Instead they were complaining; life on the overland trail was wearing them down.

> The boys seem unusually cross today — being harassed with deep waters and high mountains continually, these difficulties being on the increase daily. The boys say it is enough to make a preacher swear. After swiming streams and wading sloughs we go to bed at night wet and tired; in the morning we get up with stiffened limbs and examine ourselves for ticks, and, if any are on us they will be as

---

[11]Stewart, *California Trail*, p. 14.
[12]Marshall, *Letter to Wife and Children*.

large as a grain of corn. We travelled all day through
swarms of mosquitoes and gnats and had to hunt
for grass and water until a late hour.[13]

The overland trail was a place for losing tempers.

It was also a place for losing one's sense and perspective of time,
place, and social proprieties. That was why travel by covered wagon
beneath the big skies of the endless plains was so often compared to
an ocean voyage. "At sea or among the mountains, men completely lose the little arts of dissimulation they practice in society," a
forty-niner thought. "They show in their true light, and very often,
alas! in a light little calculated to encourage the enthusiastic believ-
er in the speedy perfection of our race."[14]

The trip itself bore hard on good nature and social order.
"Perhaps there is no situation so trying upon the infirmities of
human temper as a long trip like this," a forty-niner suggested. It
was taken "under circumstances not favorable for promoting cheerfulness and good humor."[15] An allopath explained some reasons to
his wife:

> Everything seems calculated to irritate & sour the
> disposition. Men who have hitherto sustained the
> most kind and amiable characters, often seem to
> yield to the worst propensities of their natures. This
> is to be attributed to the fatigues of the journey —
> privations, change in the customs and habits of
> their lives, and to unfortunate associations. In
> numerous instances, companies have been torn

---

[13]Entry for 22 June 1850, Pigman, *Journal,* p. 25. They were on their third day
on the Humboldt.

[14]Taylor, *Eldorado,* p. 27.

[15]Entry for 26 July 1849, Reid, "Diary," p. 44, also quoted in Reid, *Diary,* p. 97.
Also, see McWilliams, *Recollections,* p. 55.

11

asunder, enmities have been engendered between those who had long lived as friends.[16]

Other factors were the fleeting nature of acquaintances—"[M]et a Methodist friend who knew several preachers of my acquaintance formed an acquaintance pleasant though short & am sorry I have forgotten his name";[17] the weather—"astonishing what a difference there is in the tempers of men in fair weather and foul";[18] and meals—"all are alike, or at least there is scarce any variety. . . . The dishes comprise oatmeal mush, bacon-sides with pilot-bread fried in the fat, and coffee; these repeated <u>ad infinitum</u>."[19]

The heaviest burden, dulling the senses and destroying social intercourse, was the monotony of it all. "Nearly every body in camp for the past few days have been constantly wrangling & contending," a New Yorker complained only seventeen days into the trip. "[T]he reason, phylosopihically I should say, [is] because we get tired to death of our monotonous course of life & a quarrel or two or three, or ten of them makes some excitement!"[20] Another New Yorker decided that monotony was why some emigrants gambled. "The novelty of the trip appears to have worn away," he noted after crossing the North Platte in today's Wyoming, "and now many of us long for excitement of some kind and to those who indulge in games of chance, play appears the most natural resort."[21]

With the scenery monotonous—"The same boundless green, emerald prairies, seems to spread out before you, the same bright heavens are above, the same solid earth of uniform surface beneath, or if the monotony be at all broken, it is by the gradual change of

---

[16]Letter from Dr. Ormsby to wife, 18 December 1849, Bidlack, *Letters,* p. 37.

[17]Entry for 20 July 1849, Decker, *Diaries,* p. 122.

[18]Entry for 17 May 1849, Breyfogle, *Diary.*

[19]Entry for 14 May 1849, Johnson, *Overland,* p. 53.

[20]Entry for 17 May 1849, Gray, *Passage.*

[21]Entry for 5 July 1849, Searls, *Diary,* p. 43.

the broad prairie into a succession of gently rolling hills, as when the unruffled ocean is heaved into waves of the storm"[22]—and the daily routine monotonous—"The crack of the whip, the clanking of the chains and the still more disagreeable sckeuk of Wagons is all the Sense of hearing conveys to the mind"[23]—everything seemed to converge to make previously sociable people unsociable. One emigrant, complaining of the "hypnotic effect" of the Platte River valley, a kind of "emotional anesthesia," recalled being overtaken by a company on mules. "My mule kept up with them for some distance," he wrote, "but I never so much as turned my head to look at them . . . for such is the unsocial habit of nearly everybody after they have long been on this monotonous and stupefying trip."[24]

Although many emigrants complained of monotony, few said that it caused antisocial conduct. They were far more likely to blame absence of restraints, whether social or legal. "Men while travelling across this wilderness country, beyond the bounds of civilization, let loose from the restraints of civilization, and in a measure from the influence of law," a New Hampshireman observed, "show out the different phrases of their natural disposition to perfection."[25] Another forty-niner said it was "their real dispositions" that were shown. "What were 'clever fellows' at home are hard cases here where [there] are but few restraints."[26]

The restraint most missed was not the civic restraint of sovereign law, a restraint that at least one emigrant thought important for he wrote of his fellows on the overland trail: "Not being under the fear of the Law, they become careless of consequences."[27] It was

---

[22]Entry for 12 May 1850, Franklin, "Journal to California," p. 54.

[23]Entry for 1 June 1848, May, *Migrating Family.*

[24]Mattes, *Platte River Road*, p. 244.

[25]Entry for 25 August 1849, Batchelder, *Journal*, p. 40.

[26]Entry for 8 July 1849, Decker, *Diaries*, p. 114. Also, see entry for 9 August 1849, Kirkpatrick, *Journal*, p. 25.

[27]Entry for 18 June 1845, Snyder, "Diary," p. 235.

rather the social restraint of home, family, and women. During the 1849 emigration one man thought "the average of women was about one in five hundred."[28] Some trains that year traveled for two months or more without seeing a female.[29] The next year it was estimated that there was one woman for every thirty-nine men.[30] After that the differential decreased rapidly as more families crossed to California as well as Oregon. An emigrant who went over the trail in both 1850 and 1852 found a startling change. "This trip, I realized more vividly than I ever did before, the influence of women upon my own sex," he wrote of his second voyage. "There were one or more ladies in nearly every company, and the conduct of the men presented as great a contrast to that of those whom I fell in with during my former trip, as perfect civilization does to a state of savage rudeness. Few of us are aware of the mighty influence women exerts over man in all his actions."[31]

He was wrong. A respectable number of emigrant males appreciated the difference women made by just being around. In 1849, for example, a man and wife, "on acct of rude fellows," left the company in which they had been traveling and joined one that had had no women. "How strange!" a member of the second company exclaimed. "Our whole camp is quieter, obscene & improper language not heard just because a woman is in camp. . . . This is the refining influence of woman, without society men almost become desperadoes, *men care not for men*."[32]

Writing to a newspaper from the "Base of the Rocky Mountains," 8 July 1849, an emigrant from Missouri penned a

---

[28]Stephens, *Jayhawker*, p. 10.
[29]Entry for 24 June 1849, Cosad, *Diary*.
[30]Entry for 2 June 1850, Dowell, *Journal*.
[31]Udell, *Incidents*, pp. 111–12.
[32]Entry for 13 June 1849, Decker, *Diaries*, p. 95. For the best discussion of the influence of women by an emigrant, see M. Coleman's letter, *Law for the Elephant*, p. 29. Also, see entry for 22 June 1849, Reid, "Diary," p. 27.

brief summary of the interplay between social restraints and social behavior on the overland trail.

> I thought myself tolerably well skilled in judging of character, but must here confess my utter ignorance of life on the plains. It is not the same in the individual, surrounded by friends and society, and controlled by a sound public sentiment. The individual in the States may possess accomplishments, character, and sound morality; but if not possessed of a strictly sound and well-regulated mind, with a considerable amount of self-respect, with fixed and settled habits of thought and action, his character is totally changed. Cut loose from society, uncontrolled by public sentiment, if there is a black streak in the mind of an individual, it is sure to show itself. He becomes reckless, thoughtless, and troublesome. He disregards himself and the rights and feelings of others. With nothing to restrain him, he becomes a demon in human shape, until again restrained and controlled by society and a sound public sentiment.[33]

The behavior that bothered most of those emigrants who have left us their thoughts was quarreling. "The greatest difficulty we have is the petty quarrels and contentions among the company," a forty-niner wrote from Fort Kearny on the Platte River.[34] The word to note is "petty." The next year another emigrant complained about members of companies becoming upset "at Little Difficulties,

---

[33]Augustus M. Heslep, letter from Greenhorn Village, Base of the Rocky Mountains, 8 July 1849, in *Daily Missouri Republican*, 12 September 1849, in Bieber, *Southern Trails*, p. 377.

[34]Letter of 17 June 1849, Moxley, *Correspondence*.

they would be ashamed of at home."[35] This "personal bickering and discontent," the writer at Fort Kearny explained, emanated "from hardships to which they had been strangers. Those store sweeps Clerks and Gentlemen are littel [*sic*] fitting for a trip of this kind."[36] Life on the trail was just too new and different from anything they had experienced. They had never slept on the ground before, cooked at a camp fire, and a surprising percentage of them had never ridden a mule or cared for a horse.[37]

Life was not only different but at times it was nearly too much. "While traveling we are necessarily constantly exposed to the vexing, harrassing influences, incident to the road, and which has done much to deprave and dehumanize those who have gone over it," an emigrant told a Wisconsin newspaper.[38] Among the other things they constantly encountered "sickness, death & a great loss of property."[39] Almost as bad were the physical discomforts which overlanders realized made them irritable and antisocial. "The fatigue and length of the journey, the exposure to a variety of weather in a strange climate, and the absence of civilized society, all tended to irritate, and begat within the human heart partial inhumanity and desperation" was how an 1852 emigrant described the experience.[40] For a forty-niner, it was "[t]he parching winds and stifling dust, with the bountifully blotched and blistered lips that afflicted nearly every one" that "did not at all conduce to that geniality of temper that would incline men to social solace."[41]

In 1852 Jared Fox summarized one day of life on the overland trail.

---

[35]Letter of 2 June 1850, Peacock, *Letters*, p. 15.
[36]Letter of 17 June 1849, Moxley, *Correspondence*.
[37]For example, entry for 1 May 1858, Putnam, *Journal*, p. [2].
[38]Letter of 31 July 1852, Taylor, "Letters," p. 144.
[39]Entry for 29 August 1850, Parsons, "Journal," p. 265.
[40]Eaton, *Overland*, p. 227 (quoting Holmes Van Schaick, 11 July 1852).
[41]Leeper, *Argonauts*, p. 19.

The dust yesterday was hardly endurable. Now all stuck to us by rain. Eat our breakfast in the rain and mud. Slacked a little and started out. Rained again. Cold as November [he was from New York and Wisconsin]. Overcoat and yarn mitten on. Buckled around the overcoat and cap pulled down. Made some 10 miles.[42]

It was 6 July and he was on the Snake River going to Oregon.

"It almost daily happened," a forty-niner noted, writing for commercial publication, "that when the day's journey was performed, we were tired enough to sink to rest without attempting to do more; but the moment the place of encampment was reached, much labor remained to be done."[43] That fact, a physician thought—plus the weather, the novelty of the plains, the monotony, and all the other tribulations of the overland trail—was the reason why "[m]ost of [the] men here are willing to lay any burden on others to obtain a little self indulgence for themselves."[44] It was also why most of them kept a wary eye on their companions. In one mess the man who was cook for the night gave himself the biggest share of "the dried-apple sauce." Another man pushed him aside "and seated himself at the favored plate. Trifling as this affair was, the participants were never friends afterward."[45] The daily grind, anxiety, and fatigue eventually wore on almost every emigrant. "I

---

[42]Entry for 6 July 1852, Fox, "Memorandum," p. 27.

[43]Entry for 25 June 1849, Delano, *Life*, p. 103.

[44]Entry for 23 June 1850, Parker, *Notes*. Many years after he had, in the early 1850s, crossed the overland trail to California, a journalist recalled that, "the division of labor in a party of emigrants was a prolific cause of quarrel. In our own little company of five there were occasional angry debates while the various burdens were being adjusted." The company, he recalled, witnessed fights that occurred in other camps, "and these bloody fisticuffs were invariably the outcome of disputes over divisions of labor." Brooks, "Plains Across," p. 805.

[45]Leeper, *Argonauts*, p. 10.

have never regretted coming until recently," one wrote when in California, nearly at the end of the trip. "I had much rather be at hard labor than to travel as we do."[46]

On top of everything else, there were special hardships and privations that dominated certain emigrations. Every now and then there were shortages of grass, as at the beginning of the emigration of 1850,[47] and, if that was not bad enough on the animals, there were entire stretches of the trail where, if they were not watched, the horses and oxen could eat poison and die.[48] Sickness stalked several emigrations. The Gold Rush of 1849 was plagued by a cholera epidemic,[49] turning the road from Independence to Fort Laramie into a "graveyard."[50] "One who has not felt it, cannot know what it means to meet face to face with sickness and death under such conditions as surround us," a forty-niner wrote,[51] or, as a woman emigrant put it in 1852, "Sickness and death in The States is hard but it is nothing to be compared with it on the plains."[52] In 1850 some emigrants "trav[el]ed with the cholera for 100 miles."[53] Other recurring illnesses included scurvy, diarrhea, dysentery, and what they called "mountain fever."[54]

---

[46]Entry for 3 September 1850, Stockton, "Journals."

[47]*Law for the Elephant*, pp. 229, 231–32, 238, 337–38. Also, see 217–18, 235, 287; entry for 21 June 1849, Hale, "1849 Diary," p. 83.

[48]"Replenishing the Elephant," pp. 64–90; *Law for the Elephant*, pp. 53–90.

[49]Entry for 29 July 1849, Edmund Booth, p. 9; entry for 26 June 1849, Steuben, "Journal," p. 13; entry for 10 June 1849, Webster, *Gold Seekers*, p. 44.

[50]Letter from D. T. McCollum to J. H. Lund, 27 June 1849, Bidlack, *Letters*, p. 21.

[51]Entry for 18 May 1849, Benson, "Forty Niner," p. 5. Also see Rudd, "Woman's Diary."

[52]Entry for 23 June 1852, Rudd, "Notes by the Wayside."

[53]Harvey, *To California*, p. 28.

[54]Read and Gaines, "Introduction," pp. 590–91*n*113; Morgan, "Notes to Overland," pp. 372*n*32; *Boston-Newton*, p. 152*n*7.

Sickness did more than wear on the nerves and cause anxiety. It led to friction between traveling companies. One 1850 train was particularly disturbed by a company afflicted with smallpox.

> The Small pox train came up very near. Some of the men came among us. In being kindly reproved for such conduct they became offended & said they had a right to go where they pleased. Our train then halted, and resolved that it was just as much our duty to defend ourselves (as much as possible) from such a contagious disease as it was from an enemy & that we should do it. The captain informed the other company that they could go by if they chose, but that they must keep a proper distance away. We then passed on & they remained behind.[55]

When there were sufficient patches of grass far enough apart, as was usually the case, the companies could and did keep separate. Conflict as a general rule, therefore, did not occur in camp but on the road, where it was common for wagons to push "ahead as fast as possible to get past the sickness in the thousand trains behind us and just ahead the cholera was bad."[56] More often companies fought for the advance position for reasons of comfort and convenience.

> [W]e had calculated to lay still to day but early in the morning we found we were camped just between two large droves of cattle   Baker[57] a head

---

[55]Entry for 28 May 1850, Grow, *Journal,* and Grow, *Letter Diary.*

[56]Dickinson, *Overland Journal.* Between May 15 to August 19, 1852, the writer was temporarily blind.

[57]Often companies were referred to by their captain's names. Here "Baker" means "Captain Baker's company."

and Pomeroy close behind. about 3 o'clock in the morning we heard pomeroys cattle comeing, and in 15 minutes we were out of bed and under way as we were determined not to take the dust and the leave-ings of two droves of stock and it is almost impossible to pass a drove on the road and to be behind they raise such a dust you can hardly live and muddy every spring & branch.[58]

Clear air and clean water were frequent causes why emigrants fought for the lead. So too was the chance to appropriate the best camp sites or to be the first at the ferry.

[W]e started about sun rise because we was fol-lowed close by 50 large teams   we herd the noise of them in geting their teems up so we herried with all our mite to hich up ours   some was geting break-fast but we saw them acoming   put every thing in the waggons and put [off]   an[d] by the time we got in the road some of their teams had come up to us all doing their best to get to the river first   we had 3 miles [to] go but we beat them slick   we got to the [river] first and they waited till we got over.[59]

As one forty-niner put it, there "was some exciting scenes" when companies competed for the lead.[60] "A race sometimes con-tinues for half a day & the cracking of the whips & the hallooing to 'Close up' 'Close up' makes no little noise," a second forty-niner had written two weeks before. "After a while the race is terminated by coming to a place where but one wagon can go at a time, when

---

[58]Entry for 4 July 1852, Snodgrass, *Journal*.
[59]Entry for 13 May 1849, *Granville Company Journal*.
[60]Entry for 9 June 1849, Hixson, "Diary."

the train which strikes first if well closed up prevails & the other goes behind. I have heard no quarrelling over the matter, but almost wonder that there has been none."[61]

He wrote on the 24th of May when he had just started on the overland trail. Before long he undoubtedly did see quarreling. After all, as another forty-niner wrote from Salt Lake City, "a small patch of grass is worth quarreling for."[62] And quarrels were no small matter since almost every man had a weapon. The company of a woman going to Oregon found itself behind two large droves of cattle and about fifty wagons, "and we either had to stay poking behind them in the dust or hurry up and drive past them. It was no fool of a job to be mixed up with several hundred head of cattle, and only one road to travel in, and the drovers threatening to drive their cattle over you if you attempted to pass them. They even took out their pistols."[63] On a similar occasion when "the bright barrels of a number of Colt's persuaders glistened in the sunlight," word "was passed along their line that our crowd were Texas rangers, and it would have done you good to see them fall back and let us pass."[64]

These trail conflicts were potentially explosive and, although it did not happen often, there were homicides.[65] Interestingly, the most likely place for trouble to occur was at the very start of the overland trail. Because in 1849 the ferry at St. Joseph could take only about thirty-five teams a day,[66] there was a two- or three-day

---

[61]Entry for 24 May 1849, Wood, *Diaries.*

[62]Letter from John Thomas Kinkade to James and Hannah Kinkade, 11 July 1849 (ms. HM KI 85, Huntington Library).

[63]Entry for 31 May 1853, Knight, "Woman's Diary," p. 206. Also, see Mattes, *Platte River Road,* p. 55.

[64]Entry for 9 June 1849, Hixson, "Diary."

[65]One to be discussed below, the killing of Snyder by Reed occurred after two ox teams became entangled in passing on a sand hill along the Humboldt River. See below, pp 220–21.

[66]Entry for 3 May 1849, Tate, "Diary," p. 4.

wait to cross the Missouri.[67] "Fighting for precedence was quite common," the captain of a company reported, and "2 teamsters, in one of these disputes, killed each other with pistols."[68] Another emigrant explained the event using interesting, if puzzling, concepts. "[T]here was two men killed," he wrote, "in a conflict for their rights."[69]

We should marvel that there were not more killings. Despite all the extremes of anxiety, fear, and despair driving them to the limits of their endurance and fortitude, the emigrants who traveled across America's overland trails not only respected each other as human beings, they conducted themselves by a morality of trail life. If that morality was not always based on the precepts of religion and home, it was, at least, a morality of secular law.[70] They did think that people waiting to cross by ferry had "rights" to their place in line. And yet there were many excruciating anxieties encouraging antisocial behavior. No one better summed up the lessons of this chapter—the pressures of trail life—than an emigrant of 1850.

> [H]ere men are away from all influence of society, friends, or law. You cannot tell what a man is till you get him fairly on this trip. There are many things calculated to raise disputes. The majority of them are unaccustomed to this manner of living and are very apt to think they have a hard time & their companions should assist them. They perhaps think that they are required to do more than their share of the labour, or more loading put on their

---

[67]Entry for 2 May 1849, Banks, *Diary*, p. 4.
[68]Entry for 7 May 1849, Bruff, *Journals*, p. 7.
[69]Entry for 3 May 1849, Tate, "Diary," p. 4.
[70]This is the theme of *Law for the Elephant*.

horses than there ought to be, and if any man should do any thing wrong as wasting grain or the like, accidently or otherwise, every man in the company takes it upon himself to reprimand or offer advise, & it generally happens that the unfortunate man is not in humour to receive it.[71]

Add little annoyance to little annoyance and soon there are grievances. Life on the overland trail was a culmination of small things. "In camp," a correspondent wrote the *St. Louis Weekly Reveille*, "every man must stand upon his own basis, without the gloss of false reputation or fictitious influence which he may require by one means or another at home. Sooner than anything else it brings all men down to their proper level, and teaches them what actually is their proper station." That was why the overland trail was "a great school of human nature."[72]

---

[71]Entry for 7 May 1850, Thompson, "Letters."
[72]Letter of 2 May 1849, "Reveille Letters."

# 3 | ROBBERY, LARCENY, AND ABACTION

To explore the milieu of crime on the overland trail is to seek more than antisocial behavior on one side or vigilantism on the other. The migration to Oregon and California was a unique moment in America's social history, and surviving documents provide evidence of ideas and values unavailable from any other source. The emigrants knew they were experiencing a singular, never-to-be-repeated adventure, and this was one reason why they left us so many journals, and wrote such detailed accounts of their experiences. More to the point, they were acutely aware that once across the Missouri River they had passed beyond the pale of police protection, courts, judges, and even of government itself.

After they had crossed to the western side of the Missouri River, it was common for emigrants to say "we are now outside the United States"[1] or to speak of having "left the states."[2] "We were now out of reach, and beyond the arm of law and order," a husband and father later recalled of his 1853 crossing with his wife and five children, "and the only law we had was that formulated unto ourselves."[3] Three years earlier emigrants traveling along the Platte had admitted three wagons to their company. "Our new associates appear like upright men," a member wrote, "men who would respect justice where there is no law."[4] Even army officers leading troops across the plains spoke that way. The commander of the Mounted Riflemen in 1849 was a bit concerned after dismissing

---

[1] Mattes, *Narratives*, p. 349 (quoting J. C. Coupler).
[2] Entry for 17 May 1863, Yager, "Diary," p. 6.
[3] Ellmaker, "Autobiography," p. 11.
[4] Entry for 14 May 1850, Smith, *Journal of a Trip*, p. 29.

incompetent teamsters on the North Platte. "Although their threats were regarded of no importance," he noted, "still we were in a country where there was neither law nor order."[5]

It was this awareness that they were pushing beyond law's rule that, in part, makes the diaries, letters, and reminiscences of the emigrants the very best source we have for learning what average nineteenth-century Americans understood about the nature of crime and the justification for punishment. These people were the one large group of ordinary citizens in our history who had to join theory to action when coping with antisocial behavior. What they have to say about robbery, battery, arson, and intentional homicide is unique, so that we should study every word. We simply have no comparable material from which we can learn the values, expectations, prejudices, and beliefs of anonymous individuals—the so-called "inarticulate"—who generally were not asked, and did not write, about the theoretical limits of social deviance and the philosophical justifications for civic retribution.

Their writings tell us more than we can learn by any other means but we must be cautious and not expect too much. As the following pages show, we are told a great deal but seldom are we told what we need to know. Consider, for instance, the evidence left us by a physician writing in 1849. As the Gold Rush passed through the southern corner of today's state of Idaho, he wandered about for part of a day, completely lost, finally stumbling upon a valley in which he spied his wagons corralled with others far below. In the twilight he beheld a scene so pleasing that he took time to describe it for readers of the *Western Christian*, a newspaper printed in Elgin, Illinois.

> There almost under my feet was a grand encampment. Several hundred human and inhuman beings

---

[5]Entry for 23 June for 23 June 1849, Cross, "Journal," p. 100.

were congregated in one of the most delightful spots
on the route. A deep valley . . . the lamps and can-
dles and huge bonfires turning night to day — a
group there laughing and swearing and gambling —
another trying a criminal for a murder recently
committed — a hundred males and half a dozen
females dancing cotillion on the base rock to the
music of flute and hautboy and clarionet [*sic*] and
violin and horn — the loud laughter from that little group where some wag is retailing some
ridiculous misadventure comes up here distinct and
clear and quite refreshing — and yonder little squad
sure as I live it is a prayer meeting.[6]

If this forty-niner was more poetic than most emigrants, he was
in one respect typical of travelers on the overland trail—he felt no
urge to analyze events of interest to the legal historian. An educated man writing for publication, he mentioned the fact that "a
criminal" was being tried for "murder" but offered no comment.
He did not ask by what authority the person was charged, who
appointed the judge, whether there was a jury, how it was selected, or if counsel was permitted.[7] Even the outcome is passed
over—whether "the defendant" was found innocent or, if guilty,
how punished and by whom. Even though a devout Christian
addressing fellow Christians, the writer considered neither the
legality nor the morality of "justice" administered by self-appointed law enforcers.

---

[6]Entry for 11 August 1849, Lord, *Journal.* See also "Prosecuting the Elephant,"
p. 327.

[7]In fact, most diaries ignored these questions. The following account is typical: "June
the 1, 1850. to day one mess had a fracus. one man stab[b]ed another  it is thought he
will die before Monday. Monday he is to be tried.  it is thought he [we?] will hang or shoot
him if the man dies. June the 1st 1850. Traveled 16 miles.  rained last night." Rhodes,
"Journal," p. 64.

There is no need to criticize the writer: the sentence he wrote is typical of overland literature. Our lesson is not that he told us too little but that we have to take into account the context in which he wrote. "There is a man to be tried for murder tomorrow," another physician had written about a month earlier just beyond Devil's Gate in today's Wyoming. "Of course 'Judge Lynch' holds the Court out here."[8] Again, no details are provided. We are left to wonder how "murder" was defined and who defined it, and whether the reference to "Judge Lynch" was intended by the writer to describe the event or to express a moral judgment.

The action that tells us the most about overland attitudes toward crime and punishment is intentional homicide. All too often, however, we cannot reconstruct the cases analytically because, even when the event is clearly reported, relevant facts are omitted. After observing that there had been a number of deaths by drowning, an emigrant mentioned another, different kind of death—a man had been "shot through the heart in a quarrel." Two days later, near the North Platte crossing, the same writer reported: "one shot accidently and two intentionally."[9] In both instances killings occurred that possibly could have been prosecuted as murder in the states, but we cannot be certain. In the first we need to know if the victim was armed when quarreling with the manslayer, whether he had been shooting at the manslayer, whether the victim and the manslayer were advancing or retreating, and what the quarrel was about. In the second, we have to know something of how the writer used the concept "intentionally." Did it exclude the possibility of such mitigating factors as heat of passion or self-defense? Even less helpful are accounts of shootings that give no hint of culpabili-

---

[8]Entry for 2 July 1849, Parke, *Notes*. See also "Prosecuting the Elephant," p. 328.
[9]Entries for 22 and 24 June 1849, Foster, "First Diary," pp. 33, 35.

ty. "Passed an encampment where a young man by the name of McCoy was dying," a forty-niner wrote. "He was shot this morning by one Williams."[10] We know McCoy was shot by Williams but was it accidentally, in self-defense, or with malice aforethought?

Too many accounts are simply not clear. Several emigrants reported that while traveling along the Sweetwater they passed a headboard that read either "To the memory of Columbus found here with his throat cut and his knife in his hand,"[11] or "To the memory of Columbus who was found with his throat cut, having in his hand with a death grip his pocket knife."[12] One might assume that the epitaph meant "Columbus" had been killed by another person and add his death to the statistics of homicides committed on the overland trail. Actually, we know that he was a suicide who, according to another account, "had become discouraged in prosecuting one long journey, and had entered upon another longer journey, with perhaps, less preparation than upon the first."[13]

Writers were also careless with terms, especially the word "murder" which many used so loosely it often has no meaning. Writing from Bear River Valley an emigrant told her grandfather of a "murder" trial at which men from her wagon train served on the jury. The defendant was found to have acted in self-defense. "This is the ninth case of death by violence on the route," she reported, "three of whom were executed, the others were murdered."[14] Among the "murdered" she was counting the person killed by the

---

[10]Entry for 22 June 1849, Burrall, "Trip," p. 31.

[11]Entry for 24 June 1850, Paschal, "Diary," p. 28.

[12]Entry for 24 June 1850, Newcomb, *Journal*; entry for 20 June 1850, Sheperd, *Journal*, p. 17.

[13]Entry for 20 June 1850, Ingalls, *Journal*, p. 26.

[14]Letter from Abigail Jane Scott to Grandfather, 18 July 1852, Scott, "Letters," pp. 153–54.

man who had been acquitted by reason of self-defense. If the slayer killed in self-defense the homicide was not murder.[15]

Often evaluations were made that simply bore no relation to reality. "A large majority of the Californians are desperate Fellows," a forty-niner told his wife, "and they practice most all kinds of crime."[16] He was writing from St. Joseph where there was a greater amount of crime than was to be found on the remainder of the journey. Once across the Missouri, antisocial behavior was not common. As one of the leading historians of the overland trail has pointed out, "the incidence of crime along the Platte was low, much lower for the floating population of some 350,000 over a period of some twenty years than in many Americans cities of comparable population today in one year."[17]

Certainly there is one defensible historical conclusion: there was, proportionally, little stealing of property on the overland trail,[18] whether larceny, burglary, or robbery. True, it happened frequently enough to be mentioned in a high percentage of diaries, at least as rumors—larceny by passengers,[19] burglary of the contents of wagons,[20] or the robbery of animals.[21] The property most

---

[15]Admittedly, some western historians use terms as loosely as did emigrants. One wrote that a "murder" went "unrequited." Mattes, *Narratives*, p. 347 (no. 1135). He was referring to a killing in which an employer wielding a weapon, a neckyoke, was attacking an employee. While retreating, the employee pulled a gun and shot his attacker. Cole, *Early Days*, pp. 48–49. How does the historian know that this act was murder, and not justifiable homicide, self-defense, or manslaughter? See below, pp. 154–55.

[16]Letter of 3 May 1849, Hinman, *Pretty Fair View*, p. 11.

[17]Mattes, *Platte River Road*, p. 77. However, the same historian also wrote, "In 1852 crime was rampant on the California Road." Mattes, *Narratives*, p. 361.

[18]*Law for the Elephant*, pp. 335–64.

[19]Entry for 25 July 1849, Hutchings, *Journal*, p. 130.

[20]Entry for 16 July 1850, Gardner, *Journal to California*.

[21]Entry for 5 August 1853, Luark, *Diary*, p. 53.

easily taken were horses,[22] mules,[23] or oxen.[24] Their conversion by others could greatly inconvenience the owners, and might prove costly if replacements had to be acquired out on the trail. The loss of cattle, either from theft or—more often—from death, seems not to have resulted in human fatalities because when travellers were left destitute of draft animals other emigrants took them in. There is, however, the case of a company that "lost all their cattle supposed to have been stolen by emigrants. They were compelled to proceed on with their provisions upon their backs on foot."[25] One reason they may not have acquired new transportation was that they did not need it for survival. They were already in California, on Lassen's cutoff.

The point is worth considering, for it is not what would have been expected. When cattle were converted on the overland trail the danger to the emigrants was not the loss of the animals, for emigrants were not left behind to die. The dangers occurred when those robbed of their cattle pursued the robbers and confronted them, and there were pursuits with emigrants threatening emigrants. Remarkably, in those cases that we know about it was always the thief who was reported killed. Just before a company got to Independence Rock in 1854, "a thief [was] shot in the back, dead, while on a stolen horse, by the owner in pursuit of him."[26] Six years later there was a blacksmith shop at Independence Rock. Some emigrants visited it "and two of them rogues — one stole a pair of shoes  the other a butcher knife. The frenchman followed and over

---

[22]Entry for 19 July 1852, Dickinson, *Overland Journal*; Mattes, *Narratives*, pp. 296, 406, 453.

[23]Entry for 13 August 1864, Rahm, "Copy of Diary," p. 8.

[24]Entry for 4 October 1849, Austin, *Diary*.

[25]Ibid.

[26]Entry for 13 June 1854, Sutton, "Diary," p. 10. Similarly, see entry for 29 May 1850, Hough, "Overland Diary," p. 212.

took them shot at them 3 or 4 [times?]   The first shot took effect in the foot of the one who stole the shoes. The company all was from Wisconsin, a very rough set too. and don't no yet how it will terminate."[27]

Just as often there were no weapons involved in these disputes. Despite being heavily armed, emigrants avoided their use. In 1850 some emigrants looking for a missing mule found it "in the possession of a fellow who was very much disposed to act the rascal — refusing to let them see it after they had described it. They talked pretty plainly to him and took possession of the mule, which they [he?] had evidently stolen."[28] The captain of one of the largest companies traveling in 1849 may have pulled out a firearm but was happy not to use it. "A young man of the company, as reckless as unprincipled, backed by several scoundrels, attempted this morning to take my horse, prompt determination frustrated them. — The recollection of their parents stayed my hand, as I was on the eve of making a bloody example. — Glad that I checked myself."[29]

The captain's restraint is no surprise. He was an educated person who had held a responsible position with the federal government. But something that we must appreciate if we are to understand nineteenth-century attitudes to common theft is that, if the young man and his companions were really taking his horse, had the captain shot any of them he would, in the opinion of just about every emigrant, have acted with legal justification.

It was widely, perhaps universally, accepted by people on the overland trail that it was legal and proper social behavior for the owners of property to employ whatever violence they pleased to protect or retain possession of that property. That is, they were

---

[27]Entry for 5 July 1860, Guill, "Diary," p. 7.
[28]Entry for 18 August 1850, Moorman, *Journal,* p. 69.
[29]Entry for 21 September 1849, Bruff, *Journals,* p. 183.

entitled to employ what force they chose to, not what force was necessary or reasonable. Moreover, it was proper social behavior to use violence to punish the conversion of property—even if that meant a private person took the responsibility for assuming this task, making himself police, prosecutor, judge, and jury. An 1850 emigrant belonged to a company that suspected its stock was being stolen as they traveled along the Green River.

> The first thing that attracted my attention this morning was a man driving one of the cows belonging to our train from the river by our camp. The captain hailed him and enquired of him where he got the cow. His reply was, he had owned her for 5 or 6 days. The captain gave him the lie, and took up a brush and gave him a good thrashing and drove him off without the cow.[30]

The telling fact is not that the writer apparently approved of his captain's battery of the stranger, for all emigrants would have accepted it and most would have justified it. What should be marked is that the writer was a lawyer. His training might at least have led him to question the captain's justification in using violence on his own authority or to have employed violence even though he knew the cow could be repossessed without using force.

Two points may by now be obvious, but it will do no harm to restate them to be certain they are not missed. Overland travelers had no tolerance for persons converting property owned or legally possessed by another emigrant. And overland travelers did not criticize emigrants who appointed themselves police, judges, and

---

[30]Entry for 31 July 1850, Dowell, *Journal*, p. 31; entry for 21 July 1850, Dowell, *Letter Journal*.

punishers of those they regarded as thieves. Consider this account of two horse thieves. Unfortunately, the story is not told as clearly as we could wish. One thief was shot riding a stolen horse. The other "was caught & burned as long as he well could be and live." We may assume that the writer, even if he would not have participated in the punishment, did not condemn it, for he concluded: "Horse thieves are shown but little mercy by Californians."[31] Again, consider the education of the commentator. He was a physician. "There is a man laying very low here," a nineteen-year-old emigrant, traveling the Platte River, wrote nine years later. "Was shot twice, once in the back, and again in the breast. . . . The poor man will probably die. He stole some money of the men who shot him. I asked one of the company if he had any friends and he said no, and he didn't deserve any."[32]

There were some peculiar aspects to conversion on the overland trail which caused both confusion and special concern. One was that emigrants could not always tell if a company's animals had been run off by third parties: frequently, when theft was suspected, the horses or oxen had merely wandered away on their own looking for grass or had stampeded.[33] A particularly vexing problem for many emigrants was that the most likely time to lose animals was at night.[34] Horses especially had to be hobbled or corralled, and a few members each night had to stay up, to take turns guarding them. Guards were maintained to keep the stock from wandering or to keep a lookout for Indians. It was seldom, if at all, thought they might be stolen by fellow emigrants. Still, to whatever extent that possibility contributed to the caution, it

[31]Entry for 6 May 1850, Grow, *Letter Diary*.
[32]Entry for 12 May 1859, Williams, "Original Diary," p. 12.
[33]For example, entry for 30 May 1850, Griffith, "Diary of 1850," p. 44.
[34]For example, entry for 9 July 1851, Jones, "Diary," p. 10.

would have caused emigrants special anger, because guard duty was just about the most unpleasant assignment when traveling on the overland trail.

Starving times were another worry. Again, conditions along the Humboldt River in 1850 illustrate the point, for there was no other place or year when so many emigrants over such a long period of time experienced acute hunger.[35] "I never saw such hungry men," an emigrant wrote of the Humboldt that July. "[M]any talk seriously of killing their horses and eating them and running the risk of getting through on foot."[36] A second man was more concerned about the risks of contaminated food than the risks of packing. "I have noticed several dead horses, mules and oxen, by the road side, that had their hams cut out to eat by the starving wretches along the road," he wrote; "for my own part I will eat the lizards which infest the sage bushes, before I will eat the stock that died from the alkali."[37]

Not all emigrants were so cautious and a few even converted the animals of others rather than go hungry. It happened far less often than we might think from reading the fiction of the American west, but it did occur. As early as the American Falls on the Snake River, people woke up mornings to hear that stock had been killed for food. One company had several horses and one steer taken at night, "& one of their steers had been shot in the head & skin[n]ed within 250 yds of the camp."[38] Far down the Humboldt a man from Michigan saw a more dreadful sight.

> Here, indeed, was a picture of misery, which, if I
> had witnessed before being hardened to scenes of

---

[35] *Law for the Elephant*, pp. 338–44; Unruh, *Plains*, pp. 146–47, 213, 280.
[36] Lemuel Clarke McKeeby, 15 July 1850, quoted in Webb, *Trail*, p. 162.
[37] Entry for 31 July 1850, Ingalls, *Journal*, p. 39.
[38] Entry for 17 July 1850, Gundlach, *Minutes*.

the like character, would have made my heart's blood run cold; and even now the chill of horror ran over me like electricity. Dead horses and oxen, in great numbers, with steaks cut out of their flesh, long scattered over the land; and men, without a morsel to eat, were begging from wagon to wagon, offering all they had for a little dry bread. The more dishonest, however, were practising the crafty scheme of theft.[39]

The danger was nowhere as acute as we might think or as some emigrants believed,[40] but it was compounded by the fact that an unusual number of teams died in the harness that summer and people needed new animals to pack what few provisions they still possessed the remainder of the way to California.[41]

---

[39]Entry for 15 July 1850, Clapp, *Journal,* p. 39.
[40]For discussion, see *Law for the Elephant,* pp. 335–36.
[41]Entry for 21 July 1850, Gundlach, *Minutes.*

*Harassing the Elephant*

# 4 | OVERLAND MALFEASANCE AND ORGANIZED CRIMINALITY

We should dwell on the peculiar as well as the familiar. There were crimes or antisocial actions unique to the overland trail. At least two were highlighted when emigrants threatened to hang the culprits. When the 1845 emigration to Oregon approached Fort Boise, a small Hudson's Bay Company trading post in the Snake River country, it was met by an experienced mountain man and fur trapper, Stephen Meek, who contracted to guide the wagons to the Columbia River by a new, shorter route. Soon the expedition was hopelessly lost. "There was so little grass, the loose cattle frequently turned back," a historian has written. "Stephen Meek, to get them away from this hard land guided the train farther south only to find hotter days, colder nights, desert country and alkaline water. There was Mountain Fever and there were deaths in many families. Meek finally realized he was at the mercy of frenzied people."[1] His biographer says that "[h]e was forced to hide, and finally to flee."[2] It seems that "[a] group of men raised the tongues of three wagons, tied them at the top and threatened to hang Meek from them. The level headed ones in the train dissuaded them and begged that he be spared so that he could have a chance to seek help."[3]

Seven years later another hanging was talked about. As he traveled down the Humboldt, an emigrant heard "loud screaming for

---

[1]Bowers, "Account," pp. 6–7.

[2]Harvey E. Tobie, "Stephen Hall Meek," in *Mountain Men*, 2:235.

[3]Bowers, "Account," p. 7. Another writer said that some of "the party had put a rope around Steve Meek's neck and were about to hang him." Lockley, *Captain Tetherow*, p. 6. A quite similar incident occurred in 1849. However, perhaps because much of the company came from law-minded New Hampshire, there seems to have been no talk of hanging. Entries for 1–12 August 1849, Webster, *Gold Seekers*, pp. 65–71.

help." "I saw a man in the river struggling with a span of horses to which was still attached the running gear of a wagon. A few rods below him were his wife and two children about five and three years old, floating down the strong current in the wagon bed." The emigrant, at some risk to himself, saved the woman and children while the husband got his horses ashore.

> By this time the rest of our train had crossed the river and were with the man and his horses. When they learned just what had happened, they became very indignant because the man had apparently abandoned his wife and children to the mercies of the river, while he exerted himself to save his team. Quicker than I can tell it, the tongue of the man's wagon was set up on end, and hasty preparations being made to hang the man from the end of it. Almost frantic with what she saw, the wife again threw herself at my feet and begged me to save her husband. Her tears and entreaties, probably more than all I said, finally quieted the men, although some of them were still in favor of throwing him in the river.[4]

Spousal abuse was hardly ever mentioned in overland diaries,[5] but on the few times it occurred emigrants treated it as a matter of public concern. Along the Little Sandy River in 1850 a large train camped about a mile from a second company.

> their a rose a quarel with them and what quareling
> I never heard the like   they were whiping a man for

---

[4]Cole, *Early Days*, p. 96.
[5]For one incident, see entry for 29 October 1849, Bruff, *Journals*, p. 246, and Read and Gaines, "Introduction," pp. 584–85 *n*93.

whiping his wife   he had whiped her every day since
he joined the company and now they thought it was
time for them to whip him   and they caught him
and striped him and took the ox gad to him and
whiped him tremenduous    she screamed and
holler[e]d for him till one might have hare him [*sic*]
for three miles.[6]

Although family violence seems to have been virtually
unknown, there were occasions when the stresses and strains of the
journey produced domestic discord. In 1853, when they were just
beyond the Continental Divide, a husband decreed an overland
form of divorce by putting his wife out of their wagon. "The husband say she was ugly to his children she being his second wife."
The woman had little difficulty getting through to Oregon.
"Another Co[mpany] took her in & like her very much."[7]

What may have been the only other serious case of domestic
discord to be recorded in a diary occurred along the Snake River
in 1847.

> This morning one [our?] company moved on except
> one family. The woman got mad and would not
> budge, nor let the children go. He had his cattle
> hitched on for three hours and coaxing her to go,
> but she would not stir. I told my husband the cir-
> cumstance, and he and Adam Polk and Mr. Kimball
> went and took each one a young one and crammed
> them in the wagon and her husband drove off and
> left her sitting. She got up, took the back track and
> traveled out of sight. Cut across, overtook her hus-

---

[6]Entry for 28 July 1850, Davis, "California Diary," p. 186.
[7]Entry for 15 August 1853, Hines, "Oregon Diary," p. 111.

band. Meantime he sent his boy back to camp after a horse he had left and when she came up her husband says, "Did you meet John?" "Yes," was the reply, "and I picked up a stone and knocked out his brains." Her husband went back to ascertain the truth, and while he was gone she set one of his wagons on fire, which was loaded with store goods. The cover burnt off and some valuable articles. He saw the flames and came running and put it out, and then mustered spunk enough to give her a good flogging.[8]

Again the extant account does not tell us things we need to know. Did the woman actually assault John and did the husband's patience snap after finding the boy dead or injured? Surely the wife was suffering acute trail stress but that fact won her no sympathy from her fellow emigrants.

One antisocial action that might not have been considered a major crime in an eastern state was very serious when committed on the overland trail. Burning grass was an offence that emigrants spoke of as if it merited capital punishment. The idea was that fires were set in the hope of slowing down those behind by destroying the forage.[9] Of course, fires most often started accidentally.[10] These would sometimes race across the prairie and threaten emigrants camped nearby, who might have "to burn a circle around our camp" to keep their wagons, tents, and provisions from being destroyed.[11] In 1850 fur trappers going back over the trail to St.

---

[8]Entry for 15 September 1847, Geer, "Diary," pp. 165–66.

[9]Becker, "Introduction," p. 5. But see the doubt expressed in entry for 26 September 1849, Burbank, "Diary and Journal," p. 127.

[10]Entry for 27 July 1849, Wood, *Diaries;* entry for 14 May 1850, Zieber, *Diary,* pp. 14–15.

[11]Entry for 1 June 1850, Newcomb, *Journal.*

Louis told travelers that the grass was being burnt by a man named Dennison, captain of a company from Wooster, Ohio.[12] But when emigrants complained to the officers at Fort Laramie, the commandant told them that he had found Dennison a gentleman and did not think him guilty. Not only had his companions spoken highly of him, but the companies that were first behind him had not reported any burnt grass. "It is supposed that the Pawnees burnt the grass."[13]

The year before, 1849, there had been no doubts. People then had been convinced the grass was set deliberately "by a company ahead which was threatened by almost every one that saw it with linch law."[14] One emigrant learned about these fires after arriving in California.

> I was told of one man who, with a refinement of malice and cruelty which it would be impossible to surpass, set fire to the meadows of dry grass, for the sole purpose, it was supposed, of retarding the progress of those who were behind and might else overtake him. A company of the emigrants, on the best horses which were to be obtained, pursued him and shot him from the saddle as he rode — a fate scarcely equal to his deserts.[15]

---

[12]Entry for 11 May 1850, Parker, *Notes.* At least one other emigrant made the same accusation: "Dennison's train is a few days ahead of us burning the grass at every camping." Entry for 5 May 1850, Pigman, *Journal,* p. 9.

[13]Entry for 26 June 1850, Parker, *Notes.* Another company suspected of setting fires that year was from Chicago, led by Captain Clark. Entry for 13 May 1850, Christy, *Road.*

[14]Entry for 16 August 1849, Castleman, *Diary.*

[15]Taylor, *Eldorado,* p. 214. Similarly, see White, *Forty-Niners,* pp. 70–71.

An emigrant on the Humboldt River probably heard of a different case when told that "Captain Harding of Kentucky had a few miles back shot a man who set fire to the grass after leaving camp & would not allow him to be buried."[16]

Another special circumstance of trail life that could lead to trouble was emigrant fear of Indians. This study is concerned only with emigrant antisocial behavior toward one another, not toward Indians, and conflicts with Indians and acts of violence committed against Indians are not relevant to the thesis. But the ingredients for violence, that on any day might have endangered an entire year's emigration, were certainly present: the movement of so many people, way out beyond the frontier, unfamiliar with firearms, who had never before dealt with native Americans. Remarkably, few incidents occurred. People who in fiction or in the movies would surely panic and fire when unexpectedly seeing Indians did not do so in real life. Coming to the Big Blue in 1852, a wagon company sent two young men ahead as advance guard. Part way across the river they spotted Indians. Turning their horses they went back to the main party. After preparing the wagons for defense, the company proceeded. "We walked up to the Indians and said 'How,' and gave presents of copper cents and tobacco," one of the advance guard wrote. "We soon saw that they were merely looking on to see us ford the stream. They were Pawnees, and were gaily dressed and armed with bows and arrows."[17]

That encounter with Pawnees is an important event for it helps explain why there was relatively little violence on the overland trail. The company had anticipated trouble with Indians and that day the men and older boys had been ordered to be armed

---

[16]Entry for 20 July 1849, Decker, *Diaries*, p. 122. Also for 1849, see entry for 17 July 1849, Bryarly, *Diary*, pp. 158–59.

[17]Cole, *Early Days*, p. 20.

at all times.[18] The Pawnees appeared suddenly and—just by being there, on the other side of the Big Blue, apparently blocking the crossing—looked menacing. These young men easily could have fired a shot or two, either in panic or by racial reflex, as we would expect if we accept the currently fashionable social theory that events must be explained by racial antagonism. That they and so many like them restrained their trigger fingers tells us why the elephant enjoyed much peace. True, there was a minority who did shoot, but usually after giving vocal warning. An emigrant of 1850 "left his own train and went down some distance to another train with a blanket around him and a gun in his hand in an Indian manner. The guard hailed him several times and got no answer. He still advanced. The guard then fired being within a few feet of each other. The ball went through his right shoulder. . . . His intention was not known."[19]

Violence to or from Indians touched few emigrants on the overland trail. Only a tiny minority witnessed it. If overlanders saw violence at all it was fights between fellow emigrants. Sometimes it occurred between strangers—members of different companies— and the chief cause, as has already been mentioned, was that one train would suspect another of violating some rule of the road. Just the question of priority at a crossing could lead not only to fighting but to death.[20] Three incidents involving an 1853 train of eight wagons illustrate how emigrants could get their way by intimidation and threats of force. At Kanesville, a member of the company "register[ed] our names for crossing the Missouri

---

[18]Ibid., p. 17.
[19]Entry for 18 May 1850, Wilson, "Chronicle."
[20]A good detailed illustration is in Luark, *Late Diary*, pp. 26, 28 (1853 emigration). Briefly, see Mattes, *Narratives*, p. 378.

River."[21] They were assigned a time four days later, but once in line became impatient.

> There were over one hundred waggons waiting to cross ahead of ours, but by cunning management we got aboard of the steamer Hindoo, and were ferried over before our turn. . . . We came near having a rowe before crossing the river with some emigrants. They wanted to cross before us, which we refused to let them do. Pistols were drawn and hard words passed but no one hurt.[22]

Over a week later they were behind fifty wagons waiting for the Loup Fork ferry. "We formed a corrall on the bank of the river and drove our cattle about 1 mile to grass. A train came up and drove into our corrall and said they would camp there. We ordered them out. They at first refused but they found out that we meant what we said and they soon moved out, thinking that it would be bad policy to stay."[23] Finally, arriving just outside Salt Lake City, the company "came by near having a row with some other emigrants. They stopped in the road and said if we passed them we would get into trouble. We passed them pistols and knives in hand and were unmolested."[24]

These men were not typical emigrants. They were more aggressive than most. But just by their insistence on their own "rights" and their disregard of the rights of others, we see how rules of the road, accepted by most travelers as customs for avoiding conflict, could become the cause of violence.

----

[21]Entry for 15 May 1853, Brown, *Wagon Train Journal*, p. 17.
[22]Entry for 19 May 1853, ibid., p. 19.
[23]Entry for 28 May 1853, ibid., p. 24.
[24]Entry for 1 August 1853, ibid., p. 58.

Were we able to compile accurate statistics of violence on the overland trail they probably would reflect statistics of violence, or at least homicide, in representative contemporary American communities. The major lesson we would learn is that most known stabbings and shootings occurred between people who knew one another. This fact is important for it means that killings between strangers were secondary to those between traveling companions. Stranger homicides were more likely to be intentional, or felonious, and were more dangerous as they threatened everybody, since anyone might be hurt. As a general rule, however, the victims of most reported violence belonged to the same traveling train as did the attacker, although a few quarrels, even an occasional homicide, occurred within families or between several members of a family. In 1852, at the Humboldt Meadows where emigrants prepared to cross the perilous Forty Mile Desert, "a man by the name of Ross from Sacremento [*sic*] fired twice with a Colt's revolver at a man by the name of Williams, his father-in-law, but neither shot took effect. Williams' daughter braught [*sic*] him from the tent, a double barrel shot gun to defend himself when Ross' brother rode up and got his revolver away from him."[25]

Much more common than family scraps were fights between people in fiduciary relationships. Passengers became dissatisfied with their fare or the speed of travel and either complained to excess or attempted to rewrite the contract by taking a horse and provisions and breaking away from the train.[26] Hired hands became disgrun-

---

[25]Entry for 8 September 1852, Gee, "Journal of Travels." In a Mormon train: "At night, old Zabriskie and his wife had a tremendeous fight." Entry for 15 September 1849, Morgan, *Trip*, p. 10.

[26]Ness, *Journal*, p. 6 ("Express Company" of 1849); entry for 27 May 1852, Coupler, "Crossing the Plains," p. 8 (a man put out without clothes or provisions attempted to recover property and one man was shot). Also, see Reid, "Diary," p. 17 (passenger fighting with a "trainman"). Also entry for 7 June 1849, Reid, *Diary*, p. 48.

tled with the hard work or harsh treatment and tried to leave.[27] A particular cause of violence arose when employers reached the limits of tolerating their hired hands' laziness or incompetence. As he approached Fort Hall in 1850, an emigrant met what he called "some sporting fellows": "A man & his driver fell out   the owner threw a ladle & then an axe at the driver   the driver then shot at the owner but missed him & then fell to cutting him with a knife but not very dangerous."[28] Two years later we learn of another hired man who was a better shot. His employer, a doctor, was chasing him around the wagon with a neckyoke when the man "whipped out an Allen revolver and turning shot the doctor in the mouth, the charge coming out nearly under the ear."[29]

An eyewitness to this last shooting thought that "many instances of this kind" occurred on the trail, "the quarrels usually arising from the owner of the wagons constantly brow-beating and finding fault with the hired man."[30] If he meant that employer-employee disputes caused most violence between people who knew one another, he was wrong. Fights between partners and between members of traveling companies were more often reported. The claim that "nearly every diary recorded at least one" fight is an exaggeration,[31] or depends upon how you define the word "fight." What was true is that when fights occurred they most likely would be between people traveling in the same wagon train. There were very few "Partnership companys," an emigrant of 1852 wrote, "but what Quarrels among themselves, some of them

---

[27]Entry for 2 June 1849, Decker, *Diaries*, p. 86 (hired men shoot their employer: "they would not work & after the affray [they] passed on with his team (this is life on the plains)").

[28]Entry for 6 July 1850, Watts, *Diary*.

[29]Cole, *Early Days*, p. 48.

[30]Ibid., p. 49.

[31]Schlissel, *Women's Diaries*, p. 74n19.

divideing teams making 2 carts of 1 wagon — some even fighting and stab[b]ing &c."[32]

Near the end of the trail, in September 1849, a physician was "called to see a man [who] was shot, a ball had pass'd into the side by the 5th rib & ranged in the umbilical region. Another ball had gone in at the corronal suture & ranged below the occipital protuberance. — This was done in a fray between two partners, and this the result."[33] Another forty-niner was in a three-way partnership, owning a wagon and oxen with two other men. The other two had a falling-out and divided the property, one taking the wagon and the second the oxen, leaving the third man at Salt Lake City with no means of transportation. "Sam (I mean Mr. McFadden) took away 2 yoke of Oxen without saying by *you[r] leave sir* but said to Doct Downer he would either have them or my life   not wishing to die now I made no objection to his having them as this is in California."[34] By "in California" the writer meant the overland trail where there was no law enforcement.

Further west, on his third day on the Humboldt River, an emigrant of 1852 for the first time in his life "saw men draw pistols on each other." About six weeks before, his company had picked up a Frenchman named Peter whose partner had "ran away from him carrying off one of his horses & most of his possessions." Now, on the Humboldt, Peter spotted his former partner.

> [L]ast night he camped within a hundred rods of us, & this morning as we were hitching up he unexpectedly to both drove by us. Peter at once recognized him, borrowed my Pistol & went after him, as soon as the other chap saw Peter he mount-

---

[32]Entry for 30 July 1852, Lewis, *Notes.*
[33]Entry for 6 September 1849, Caldwell, "Notes," p. 1264.
[34]Letter of 2 September 1849, Swan, "Letters," p. 70.

ed his stolen horse drew his Pistol & defied Peter, but he was careful to keep at some considerable distance. Peter very courageously followed him up and fired at him, when the two companies interferred & put a stop to further firing. but Peters enemy rode off with the horse.[35]

Partners and company members did not usually fight over who owned what property or other matters of weight and substance. More often, they fought over a triviality—"as to which route was the better,"[36] "about who shall drive ahead,"[37] and, in 1852, two men "fought about a biscuit."[38] The consequence could be much more serious than the cause. On the Little Blue a forty-niner came across evidence of "a company that got into a fight among themselves . . . burnt fragments of wagon, stoves, axes, etc., with a great quantity of harness cut to pieces; with a quantity of torn shirts, coats, hats, etc. all besmeared by blood."[39]

Some emigrants were as puzzled by these fights as they were angered. Between Fort Laramie and the North Platte crossing a physician witnessed the members of a train make "a regular dog time" fighting one another. "[S]uch actions belong to brutes, not men," he complained. "While men act like men, especially when on a trip like this, they always find enough to do, to the entire exclusion of such senseless brutality, alas, but few seem to appreciate this truth."[40] Other emigrants knew what was to blame. The cause, Edwin Bryant wrote, was the overland trail itself and the pressure it put on people.

---

[35]Entry for 17 August 1852, Anable, *Journal*, p. 32.
[36]Cole, *Early Days*, p. 106.
[37]Entry for 6 August 1863, Crawford, *1863 Diary*.
[38]Entry for 13 June 1852, Johnston, "Diary," p. 6.
[39]Mattes, *Platte River Road*, p. 72.
[40]Entry for 9 June 1852, Wayman, *Diary*, p. 48.

> A fisticuff fight, in the progress of which knives
> were drawn, took place near the river bank, between
> two drivers, who ordinarily were very peaceable and
> well-disposed men. . . . The pugnacious and bel-
> ligerent propensities of men display themselves on
> these prairie excursions, for slight causes and provo-
> cations. The perpetual vexations and hardships are
> well calculated to keep the nerves in a state of great
> irritability.[41]

No words better explain the cause for most overland fighting
than those: "great irritability." In 1852 a seventeen-year-old girl,
destined to become the west's leading suffragette, said much the
same when writing a letter beside the Bear River. "This route is the
greatest one for wrangling, discord and abuse of any other place in
the world," she told her grandfather. "Tho we have had less difficulty than any other train we hear of, but we sometimes feel a little
ill-natured."[42] Even so, the people who were crossing on the overland trail came from towns and villages where they had seen little
quarreling and fighting, and they could not get used to it. Besides,
there was something particularly unsettling about such violence
when it happened out on the trail. Fighting struck some emigrants
as out of place on the overland trail, and the fact that it occurred
more frequently during the trip west than it had back home was
particularly unsettling. Bryant may have meant what he said when
he said that quarreling or fighting on the trail had to be anticipated, yet when it took place he was surprised. After breaking up a
fight between two men belonging to his small, isolated party—a
fight in which guns were drawn—he wrote: "It was truly a startling

---

[41]Entry for 31 May 1846, Bryant, *Journal,* p. 65.
[42]Letter from Abigail Jane Scott to Grandfather, 18 July 1852, Scott, "Letters," p. 154.

spectacle, to witness two men, in this remote desert, surrounded by innumerable dangers, to guard against which they were mutually dependent, so excited by their passions as to seek each other's destruction."[43]

We are interested in how ordinary people defined and responded to antisocial actions and to punishment of those actions. Our evidence is therefore best confined to the emigrants themselves: to emigrants who committed antisocial acts against other emigrants, and emigrants who punished other emigrants for "crimes." There is a bigger picture, however, that embraces nonemigrant offenses, and this deserves brief mention if we are to understand the conditions of criminality on the overland trail. It was known that organized bands roamed the trail, preying on the emigrants. None the emigrants thought better organized, and none was more feared, than the Mormons.

"A great many stock have been stolen or strayed from this point," a lawyer wrote, while at the Green River in 1850. "It is supposed by the emigrants that the Mormons and Indians are stealing every day."[44] Seven years later another emigrant was even more certain of the culprits. "The Mormons is stealing a great many sto[c]k," he claimed. "They are a great deal worse than the Indians."[45] As he was writing at Fort Laramie, relatively early on the trail, he must have been referring to organized Mormon emigrant companies stealing from nonMormons. There is at least one account that asserts that Mormons, traveling in Mormon trains, were caught with stolen animals.[46] It was, however, much farther west, in the area of today's northern Utah and southern Idaho, that

---

[43]Bryant, *Journal*, p. 188.

[44]Entry for 21 July 1850, Dowell, *Journal*, pp. 30–31; entry for 19 July 1850, Dowell, *Letter Journal*.

[45]Mattes, *Narratives*, p. 473 (quoting P. H. Ferguson).

[46]McMillan, "Reminiscences" (1852).

emigrants felt they had to be on guard. They were especially apprehensive of Mormons who collected in small trading bands beyond
the authorities in Salt Lake City. One encounter occurred in 1854.

> There were forty of them in number and all had a
> predatory and roguish appearance. All were armed
> to the teeth. When we counted our cattle the next
> morning, we found that five oxen and two horses
> were missing. We found the horses in a gully while
> a front and a hind leg were so tied together that they
> could scarcely move from the place. We did not find
> the oxen as the thieving Mormons had undoubted-
> ly driven them off.[47]

It has been suggested that "a plethora of rumors" was responsible
for the many stories of Mormon criminality.[48] There may be something to that, but the Mountain Meadows massacre did not help
emigrant impressions. There more emigrants were killed than in any
other incident connected with the history of the overland trail. And
emigrant fears were not unfounded since, even without that mass
killing of nonMormons, there seems to have been a disproportion-
ate amount of violence occurring in the vicinity of today's Utah. As
long as eight years before the massacre, a Presbyterian minister passing through Salt Lake City believed a serious amount of criminality
was going on. "Brigham Young," he claimed, "told the saints if any
emigrants stole any of their horses and cattle to kill them dead on
the spot and emigrants to do the same to the Mormons if they stole
ours, and he would absolve them."[49]

---

[47]Entry for 24 July 1854, "Kleinsorge Diary," pp. 440–41.

[48]Unruh, *Plains*, p. 194. The editor of the local newspaper at the Mormon winter
gathering place printed stories of how emigrants robbed emigrants, rejecting the implication that some thieves might be Mormons. For example, see *Frontier Guardian*, 12 June
1850, p. 2, col. 1.

[49]Entry for 24 July 1849, Foster, "Journal," p. 57.

We should wonder at this report. Not at whether Young really made the statement or at the fact an ordained clergyman recorded it. What is striking is that the minister, who was also a lawyer, did not comment on it. One might expect him to criticize it. Did he really accept a law that permitted owners of "horses and cattle to kill" thieves "dead"? Even if the owners' lives were not in danger? What if the property could be recovered by using nondeadly force? Young's legal formula was a license to kill—with cause to be sure, but not enough cause to have justified homicide in any European legal system.

Young may have been thinking of apostate Mormons who, fleeing from Deseret, collected on the trail in armed bands and preyed on the emigrants. They were much like those army deserters who had tried to join the Gold Rush but, having got no farther than across the Continental Divide, became members of armed gangs to rob, rape, and occasionally kill.[50] As early as 1849 the renowned mountain man Robert "Doc" Newell had warned the government about the danger of organized attacks on the overland trail. Along the Snake River, he advised, emigrants should travel in disciplined groups, perhaps even with an Indian agent to deal with natives. He was not, however, thinking only of danger from Indians. "[I]f some kind of system is not adopted," Newell predicted, "a band of freebooters can comfortably sustain themselves anywhere on the route and get protection from many of the Indians for a small share of the booty."[51]

Writing from experience,[52] Newell's concern was only with the Snake River Country. Had it been with the entire overland trail, he

---

[50]Below, pp. 57–59.

[51]Newell, "Report on Indians," p. 155.

[52]Eleven years earlier, on the south fork of the Platte, it was reported that a Dr. Saterlee had been killed by Pawnees. "Mr Newel . . . says he does not believe a word of it. The Pawnees did not kill Dr. S," rather "Doct Saterlee died by the hand of a white man." Entry for 21 May 1838, Gray, "Oregon Journal," p. 281.

would have had to report that organized crime had already commenced. It would become a problem in at least four regions.[53] Two of these were to be found at the ends of the California part of the trail. The start—across the Missouri River from either Independence or St. Joseph—experienced criminality in the first year of the Gold Rush.[54] This was because nonemigrant, professional criminals were naturally attracted to the frontier and some then organized themselves into gangs.

There was a name for such gangs on the overland trail. They were called "white Indians." "There is a tribe of white Indians upon these plains at this time that are more dangerous than Pawnees," a correspondent reported. "They carry on horse and mule stealing pretty extensively and even oxen do not escape their attention."[55] "Stood guard last night, more for fear of white thieves in guise of Indians, than of Indians," an emigrant camped at the Elk Horn wrote.[56] It was, in fact, to look out for white rustlers more than for Indians that most guards were posted during the first week or two of the trip.[57]

At the other end of the trail, in California, there was less organized criminality during the early years. True, there were suspicions of white gangs along Lassen's cutoff, a somewhat isolated spur of

---

[53]Unruh, *Plains*, p. 194.

[54]Entry for 4 May 1849, Stackpole, *Journal;* entry for 24 May 1849, Burbank, "Diary and Journal," p. 21.

[55]Mattes, *Platte River Road*, p. 77. Whites "are worse than Indians the[y] steal here & take back & sell again to emigrants." Entry for 11 May 1849, Chalmers, *Diary.*

[56]Entry for 20 May 1853, Allyn, "Journal," p. 389. Also, see entry for 19 May 1853, ibid., p. 389.

[57]Entry for 19 April 1849, Decker, *Diaries*, pp. 54–55; letter to Edward Thompson, 29 April 1850, Thompson, "Letters"; entry for 14 May 1852, Richardson, *Journal*, p. 28. For actual attacks by whites, see entry for 31 May 1853, Handsaker, "Journal," p. 7; entry for 2 May 1854, Woodhams, "Diary," p. 52. In the era of the Civil War the danger would greatly increase. Entry for 16 May 1862, Hewitt, *Across*, pp. 37–38; entry for 6 June 1864, Loughary, "Diary," p. 132.

the trail that was traveled only in 1849.[58] Before long, however, there were a few, small, scattered groups of thieves from California operating well east of the Sierras.[59]

There was a third area of organized criminality on the overland trail: those stretches of the road coming east toward, going west from, and passing north of the Great Salt Lake.[60] A San Francisco newspaper in 1852 reported the area infested with "systematically organized bands of thieves," and Brigham Young used a newspaper editorial to warn of "a numerous and well organized band of <u>white</u> highwaymen, painted and disguised as Indians" who robbed emigrants of their stock "by wholesale" and even murdered their victims.[61]

The fourth area of organized criminality on the overland trail was not a geographical unit but found in several scattered locations. It was concentrated mainly around trading posts, most notably on the Green River[62] and along the stretch between Goose Creek Valley going into Nevada[63] and in Carson Valley going into California. During the 1850s that area was frequented by "the dregs of the Gold Rush who had failed to strike it rich in the diggings and who now sought easy wealth from raids on emigrant trains."[64] Emigrants, newspapers,[65] and the government agent

---

[58]Entry for 7 October 1849, Middleton, "Across the Plains," p. 153.

[59]For example, in 1856, Burroughs, "Reminiscences," pp. 46–47 (cattle thieves from California. *Law for the Elephant*, pp. 25–26).

[60]Unruh, *Plains*, pp. 195–96.

[61]Madsen, *Shoshoni Frontier*, p. 47 (San Francisco *Alta California*, 27 July 1852), p. 60 (*Deseret News*, 13 July 1854); Unruh, *Plains*, p. 195.

[62]Entry for 27 June 1849, Tiffany, *Diaries*.

[63]Entry for 16 July 1854, Burrell, "Diary," p. 245.

[64]Madsen, *Shoshoni Frontier*, p. 55.

[65]The San Francisco *Alta California* claimed: "Even greater thieves, perhaps, were white traders who rivaled the Digger Indians in robbery exploits." Ibid., p. 47.

responsible for the Humboldt River Indians,[66] all complained that "to a man" proprietors of trading posts were "worse for stealing than the Indians."[67] The Indian agent summed up the evidence he had collected in 1852:

> By unkind treatment to the Indians they make them unfriendly towards the emigrants; schisms arise which they take advantage of, and steal, and commit more depredations than the Indians, all of which they manage to have charged to the Indians. I was told by the Indians that some of these traders had proposed to them to steal stock from emigrants, and run them off into the valleys in the mountains, and after the emigration had ceased passing, they would bring out guns, ammunition, blankets, &c., and trade with them for the stock stolen.[68]

If that is true, we can understand an emigrant of 1854 who concluded, "The Indians are better than the whites in my estimation."[69]

On balance emigrants on the overland trail experienced greater difficulties with "white" than with "red" Indians. "White Indians" were more desperate, better disciplined, better armed, and, probably because they were more fearful of recognition and of punishment, or because they felt they had to act as they believed Indians acted, they may have been more cruel.[70] In return, the

---

[66]Ibid., p. 53.

[67]Letter from Wesley Tonner, 10 September 1854, printed in 6 *Covered Wagon Women*, p. 257.

[68]Unruh, *Plains*, p. 196 (quoting Jacob Holeman).

[69]Entry for 15 June 1854, Sutton, "Diary."

[70]See discussion, Unruh, *Plains*, pp. 192–97; Madsen, *Shoshoni Frontier*, pp. 78–79.

emigrants treated them more harshly than any other criminal element encountered on the trail.

In 1862, on Landers' cutoff through the Bear Mountains, some Indians rode into the camp of an overland train and were fed. "Mrs Oppenheimer pointed one of the Indians out as a white man and we all laughed at her." After midnight the Indians attempted to stampede the stock and failed. In the morning, however, they ran off some cattle from another train. "The immigrants followed the Indians, recovered the cattle, and killed three Indians, or two Indians and a white man." The white man "hollered, 'For God's sake don't kill me,' and the men asked him what he was doing there and he replied, 'This is the way I make my living.' They gave him a bullet and sent him to his long home." It was, the writer noted, "the only accident we had" crossing the plains.[71]

---

[71]Burgunder, "Reminiscences," pp. 1–2.

*Protecting the Elephant*

# 5 | SOLDIERS AND EMIGRANTS

There were two United States military posts on the overland trail: Fort Kearny on the Platte River, established when most emigrants were headed for Oregon, and Fort Laramie on the North Platte, purchased from the American Fur Company during the first month of the Gold Rush. There was also Fort Hall, guarding the Oregon trail at the Boise River. The government acquired it from the Hudson's Bay Company but stationed troops there for so short a period that it played no military or policing role in the history of the overland emigrations.

Army officers stationed at the forts watched out for what they called "white Indians." "Judging by the events of last summer," the acting adjutant general wrote a commander patrolling the emigration of 1860, "there is a tribe of Indians who have blue eyes and light hair, who wear whiskers, and speak good English. They may always be regarded as so hostile that no terms are to be made with them."[1]

Military officers had to be concerned about white crime. During the first year of the California Gold Rush the ranks of the banditry had been swelled by army deserters. Like the naval ships then at anchor in San Francisco harbor, military units west of the Mississippi in 1849 were plagued by desertion. "The dragoons are continually deserting," a forty-niner wrote of Companies G and B then on their way to occupy Fort Hall. "20 out of 60 having absconded & they are on the look out (for they say so openly) to do so continually & it is almost impossible to prevent it."[2] By the

[1]Unruh, *Plains*, p. 193.
[2]Entry for 26 June 1849, Gray, *Passage*.

time the forces reached Fort Hall, a second forty-niner reported, "62 had deserted and gone after" the first twenty. The commanding officer sent men to arrest them "but it is of no use," the emigrant thought. "The pursuers will only join their comrades and all go on together."[3]

That statement summarizes the general pattern of desertion and the general attitude of emigrants. When eighteen soldiers overpowered the horse guard at Fort Laramie, taking "the best horses in the troop," emigrants doubted they would be overtaken. "A party left to-day to retake them," one wrote, "but the odds are greatly in favour of the deserters, especially if the capturing party take it into their heads to shoot their officer, and join the fugitives in the attempt to make their fortunes in California."[4] As a whole, the emigrants misjudged the military. One prediction, for example, that most troops would desert and, once through South Pass, even officers would throw up their commissions and head for the placers, simply did not happen.[5]

Emigrants occasionally aided deserters, giving them food and even old coats to replace their uniforms,[6] but as a rule they supported efforts to recapture them. An overland company of 1849 lent three armed men to an army officer to help him track down deserters.[7] The army gave emigrants an incentive by posting a $200 reward for every runaway brought back. "The object of this liberal offer," a forty-niner believed, "is not only to stop future desertion, but to prevent the deserters joining other renegades and becoming strong enough to take either the government trains or robbing bod-

---

[3]Entry for 21 July 1849, Mann, "Portion," p. 11.

[4]Entry for 26 July 1849, Coke, *Ride*, p. 156. For a similar prediction by an army officer, see Hafen and Young, *Fort Laramie*, pp. 168–69.

[5]Letter of 31 May 1849, Harker, "Letters," pp. 52–53.

[6]Entry for 6 June 1849, Austin, *Diary* ("we gave them some bacon and bread"); entry for 18 July 1849, Middleton, "Across the Plains," p. 17 ("old coats").

[7]Entry for 22 July 1849, Bruff, *Journals*, p. 51.

ies of emigrants, for the desertion has proceeded to such an alarming extent as to render either object probable."[8] Actually, it had been done "for the safety of the command," the officer who announced the reward later explained. "Many had already deserted, and I had certain information that large numbers were to follow. Every exertion had been made to avert it, [and] frequent pursuit and all other means had been resorted to without avail. Upon publishing the notice desertions immediately ceased, and although we passed several roads leading to California few or no attempts were made."[9]

The most notorious deserters were four mounted riflemen on a march to Oregon who left their unit in the area of Green River. Heading toward California, they passed a camp where they found a woman alone. "They compelled her to open her trunk and took all the money, which was $115. They then ravished her one after the other in immediate succession: then they left."[10] An army captain was immediately on their trail, offering passing companies $100 "to send on a man or men to catch them."[11] With help from members of the Boston Company he captured all four of them.[12] It was understood by an eyewitness that "he intended to take [them] back to Ft. Laramie, making them perform the whole journey on foot."[13]

---

[8]Entry for 10 July 1849, Wilkins, *An Artist*, p. 54.

[9]Loring, "Report," p. 335. Earlier an emigrant, apparently hoping for payment at Fort Laramie, betrayed a deserter whom he had hidden. "We all in camp, heartily despise him for his treachery & meanness to the dragoon." Entries for 21–22 May 1849, Gray, *Passage.*

[10]Entry for 24 July 1849, Middleton, "Across the Plains," p. 31.

[11]Entry for 25 July 1849, Staples, *Diary*, p. 144.

[12]Entry for 4 August 1849, Middleton, "Across the Plains," p. 64. Middleton, who was not a witness, says three were recaptured and the fourth shot. Emigrants who met the officer returning east said he had four prisoners.

[13]Entry for 29 July 1849, Gould, *Diary*, p. 149. Perhaps they did walk, as four days later they were only at Pacific Springs. Entry for 1 August 1849, Austin, *Diary*. Next day the officer met an emigrant company, and recognized as a deserter a man "who had joined us a few days ago," and arrested him. Entry for 2 August 1849, Hall, "Diary," p. 8.

Most emigrants, at least in 1849, expected the army to perform such a role and police the overland trail. They thought the troops would keep the trail safe by arresting wrongdoers and holding them in some form of custody. A forty-niner at the crossing of the North Platte took a good deal of comfort from meeting a party of soldiers "returning to Ft. Laramie, with some stolen cattle & horses & two of the men that stole them. The soldiers remarked that we did not need the company of the two men on this route & so they thought they would take them back & they are right."[14]

That was the expectation emigrants had had when starting west: that United States troops would track down overland travelers who by force or other means stole the possessions of fellow travelers,[15] and that officers at the forts, upon receiving complaints from victims of crime, would police behavior on the trail.[16] In 1850 an allopath from Indiana explained the emigrants' ideal.

> I left Fort Laramie with regret, not for any thing it contained, but because it was the last link that bound us to our native land. Heretofore or now, if difficulty, accident, or disease occurred, we had the friendly authorities of the Fort to rely upon. Even grievances or wrongs between one & another could be here adjusted, as the strong arm of the law, even here, protected the injured and oppressed; but after leaving here, we were without the pail of protection.[17]

---

[14]Entry for 21 June 1849, Wood, *Diaries*.

[15]For citation of two diaries reporting that troops did perform in this manner, see Unruh, *Plains Across*, p. 331.

[16]"At Fort Laramie the commanding officer daily received complaints about emigrants robbing one another." Ibid., p. 280.

[17]Entry for 31 May 1850, McBride, *Diary*.

This was not quite true. Before the day was out the doctor had evidence that the military was still watching over the emigration.

> Three soldiers came riding up to an old man who was driving a three horse team, and accosting said, "See here old man, you must go back with us to the Fort." For some time the old man said not a word, but at length replied reluctantly: "well I suppose I can" — accordingly he turned around his team & drove back. This old man had quarreled with, & mistreated a man who was traveling with [him?], who had applied to the commandant for redress. The commander of the Fort acts something as a Spanish Alcalde — settling difficulties amicably if possible, if not, he settles them equitably, but if the offenses are very grave, he sends the accused back to "the States" for trial.[18]

It would be unwise to guess how so educated a man could have concocted so farfetched a vision of dispute settlement and law enforcement on the overland trail. It is possible, even likely, that the commanding officer at Fort Laramie adjudicated a few civilian controversies, but these disputes almost certainly had to have occurred in the vicinity of the post and, perhaps, threatened to disturb the peace. But that he ever attempted to enforce judgments or ordered the incarceration of citizens for a civil offense short of violence is most unlikely.[19]

It is important to consider both the role of the military in pre-Civil War America and its authority, especially its power over

---

[18]Ibid.
[19]But see Unruh, *Plains Across*, pp. 331–32; Mattes, *Narratives*, p. 549.

civilians. We can accept stories that troops would arrest emigrants for desecrating Indian graves or attempting to violate Indian women.[20] It was quite another matter for the officer in charge of either Fort Kearny or Fort Laramie to send soldiers to arrest an emigrant for knifing a member of his train during a quarrel. It is true that some diaries tell us that they did, but none of these accounts was written by an eyewitness and none provides essential information, such as whether the fight occurred on the fort's grounds or even within the extended military reservation that the commandant considered to be under his jurisdiction.[21]

When they reported military enforcement of legal behavior on the overland trail there was a gap between what some emigrants expected the army to do and what the troops had authority to do. An indication of the expectations of some emigrants comes from the diary of an Illinois man going to Oregon in 1852. Somewhere along the South Platte a husband and wife killed another couple for their outfit and started on the back track for the Missouri River. "Within a day or two the dead bodies of the murdered couple were discovered in the brush near where they had camped," the man recorded in his diary. "The officers at Fort Laramie were immediately notified of the murder. Suspicion rested on the couple who had turned back, and the commander sent a squad of soldiers in pursuit, who soon overtook and apprehended the murderers. We heard later that they were tried at Fort Laramie on the charge of murder, convicted and hanged."[22]

We can dismiss this story as an overland rumor, an event the writer heard about long after it occurred, an account that was not

[20]Unruh, *Plains Across*, p. 331.
[21]See, for example, entry for 25 May 1852, Rudd, *Notes by the Wayside*; Rudd, *Notes*, p. 6; Mattes, *Narratives*, p. 283.
[22]Entry for 22 June 1852, Conyers, "1852 Diary," p. 444.

even hearsay but embellished by several retellings.[23] Even the most extensively documented case of a trial of a civilian at one of the forts is not persuasive. This trial occurred in 1849 at Fort Kearny and, again, the tale is told by emigrants who were not witnesses.

> A day or two previous to our arrival, an emigrant was tried here for shooting one of his comrades. He was taking his family to California, and when a few miles beyond the fort, a man offered a gross insult to his wife. In a country where there was no law — where redress could not be had by a legal process — he determined to protect his own honor, and raising his rifle, shot the scoundrel down. His companions took him back to the Fort (with his consent,) where an investigation into the circumstances was made, and he was honorably acquitted.[24]

Most accounts say that the victim was not shot but killed by a blow to his skull by an axe. He was "a man of no character,"[25] who reportedly had been tried for rape in Iowa the year before,[26] and was trying to crawl into the bed of his messmate's wife, despite having been warned to get out.[27]

The account quoted above, that says the man was shot, was written for publication and became a popular guidebook for the emigrations of 1854 and subsequent years. By saying that the hus-

---

[23]"The hanging of a couple at Fort Laramie is a most unlikely story." Mattes, *Narratives*, p. 348.

[24]Entry for 23 May 1849, Delano, *Life*, p. 50.

[25]Entry for 20 May 1849, Tiffany, *Journal*.

[26]Davis, "Introduction and Notes," pp. 171–72 (quoting the *Oquawka Spectator*, 25 July 1849).

[27]One account says that the would-be rapist was arrested by the soldiers, which would have made this a very different story. Mattes, *Narratives*, pp. 192–93 (citing Muscott, "Letters").

band "was tried" at Fort Kearny and "honorably acquitted" the author left the impression for future emigrants that the army had exercised jurisdiction over a civilian homicide. But an emigrant who heard about the affair three days earlier—yet was himself already two days' travel beyond the fort—implied that there had been no arrest and no trial. "A kind of examination was had at the fort before the officer in command," he wrote, "but the matter was drop[p]ed and the parties permitted to pass on."[28] If we combine the two accounts—one saying that the manslayer returned to the fort voluntarily and the other that there was a "kind of examination" that was "dropped"—a plausible reading of the evidence is that the manslayer asked for a pro forma hearing, seeking exoneration if not vindication. The commandant conducted it much as he would have conducted a court martial to determine that some action by a fellow officer was an accident, justifiable, excusable, or otherwise not blameworthy. Even the most liberal reading of the evidence no more than suggests that the army *may have* taken jurisdiction over the case and subjected the manslayer to an administrative investigation.

Some emigrants not only presumed that the military would pursue, arrest, and try suspected wrongdoers, but they also acted on that presumption. Along the Bear River in 1849 several travellers saw a Mormon "beat a half Breed Indian nearly to death." They took the man into custody "to hand over to the government troops when they came along."[29] Following a shooting in the area of Ash Hollow, the culprit was seized by his fellow emigrants. Apparently they conducted a preliminary hearing, not a formal trial, for the verdict was "that the prisoner be taken to Fort Laramie

---

[28]Entry for 20 May 1849, Tiffany, *Journal*. Also, see entry for 23 May 1849, Steuben, "Journal," p. 5.

[29]Entry for 13 July 1849, Mann, "Portion," p. 9.

and delivered up to the military authorities to be sent home for trial."[30] In both these cases emigrants acted on the assumption that the army could accept custody of prisoners, try them if it chose, and even punish them.[31]

Jurisdictional reality, however, was the opposite of common expectation. It is possible to believe that the army, when it passed along the trail, would offer to transport to Oregon two men convicted by fellow emigrants of attempted murder, but there was not much else the military could do. It just did not have jurisdiction or authority over civilian offenses. Even the two men whom the troops offered to escort to Oregon were set free. All the witnesses were headed for California so there was no point taking the prisoners north to be released at the end of the trail.[32] Although the laws of the United States providing "for the punishment of crimes committed within the sole and exclusive jurisdiction of the United States," were in force against nonIndians in the Indian country,[33] the army was vested with no authority to execute them. The soldiers had a duty to keep liquor out of the territory but very little else. It was not even any longer necessary for civilians to obtain passports to pass through Indian nations.[34] Emigrants might fault the military for not interfering when self-appointed courts condemned manslayers to death,[35] but the officers who stood by while executions were carried out believed they were the ones obeying the law.

---

[30]Mattes, *Platte River Road*, p. 81; Mattes, *Narratives*, p. 297.

[31]For example, entry for 9 July 1849, Banks, "Diary," p. 36; Mattes, *Platte River Road*, pp. 80–81; Mattes, *Narratives*, p. 261.

[32]They were, however, "sentenced" "to return to the States, and if caught on the road or in California, they will be shot." Entry for 20 July 1849, Banks, "Diary," p. 46. The "sentence" must have been imposed by emigrants, not the army.

[33]"The Intercourse Act," Sec. 25, 4 *Statutes at Large* 729, 733 (1834).

[34]Sec. 2, ibid., p. 729.

[35]Mattes, *Narratives*, p. 544.

Just what the authority of the military was is not as certain as we would expect. It is not known what officers were told about how to deal with and police civilians on the overland trail. Surely the army had some role in an area beyond the jurisdiction of any civilian authority, but no orders are extant. Even particular commands detailing an assignment failed to include any consideration of the issue. The commander of the Mounted Riflemen posted to Oregon in 1849 was instructed how to organize the regiment, what to carry, what civilian teamsters could be hired, and when to start, but nothing was said concerning duties to or responsibilities for emigrants encountered along the route.[36] Officers leading dragoons onto the plains were told that the "purpose" of going was for "giving protection to emigrants, and restraining and favourably influencing the Indian tribes on the plains." Nothing else was said about civilians, whether they could be furnished supplies if in need, whether disputes should or even could be adjudicated, whether emigrants could be apprehended if suspected of crime, and whether witnesses could be taken into custody and escorted east to testify in federal court.[37]

One conclusion is beyond doubt. Civilians going west over the trail thought the army was there to protect them. "The object of this garrison," a physician wrote of Fort Kearny, "is said to [be to] overawe the Indians of this region of the U.S. Territories and thus

---

[36]Orders No. 8, 9 February 1849, *Sixth Military Department*, pp. 15–17. Also, see Letter from Assistant Advocate General D. C. Buell to Colonel J. Plympton, 29 May 1849, *Sixth Military Department Letter Book*, p. 81. For the report of the commander after the march was completed, see Loring, "Report," pp. 331–43.

[37]Orders No. 10, 25 March 1850, *Sixth Military Department*, pp. 132–33. Admittedly, instructions regarding Indians were often as general. The commanders at Fort Kearny and Fort Laramie were told: "In their necessary contact with the Indian tribes, their official conduct cannot exhibit too much activity and firmness, nor at the same time, too much discretion and justice." Orders No. 44, 21 November 1849, ibid., p. 107.

protect the Emigrants."[38] The doctor was only partially correct. The year that this emigrant went overland the commandant of the post was given these orders:

> With a view to give confidence to the emigrants passing on the routes to New Mexico, California and Oregon and afford them protection as well as to diminish the chances of attack from hostile bands of Indians, the commanding officers at the several frontier stations, will cause detachments of suitable strength to be sent out from their commands, to patrol and examine the country along these routes, to such extent as will insure, as far as practicable, the security and protection designed to be afforded.[39]

Less than three months later army officers were reminded "that, while it is their duty to protect the whites against the Indians, they are also to prevent, or remedy, as far as possible, all depredations upon Indians, by Emigrants passing through their country, or by other persons."[40] What did the word remedy mean? Did it include restitution extracted from the wrongdoers, seizure of their property, or even punishment? These questions were surely discussed but there is no direct evidence of how they were resolved.[41]

---

[38]Tompkins, *Expedition*, p. 58 (1850). Foreign emigrants had the same idea. See for example, entry for 24 May 1854, Kleinsorge, "Diary," p. 433.

[39]Orders No. 7, 14 March 1850, *General Orders*.

[40]Letter from Assistant Advocate General D. C. Buell, 30 May 1849, *Sixth Military Department Letter Book*, pp. 81–84.

[41]In the one known case of a civilian held as a prisoner, the commander of Fort Laramie was reprimanded for sending him to Fort Leavenworth. The officer was told that he had exceeded his authority as he was, in effect, ordering the commandant at Leavenworth to take custody of the prisoner. It is not clear, but it appears that he was not told that he had exceeded his authority in holding the civilian in military custody. Letter from Adjutant General Irwin MacDowell to Captain William S. Ketchum, 15 April 1852, ibid., p. 174.

The one area of authority of which we can be certain concerns the commission of crimes within the jurisdiction of the forts. Two brothers got into a fight while playing cards at Fort Laramie. They both had bowie knives. One was killed. "The living one was taken into custody at the fort, also the two that were playing with them as accomplices."[42] If army horses were stolen from the post, soldiers would not only go in pursuit to recover the government's property, they would bring back "the emigrant suspected" of theft.[43] Just what the military did with the thieves, however, has to be guessed.[44] An officer described one "punishment" that occurred when his regiment passed through Fort Laramie on its march to Oregon.

> A corporal who had been sent out to find some missing horses brought in two, and with them an emigrant in whose possession he had found them. . . . [N]o proof existed on which to found a conviction of horse stealing, nor was the arrest directed by any authority. Some of the younger officers and citizens traveling with the regiment determined, however, to make some fun out of the affair and organized a drumhead court-martial on their own account. A judge-advocate, the most noted wag in the regiment, was appointed on behalf of the government and a citizen as counsel for the defense. The contest was carried on with due vehemence

---

[42]Letter from Alphonso B. Newcomb to Solurous Wakeley, 13 July 1850 (ms., State Historical Society of Iowa, Iowa City).

[43]Entry for 20 June 1849, Parke, *Notes*; Parke, *Diary*, p. 38; entry for 19 June 1849, Stackpole, *Journal*.

[44]Although a forty-niner has left a hint. At Fort Laramie he wrote: "Nothing interesting except the tying up and whipping of a white man." Entry for 17 June 1849, Caldwell, "Notes," p. 1254.

and personality, the prisoner of course convicted, and sentence of death passed upon him with awful solemnity by the president.

Given fifteen minutes to prepare for his execution, the emigrant was permitted to escape "amidst a volley of balls fired in every direction but his." The officer who wrote this account was a lawyer. The fact that he said there was "no proof" on which to convict the man suggests that had there been evidence he would have been held for trial. But where? At Fort Laramie or back in a federal court? The army would have had to send the arresting corporal to be a witness. Even the "drumhead" proceeding was improper. It had been conducted out of sight of the colonel commanding the regiment. When told about the affair, it "was censured extremely by him."[45]

There was only one category of offenses where the army unquestionably assumed jurisdiction over emigrants. It involved crimes special to the military posts. One of these was sale of liquor. "Citizens" as well as soldiers "at or near" Fort Laramie were "prohibited selling, exchanging, giving, bartering or otherwise disposing of the same at or in the vicinity of the post."[46] At Fort Kearny in 1850 civilian violators were imprisoned and may have been fined. "[T]hare was some men in encampment," an emigrant wrote, "that sold liquor to the soldiers and they were fiend and to [two] of them taken to the forte and confined and the rest of their liquor turned out of the casque."[47] By "fiend" he may have meant that some of the men were fined. More likely he meant that they were found out.

---

[45]Gibbs, "Diary," pp. 325-26. For Gibbs's other profession, see Settle, "Introduction," p. 24.

[46]Order No. 1, 1 January 1852, *Fort Laramie Orders*. Also, see Post Order No. 8, 30 May 1853, *Laramie Letters Received*.

[47]Entry for 11 June 1850, Davis, "California Diary," p. 177.

A second special offense was buying army property. "Citizens are hereby warned," an order issued at Fort Laramie provided, "not to violate the law prohibiting the purchase of soldiers clothing, arms, equipment, &c."[48] The order may have been intended for civilians working for or at the fort, but it was enforced against emigrants and caused a good deal of hard feelings. "The soldiers are very insolent to emigrants, stripping them of old soldier clothes, belts, pistols, etc.," a late traveler on the overland trail complained. "They are no protection to emigrants at all."[49] What especially upset emigrants were officers who seized animals stamped with the "US" brand. It did not matter that the possessors had made bona fide purchases or that the sellers had assured them the horses or mules had been sold as surplus by the army. Some officers insisted that any animal with government markings had been stolen and could be repossessed. "The protection afforded to emigrants by the chain of Military Posts is only another name for robbery," an emigrant objected, when a company mule was seized at Fort Laramie. "In consequence of this high-handed piece of villainy we struck our tent and drove four miles."[50]

When, however, property was stolen by one emigrant from another or by "white Indians" from emigrants, the army usually did nothing. On one occasion it refused to interfere even though the thieves were a mixture of white and red Indians and the taking occurred less than a day's wagon ride from Fort Laramie.[51] More

---

[48]Order No. 1, 1 January 1852, *Fort Laramie Orders.*
[49]Entry for 20 June 1864, Dunlap, "Journal," p. 18.
[50]Mattes, *Platte River Road,* p. 495.
[51]Entry for 4 June 1864, Epperson, "Journal," pp. 175–76. Contrary, see a very doubtful account of an army officer who not only pursued a thief but "deliberately shot him notwithstanding he begged the officer to spare his life." Entry for 28 July 1860, Fish, *Daily Journal,* p. 53.

telling were the occasions when emigrants arrested, tried, and executed suspected manslayers just outside the fort and the military did nothing.[52] In fact, the army was less likely to stop executions than to help emigrants capture suspected manslayers.[53] Or, if the troops had a suspected manslayer in custody, they would turn him over to the emigrants, knowing that the accused would be tried and, if found guilty, would be executed.[54] The army just did not have jurisdiction or authority to do anything else, unless it had been willing to set free a possible killer. Even if it had had the resources to keep the suspect in custody and to take him hundreds of miles back along the trail to a federal court, there was no point. It would have had to bring back the witnesses as well and they were all going in the other direction.[55] Without witnesses, no court would have indicted the prisoners, let alone convicted them. Except for dealing with the Indian nations, the military had no significant role to play in maintaining law and punishing offenders on the overland trail.[56]

---

[52]For example, Mattes, *Narratives*, p. 382.

[53]Entry for 3 July 1849, Delano, *Across the Plains*, p. 52.

[54]Letter of 25 July 1862, Anderson, *Letters*; Mattes, *Narratives*, p. 542.

[55]Mattes, *Narratives*, p. 261; Mattes, *Platte River Road*, p. 81.

[56]The army did exercise more authority during the turmoil of the Civil War when the Sioux and other nations were attacking along the overland trail. It was claimed that then emigrants had to comply with military regulations

> which required that we travel under military discipline, in fighting strength of no less than one hundred able bodied men in a train, and that the caravan be officered by men who had previous experience in the bad lands of the frontier, and that careful sworn reports be made to the next commanding officer of disobedience, infraction or insubordinations to be dealt with according to the code of duty as viewed by a Military Court.

Entry for 22 May 1865, McDonald, "A Story," p. 29. Also, see entry for 19 May 1864, Epperson, "Journal," p. 169.

*Killing the Elephant*

# 6 | DEATH AND HOMICIDE

It is easy to keep a focus. Several types of crimes and other antisocial acts occurred on the overland trail to the Pacific, but only one tells our story about how average nineteenth-century Americans understood the law for the trial of wrongdoing and the punishment of offenders. Emigrants were very concerned about delicts such as fighting, conversion of property, quarreling, grass burning, and violation of road rules. They seldom, however, discussed how they dealt with these matters, except to note that horse thieves were pursued and white Indians shot. The one act that mobilized travelers on the overland trail to arrest an offender, put the wrongdoer on trial, and inflict punishment was homicide or what they invariably termed "murder." It was also the crime about which they commented the most and about which, therefore, they expressed their thoughts on procedure, civil rights, judicial fairness, and the right of citizens, on their own authority, to enforce law and order beyond the pale of police, courts, judges, or even law itself.

Death was everywhere on the overland trail. Emigrants died from drowning, stampedes, falling from or being run over by wagons, suicide, occasional Indian encounters, and, most frequently, sickness.[1] Apart from disease, most deaths resulted from firearms not fired in anger. "Cox killed a rabbit," an emigrant noted on his fifty-fourth day on the trail to California, "the first living thing he ever killed in his life."[2] Cox was not unusual. Many emigrants had

---

[1] Drunkenness was not a major problem on the overland trail, but it did contribute to all the other causes of death just mentioned, for example, drowning. Entry for 2 June 1853, Allyn, "Journal," p. 395.

[2] Entry for "54th Night," 1854, Taylor, "California Journal," p. 7.

done little hunting before starting west. Even more had never been taught how to handle weapons.

Yet everyone on the trail had weapons. They may not have known how to handle them but they possessed them. "Arms of all kinds must certainly be scarce in the States, after such a drain as the emigrants must have made upon them," a newspaper correspondent wrote from Fort Kearny in 1849. "No man but what has a gun or a revolver or two, and one fellow I saw, actually had no less than three bowie knives stuck in his belt."[3] "The United States armies were never armed as these emigrants are," another correspondent reported, "every one a little afraid of the Indians has prepared himself, if necessary, to force his way through the uncivilized country . . . there is hardly a wagon but what can give out from six to thirty shots from rifles, revolvers, pistols, &c. without even halting to load."[4] "[B]etter armed men probably never went out to bloody warfare," an emigrant thought as he contemplated the start of the 1850 emigration from a bluff above St. Joseph.[5]

Every emigration, even the early ones including the family trains going to Oregon, had too many arms. "If serious accidents do not occur," an officer of an 1843 company wrote, "they will be avoided by great good luck, not precaution."[6] He was thinking about firearms in the hands of untrained and very careless emigrants. Near Ash Hollow in 1852

---

[3]To the St Louis *Republican*, 18 May 1849, Read and Gaines, "Introduction," pp. 466–67*n*104.

[4]Letter from M. L. Wisner to *The Western Christian*, 10 May 1849, loose newspaper clipping inside pocket of back cover, Lord, *Journal*. For an emigrant's description, see Goldsmith, *Overland*, pp. 8–9.

[5]Entry for 28 April 1850, McBride, *Diary*.

[6]James Nesmith quoted in Lavender, *Westward*, p. 373.

4 of us started out from the camp to hunt some stray cat[t]le perfectly unarmed    soon after there started two more that never left the camp whithout [*sic*] being armed with rifle and Pistol  When about half a mile from the camp they hove in sight one of the men that was ahead said that we would scare the other Boys and have some fun    so down we sent [*sic*] on all fours  Bang went a rifle    down went one of our men they sup[p]oseing us to be Wolves   he died in about twenty minutes   so much for fun on the Plains.[7]

Reckless firing of weapons was a minor danger. Far more deadly was careless handling of firearms. Diaries are filled with accounts of emigrants wounding or killing themselves because they did not know how to handle guns. When the mountain man Kit Carson came north to sell "Santa Fe mules" to the 1850 emigration,[8] he witnessed a young man kill himself while loading a pistol. "I have been telling you all the time," Carson scolded an acquaintance, "that these emigrants not knowing how to use fire arms ware more dangerous to them selves & everyone around [them]." In fact, he would not travel with or camp near an emigrant train. "[H]e said he would much prefer fighting Indians than traveling behing [*sic*] emigrant wagons."[9]

Plenty of emigrants had that same worry. "I confess to more fear from careless handling of fire-arms than from any external foe," a

---

[7]Entry for 4 June 1852, Anon., "Diary." Similarly, see entry for 18 July 1849, Pritchard, *Diary*, pp. 117–18.

[8]Entry for 31 May 1850, McBride, *Diary*; entry for 3 June 1850, Loomis, *Journal*, p. 35.

[9]Harvey, *To California*, pp. 41–42. For another summary of "firearms accidents" on the overland trail see, Munkres, "Plains Indian Threat," pp. 215–16.

forty-niner later recalled.[10] "I am more fearful from the carelessness of my companions than of all the indians from the borders of civilization to the Pacific," another emigrant wrote the next year, after a man was shot due to carelessness.[11] Part of the tragedy, many realized, was that there was no need for these weapons except for hunting. "So far, a gun is of little use except to fire off, clean out and load up again every three or four days," an emigrant wrote after crossing most of the Rocky Mountains.[12]

We know much more about accidental killings on the overland trail than of intentional homicide because they happened far more frequently. More to the point, the accidents generally occurred in camp and were witnessed by the writer, who recorded the event soon after in a diary or made notes for later reference. The overwhelming majority of accounts of deliberate killings, by contrast, are hearsay, second-, third-, and even fourth-hand, and are not always reliable. Occasionally the diarist got not just some, but all the facts of a homicide wrong.[13] At other times the information is more speculative than accurate. "[M]any murders are committed on the plains," a physician wrote after arriving in Oregon. "I think there were not less than 50 last year.  many of the murderers were detected, & hung, but many escaped without being detected.  we saw nothing of the kind, but I have seen many who have."[14] He was guessing. The emigration of 1852, the year he wrote about,

---

[10]Ansel J. McCall quoted in Potter, "Introduction," p. 60.

[11]Entry for 17 May 1850, Newcomb, *Journal*. "I felt persuaded that more danger is to be apprehended from the carelessness of arms among fellow emigrants, than from the hostile Indian." Brown, "Gold Seeker," p. 140; Brown, *Memoirs*, p. 13 (June 1849).

[12]Letter of 7 August 1853, Taylor, "Letters," p. 147.

[13]See discussion of an 1862 example. Mattes, *Narratives*, p. 543. We know the facts of this incident because witnesses recorded the event on a headboard near the grave of the victim, and subsequent emigrants copied its message in diaries. See, for example, entry for 13 July 1862, Cook, "Diary Letters," p. 49.

[14]White, "Oregon Letter," p. 30.

seems to have had the largest number of known intentional homicides and the largest number of executions of any emigration. But whether the total even came close to fifty killings is, at best, a guess. Perhaps it did, but if so it is unlikely it went higher.

Often our information is pure hearsay. "A man was supposed to have been murdered near the ferry, as he had a ball through the eye," is a typical report.[15] The writer was already a day's journey beyond the ferry when he learned the news. The emigrant who may have recorded the most victims of homicide—during the bloody year of 1852—did so by counting graves. She mentioned three on 29 June, one on the 30th, and next day, although she did not see the grave, "we learn that another man was found murdered near where the others were found." Ten days later she recalled passing "2 or 3 days ago another grave of a murdered man — the murderer was buried near."[16] From her account it appears that six people were killed, and it is likely that some if not all of them were killed by malice aforethought, but that is all we know.

Much more is learned when someone in the writer's company found the body. Of course, they were not always certain there had been a murder. "Today we found a part of a skeleton of some poor fellow who had been murdered or perished on his way for the Golden land," an emigrant noted in 1850 when passing through today's southern Idaho.[17] Two years later, back on the Little Blue, a body was found that had "most likely been murdered,"[18] and another that "was shot" although the discovers "could not tell if Indians done it."[19] The emigrants were not as quick to blame

---

[15]Entry for 20 June 1849, Hillyer, "Journal," p. 234.

[16]Entries for 29, 30 June, 1, 10 July 1852, Coon, "Journal," pp. 192, 194. Similarly, see entry for 21 May 1852, Hanna, *Journal*, p. 32.

[17]Entry for 15 July 1850, Griffith, "Diary of 1850," p. 73.

[18]Entry for 17 May 1852, Snodgrass, *Journal.*

[19]Entry for 24 May 1852, Laird, *Book.* For two killings on the Little Blue attributed to Pawnees, see entry for 23 May 1850, Brown, "Journal to California," p. 20.

Indians as we might think, for they usually weighed the evidence before making a judgment. In 1852 a man was found "shot through the vitals & head with a pistol," and "also scalped. But no one thinks the Indians done it. First because what Powder & Balls he had about him were not taken, his clothes were also left, things which the Indians would certainly have taken sooner than any thing else."[20]

We learn the most when the writer actually examined the evidence or found the body. Also in 1852, another emigrant passed by the place where a man had been killed eleven days earlier. "All his clothes were burnt with the exception of his shirt, which I saw myself," he wrote. "It had quite a number of holes in it, where he had been shot and stabbed, and it was all covered with blood."[21] Thanks to the eyewitness there is no doubt the man was killed by another individual, and the multiple wounds indicate the act had been deliberate. That surmise is even more certain for a body discovered a month later, just before the crossing of the North Platte.

> Soon after we drove down to the river we saw a man floating down stream, Schuyler Fowler swam in and brourght [*sic*] him to shore. . . . A whiplash tied around his body, the sto[c]k of which hung loose, has two brass rings on his left hand.  one marked with the letter F.W. and a heavy gold ring on his

---

[20]Entry for 25 May 1852, Bradley, *Daily Journal.* Five days later the writer was told that the victim had been killed by a member of his company. For other accounts of bodies being discovered, see entry for 25 August 1851, Wood, "Journal of a Trip," p. 201; entry for 16 June 1863, Yager, "Diary," p. 14; Eaton, *Overland,* p. 56. Once the body discovered was that "of a woman who had been murdered." Entry for 20 June 1852, McAuley, "Record," p. 57.

[21]Entry for 30 May 1852, Hickman, *Overland Journey,* p. 6; Mattes, *Platte River Road,* p. 77.

right hand but his fingers were so swollen that we could get but one of them off, which we will preserve for identification. We are of the opinion that he was killed and thrown in the river, his body and head having the appearances of bruises on them.[22]

Once again there is no doubt these emigrants had found a murder victim.

We often learn about homicides and executions of manslayers because eyewitnesses wrote an account of what happened and posted it along the trail for the information of later emigrants. Some of those coming along copied what was said or made notes in their diaries. It is these later diarists, who recorded what they saw posted, that are our informants. Too often it is but a short entry, telling us little except that a homicide had occurred. "We passed the grave of Mathias Beal of Boon County, Ky., who had been shot on the 12th day of June by Leon Bolsey of the same place" is a good example of the information that they copied.[23] The one thing of value that this account tells us is that the manslayer and the victim were probably not strangers. As they were both from the same county they very likely were traveling together. Not all entries are that helpful. In most instances the grave marker identified only the victim and the killer and said that the latter had been shot or hanged. An emigrant of 1859 probably copied the entire headboard when he wrote, "Saw a new grave marked 'John Snyder Shot by James Garner may 14'."[24]

---

[22]Entry for 19 June 1852, Graham, "Journal," pp. 10–11; Koch, "Big Circle," p. 55.

[23]Entry for 3 July 1852, Graham, "Journal," p. 13. For other readings of the same headboard, see entry for 4 July 1852, Thorniley, *Diary* (the writer later learned the circumstances of the killing); entry for 11 July 1852, Dalton, "Diary," p. 22; entry for 25 July 1852, Gee, *Journal*; Todd, "Forward," p. 59n48.

[24]Entry for 20 May 1859, Wilkinson, *Across The Plains*. Similarly, see entry for 18 May 1859, Chillson, *Diary* (grave of Carpenter "murder[e]d but a few day's since");

Generally the messages were more informative. A board at the north fork of the Humboldt River in 1849 read, "Samuel A. Fitzsimmons, died of a wound inflicted by a bowie knife in the hands of James Remington, on the 25th of August 1849."[25] The bowie knife implies either that the homicide was an intentional murder or that the men had been fighting and weapons were drawn. By telling how the person died, some notices indicate clearly that the victim was murdered. The 1852 emigration saw three graves on the North Platte about five days' travel beyond Fort Laramie. "A message cut into a nearby tree stated that they were the graves of a man, a woman and a boy who were found near there with their throats cut from ear to ear."[26] The next year, in the mountains near the end of the Oregon trail, there was a grave "of a man that was found murdered on the 27th August, he had been shot near the right eye the ball coming out the back of the head — by the description given on a paper put upon a tree, it is supposed that he was coming from Oregon to meet some of his friends."[27]

As a general rule, the markers over the graves of the killers told more than those over their victims. At the very least they indicated that a trial and execution had occurred. At Goose Creek Mountains entering Nevada in 1859 emigrants saw the grave of Joseph Selleck "executed for the murder of W. Humble."[28] Seven years earlier along the North Platte an emigrant from Ohio "passed several graves to day.   last one we passed was a man that had been mur-

---

entry for 25 May 1852, Moreland, *Diary.*

[25]Entry for 27 August 1849, Lord, *Journal.* Also, see entry for 4 September 1849, Bruff, *Journals,* p. 163; entry for 5 September 1849, Austin, *Diary.*

[26]Entry for 29 June 1852, Stillman, "Recollections," p. 6. For the same sighting, see entry for 29 June 1852, Coon, "Journal," p. 192; entry for 26 June 1852, Loomis, *Memorandum.* Similarly, see entry for 1 June 1852.

[27]Entry for 29 August 1853, Dinwiddie, *Journal,* p. 12.

[28]Mattes, *Narratives,* p. 497 (quoting L. D. Chillson). "Two or three days ago we passed another grave of a murdered man. The murderer was buried near." Entry for

dered two days ago in cold blood.    Murdered J. Miller    murderer
Lafaette Sale." Next day the same party passed the La Bonte River
about noon and saw "the grave of the Murderer of J. Miller before
mentioned    [he] was followed by the emigrants to this place &
hung upon the tree until dead."[29] The writer got the executed man's
name wrong. It was Lafayette Tate, not Sale, whose capture and execution will be discussed below.

Of course, the best evidence comes from the diaries, journals,
and letters written by people who saw the killing or were in the
immediate vicinity. However, it is worth emphasizing again that
eyewitnesses, although generally more reliable, often tell us next to
nothing. "Next morning at the point of leaving," an emigrant wrote
at the South Pass, "a conflict took place which terminated in the
death of E. Brown. Buried him & left at 12 A.M." The only comment the writer offered was entered in the diary after they stopped
for the night and it makes little sense. "Still not satisfied with the
justice unfortunateness of the past day, owing all the Woman's
tounge,"[30] were words that undoubtedly meant something to the
diarist. After all, he was probably writing just for himself, certainly
not for us. He had seen the killing and knew what had happened,
so he needed only facts enough to refresh his memory and was not
concerned to tell the whole story.

Traveling along the Gila River in 1849, a company "was
alarm[ed] by one John Pearson coming in our camps at full speed
calling for the Doctor saying at the same time that one Georg[e]
Hickory had stab[b]ed Elijah Davis, we learned that he died in a
few minutes, at about 5 o'clock."[31] The writer probably learned all

---

10 July 1852, Stillman, "Recollections," p. 7.

[29]Entries for 17, 18 June 1852, Sharp, *Travel Diary*, pp. 63–65. For a similar sighting of the two graves, see entries for 30 June and 1 July 1852, Gee, *Journal.*

[30]Entry for 2 August 1857, "Menefee's Travels," p. 16.

[31]Entry for 5 September 1849, King, *Journal,* p. 60.

the facts but did not confide them all to his diary. In this case, as it happens, we have not lost much since others did describe what happened. This was one of the most extensively documented homicides in the history of the overland trail.

There were not many causes for homicide on the overland trail. "[S]eldom did they occur as the result of a love triangle," for example, as the leading authority on the Platte River section of the trail has pointed out.[32] "Contrary to the impression left by novelists and scenario writers, sex crimes were not commonplace in covered wagon days. Although the relative scarcity of women on the Trail might seem to contribute to such crimes, this is not borne out by available evidence."[33] There were, however, a few homicides that can be traced to sex. Already mentioned earlier was the husband who, below Fort Kearny, killed a man "attempting to get in bed with his wife."[34] That same year another husband "got a notion in his head that the familiarity that existed between Mr. L. and his wife was greater than the nature of the case warranted." It was, however, the husband who was shot.[35] Next year an emigrant from Indiana was told "that there was a man shot to day a few miles back for interfereing with a lady."[36] The year after that, near Jim Bridger's trading post, a grave was dug for James Monroe, shot by Howard Egen "for committing adultery with his wife."[37] The following year, emigrants arriving at the North Platte crossing in today's Casper, Wyoming, heard "about the tragedy across the River. There were two men and a woman concerned. The woman's husband attacked the other man and stabbed him to death. He was

---

[32]Mattes, *Narratives*, p. 373.
[33]Mattes, *Platte River Road*, pp. 77–78.
[34]Mattes, *Narratives*, p. 209 (quoting L. Shutterly).
[35]Mattes, *Platte River Road*, p. 78.
[36]Entry for 22 May 1850, Springer, *Day Book*.
[37]Mattes, *Narratives*, p. 325.

tried, convicted and hung, and the woman was sent back to the fort,"[38] that is, all the way back to Fort Laramie.

The most talked-about love triangle on the overland trail could better be described as a love pentagon. The relationship came to a head just beyond Devil's Gate on the Sweetwater River in 1849. "Yesterday," an emigrant explained, "Mr. Jenkins was shot while out from camp & wounded badly but not dangerously. The intention was to murder him on account of his wife."[39] Four months later another emigrant met Jenkins and was told that the affair was a bit more complicated than a husband, wife, and lover: "That a Reverend gentleman and his son, of the same company, had arranged to abscond with Mrs. J[enkins] and her daughter, and turn off to the Salt Lake settlement. In order to get Jenkins out of the way, the Rev. Mr. L[ancaster] attempted his life, but only wounded him with buckshot, in the neck; . . . my informant called my attention to the fact, that the old gentleman carries his head on one side. I pity the old gentleman."[40]

There were at least two cases where fathers killed young men for being too interested in their daughters. One was a nineteen-year-old who was "Shot by the man with him for makeing too free with his daughter."[41] The other, who was said to have waited until "he was beyond the reach of law and civilization," may have attempted rape.[42] Put another way, he "crept in" with the daughter of the man who killed him.[43]

---

[38]Entry for 23 June 1852, Egbert, "Record," pp. 26–27. See also McAuley, "Record," p. 58 (same date).

[39]Entry for 5 July 1849, Howell, *Diary*, p. 18.

[40]Read and Gaines, "Introduction," p. 620*n*205 (quoting entry for 5 November 1849, Bruff, *Journals*). It was reported incorrectly on the trail that Jenkins died of his wounds. Entry for 28 July 1849, Banks, *Diary*, p. 52.

[41]Entry for 12 June 1849, Littleton, "Journal," p. 8; Mattes, *Platte River Road*, p. 78.

[42]Letter of 19 May 1850, Ayres, "Letters."

[43]Mattes, *Narratives*, p. 233.

A second minor cause for homicide was property. Just as relatively little property was stolen on the overland trail, so also few emigrants were killed by fellow emigrants for their property. Generally bodies were found and robbery was suspected either because the victim was shot,[44] "his pockets were rifeled,"[45] other property was taken,[46] or he was suspected to have had "a considerable amount" of money.[47] In a few isolated cases the victim and perpetrator were not strangers but members of the same traveling company,[48] partners,[49] or fellow passengers.[50] A young boy who was orphaned when his father drowned continued overland with two Germans. "There is no doubt in the world [they] killed the boy last night and threw him in the river for the sake of getting the wagon and team!"[51]

We cannot be certain how many other homicides were committed to obtain property. They could have been concealed or not recorded in diaries. But even so—even if ten times the known cases took place—the number would still have been small. In fact, as Merrill Mattes has pointed out, writing of homicides which he calls "murders," "[t]he most common motive of covered wagon murders was not robbery but unleased antagonisms, small personal matters greatly magnified."[52] There may be no typical incident but one that happened on the southern branch of the overland trail, through Texas and today's New Mexico, comes close.

---

[44]Entry for 22 July 1852, Gee, *Journal.*

[45]Entry for 26 August 1853, Washburn, *Journal,* p. 28.

[46]Entry for 2 July 1852, Chadwick, *Travels;* Davis, "Introduction and Notes," pp. 198–99; Mattes, *Narratives,* pp. 303, 342, 378.

[47]Entry for 18 June 1852, Sawyer, "Notes from a Journal," p. 12; Sawyer, "Journal," p. 97.

[48]Froncek, "Winterkill," p. 37.

[49]Entry for 4 July 1849, Mann, "Portion," p. 5.

[50]Eaton, *Overland,* p. 150.

[51]Mattes, *Platte River Road,* p. 77.

[52]Ibid.

> On the 9th June [1849] two young men of the com-
> pany from Shelby County, Texas, named <u>Walter
> Beard</u> & <u>Byron B. Lee</u> belonging to the same mess
> had a dispute about a very trivial affair (a mess of
> beans I think) when <u>Walter</u>, the larger of the two
> jumped up after finishing his breakfast, while Lee
> was still in his hand cooking something for himself,
> which made the first attack I am unable to say as I
> did not see it. <u>Lee</u> however arose with his knife in
> his hand stabbed Walter in 3 places in consequence
> of which Walter died the next day.[53]

It was a quarrel like many others on the overland trail, not so much
about beans but growing out of irritations without end and an
accumulation of vexations. The only thing different in this affair
from thousands that are not reported in diaries is that when it started Lee had a knife in his hand.

Although fighting was the major cause of homicides on the
overland trail, few seem to have occurred between members of different companies. The sources are difficult to interpret on this
point, however, because our accounts generally say that two men
engaged in mortal combat, or had a gun fight in which one or both
were killed, but indicate nothing else except that they were not
known to the writer.[54] One report was written on the Humboldt
River. "While crossing the desert today," it said, "close to our camp
two men got into a quarrel and one stabbed the other three times.
The doctor supposed the wounds were mortal."[55] If the two fighters had been in "camp" as the writer seems to have been—that is,
stopped for the day or for the noon meal—then it is more likely

---

[53]Pownall, *Letter Book*, p. 4a. Also, see Cleland, "From Louisiana," p. 25.
[54]Mattes, *Narratives*, pp. 190, 214, 303.
[55]Entry for 24 August 1852, Richardson, "Diary of 1852."

that they belonged to the same traveling party. But if they were "crossing," that is, on the move, and some conflict arose on the road, they could have been strangers. "This day a man was shot in a fray & killed," a forty-niner wrote in his diary.[56] The fact the incident took place at the Green River ferry suggests they could have been from different companies,[57] but it is not certain. Most of the few homicides resulting from fights while emigrants were on the move occurred within companies, between men who knew each other and had been getting on one another's nerves for weeks. "In driving across the Mudy Run, or slew where we broke down," an emigrant wrote on the day he abandoned a wagon, "the driver of Dunmore's wagon broke the tongue. This ag[g]ravated Dunmore so he drew his pistol & shot Dunbar dead."[58]

Most homicides resulted from quarrels, and so the incidence of homicides followed the pattern that we have seen for quarreling and fighting. The majority that are reported in diaries occurred between people belonging to the same company, not between strangers.[59] And, of course, as with quarrels, the manslayer might be the victim's partner,[60] a member of his mess,[61] passengers paying him for their passage,[62] or either the victim's hired man[63] or his

[56]Entry for 2 July 1849, Drake, *Diary*.

[57]For two fights that ended in homicides at the North Platte ferry, see entry for 19 June 1852, Clark, *Guide* (also in Eaton, *Overland*, p. 154); entry for 30 May 1862, Clough, *Diary*, pp. 105–106. For a stranger killing that occurred on the road, not at a ferry, see entry for 17 June 1853, Luark, *Diary*, p. 35.

[58]Eaton, *Overland*, p. 165.

[59]Some of these reports are: entry for 7 June 1849, Stitzel, *Diary*, p. 112; entry for 10 June 1849, *Granville Company Journal*; Ingrim, "Gold Mines," pp. 6–8; entry for 19 July 1850, Gunlach, *Minutes*; entry for 30 May 1852, Bradley, *Daily Journal*; entry for 10 July 1862, Stites, "Journal of Travels," pp. 7–8.

[60]Entry for 6 September 1849, McLane, "Leaves," p. 1270.

[61]Entry for 1 June 1850, Rhodes, "Journal," p. 64.

[62]Entry for 12 August 1850, McKinstry, "Diary," pp. 104–105; entry for 12 August 1850, McKinstry, *Diary*, p. 254.

[63]Letter from Erasmus Taylor, 11 September 1853, Taylor, *Letters*; Mattes, *Narratives*, p. 422.

employer.[64] In fact, the likelihood that the manslayer and the victim knew each other was so strong that, on finding a body, emigrants sometimes guessed that the person had been killed by traveling companions. "He had probably got into some effray with his company who served him in this manner," one wrote on seeing the grave of a man stabbed to death with a bowie knife,[65] while another emigrant wrote, "found the body of a man to day that had most likely been murdered by his companions."[66]

At least one intra-company homicide may have resulted from liquor,[67] and others were because of arguments about property.[68] But almost every one of which we have sufficient facts to know what happened shared a common feature. It was that, as one emigrant put it, the parties "had frequently quarreled on the way."[69] Although the resulting animosity might motivate a manslayer to plan the killing,[70] most fights and homicides were spontaneous. An emigrant of 1850 described what has been called "a classic case."[71] It is, however, a secondhand tale about an event that occurred "a few days since," and related to the writer by two strangers.

> Two men who prepared their outfit in company at Independence, had frequent quarrels in regard to their traveling and camping arrangements. Going into camp near Chimney Rock, the quarrel was renewed, and one of the company with which they traveled, no doubt tired of the contention but prob-

---

[64]Entry for 7 June 1864, Ringo, "Journal," p. 206.
[65]Entry for 26 May 1852, Scott, "Oregon Journal," p. 56.
[66]Entry for 17 May 1852, Snodgrass, *Journal.*
[67]Entry for 26 May 1849, Breyfogle, *Diary.*
[68]Entry for 6 September 1849, McLane, "Leaves," p. 1270.
[69]Entry for 21 October 1849, Forsyth, "Journal," p. 87.
[70]Entry for 30 June 1852, Scott, "Oregon Journal," p. 79.
[71]Mattes, *Platte River Road,* p. 78.

ably in jest, proposed that they fight it out and quit. Whereupon, in the heat of passion, they drew their hunting knives and closed in mortal combat. In a few minutes one fell and almost instantly died; the other, fainting from loss of blood was carried into the shade of a tent where, within an hour, he too expired; and with the grim irony of fate, at sunset they were laid side by side in the same grave.[72]

We have an eyewitness account from 1852 of another homicide. The men involved, Holmstead and Dunmore, had been neighbors in Illinois and quite possibility had been friends for "Dunmore had hired his pas[s]age with Holmstead." After starting on the overland trail, however, they "had had other disputes before" the fatal one. As the company was hitching teams to wagons in the morning,

> Dunmoore and Holsted was a quarreling pret[t]y hard the[y] swore prety hard at one another and final[l]y Dunmore pitched on to Holmstead whilst [he] sat eating breakfast in the tent and they was scuffing together in the camp about a minute and when they had just left of[f] one another Dunmore said that Holmstead had stab[b]ed him. . . . we asked him where he had stabbed him and he put his hand on his belly but did not say anything then we unbuttoned his pants and vest and looked and sure enough he had the knife in his belly . . . he did not live more than 10 or 15 minutes.

Again, circumstances and timing transformed a quarrel into a

---

[72]Steele, *Across the Plains*, p. 67.

homicide. Holmstead had rounded up the cattle for the company and was having breakfast while the others were hitching the teams. He was eating "when Dunmore pitched on him   consequently he used his knife that he was eating with."[73]

In summing up the meaning of these homicides, a leading authority on the history of the overland trail has framed both the perspective from which we should view them and the issues that they pose for us. "The usual human weaknesses aside, emigrants were subjected to extremes which tested to the limit their endurance and fortitude. Under the circumstances the vast majority behaved admirably."[74] That observation tells us the true story of the overland trail. It is not that the fearsome toil, anxieties, hardships, and pressures of the overland journey forced men like Holmstead to break under the strain and, in the heat of passionate animosity and frustration, commit homicide. The story of social behavior on the overland trail is that few people broke. Even those who, on the trail, did what they had never done at home—fought with their companions once, twice, or several times on the trip— did not as a general rule draw weapons, and did not wound, or cripple, or kill.

There is, of course, yet another story that can be told, as the historian just quoted suggested when he praised "the vast majority" of overland emigrants for behaving "admirably." They did so, he added, where there were no law, no sheriffs, and little military to protect them. "The only effective law was the inward sense as well as the outward form of justice habitually observed by the emigrants. Under trail circumstances this informal justice was sometimes brutal, sometimes fickle, but its unseen presence doubtless served as a

---

[73]Entry for 14 July 1852, Chadwick, *Travels.*
[74]Mattes, *Platte River Road,* p. 77.

powerful deterrent."[75] There is more rhetoric than proven analysis in this statement, and we must ask how much of it is true. Was there an inherent sense of law obedience shared by emigrants on the overland trail? Was there justice? And if so, considering "trail circumstances," how could it be a "deterrent"? These are questions that have to be answered, not assumed, if we are to use the experience of the overland trail to learn about legal understanding or social behavior in the nineteenth century.

---

[75]Ibid.

*Arresting the Elephant*

# 7 | COLLECTIVE SOCIAL DEFENSE

Even before they started on the trail, overland emigrants anticipated being their own police, their own courts, and their own hangmen. Once on the trail they were to learn that although some "crimes" might go undiscovered, might have to be tolerated,[1] or left to self-help,[2] most—at least of those of which we have learned—were met with collective response. Few facts more graphically demonstrate the degree of nineteenth-century Americans' attachment to the principle of rule by law than the attitude of overland emigrants toward that response. All available evidence from the overland trail indicates that Americans at that time were prepared to join in, or approved of those who joined in, the pursuit and arrest of "criminals."[3] Moreover, if matters could not otherwise be resolved, they agreed that someone not only could but should put the suspects on trial and, if guilt was established, punish them.

Theories supporting criminal-law enforcement by citizens acting on their own, without authority conferred by the sovereign state either directly or by implication, will be the subject of chapter fourteen. Closely related to the theories of justification were the principles of criminal-law jurisprudence which guided emigrant actions. There were several objectives of penology—such as retribution, making an example of the wrongdoer, and deterrence —which emigrants mention as reasons for inflicting punishment; but, due to the transitory nature of overland life, reformation, of course, was not included. One important principle deserves mention as it is less

---

[1] For example, see the case of "Sam," above p. 47.
[2] For example, cases of horse thieves shot from the saddle by pursuers.
[3] For example, entries for 24 July and 25 August 1849, Gould, *Diary*, pp. 143, 172–73.

apparent than others. It is the doctrine of social defense and is best illustrated by considering specific applications. "This afternoon," an emigrant of 1862 wrote, "a suspicious looking chap, acting suspiciously made his appearance in camp and fearing treachery on behalf of the Indians and himself against the emigrants we took him custody and kept him under guard until next morning when we set him adrift."[4] The party was camped on the Sweetwater River at a place where two emigrants had been killed by Indians about fourteen days before. "Last night had a 'court' trial," an emigrant of 1844 wrote in his journal. "Young Eades was charged with attempting to shoot a man in a quarrel. The court ordered him bound over for good behavior." The trial had been more precautionary than punitive. Eades had raised an ordinary quarrel to a dangerous level by threatening the other party. To preserve the peace, the company bound Eades to better conduct. The members were protecting themselves as much as they were preserving law and order.[5] In a third case the element of social defense was more evident than was the crime. Along the Humboldt River in 1852, six Indians visited a camping ground. "The emigrants wanted to trade a rifle for an Indian pony," a German, not an American citizen, wrote, "but we prevented them from doing so."[6]

Social-defense measures were sometimes codified in the constitutions and bylaws of overland companies. An example that is unrelated to crime and punishment comes from the bylaws of an 1847 company bound for Oregon.

> 4th. Camp Master Shall see that no guns Pistols or other [fire] Arms be discharged in or nearer than 20 steps of the Camp.

---

[4] Entry for 13 July 1862, Stites, "Journal"; Stites, "Journal of Travels," p. 8.

[5] Entry for 5 June 1844, Parrish, "Crossing in 1844," p. 87. This company had a constitution authorizing the court.

[6] Entry for 26 August 1852, Schneider, *Memorandum.*

5th. Camp Master Shall Se[e] that no guns shall be
Carried [with] Caps on or with Primeing in the Pan
or Put in [w]aggons in Such Condition and in handling guns [in] Camp the Mussles [shall] be kept
upwards.[7]

It is possible that all emigrants—apart from those who found
themselves subject to police action—believed that legitimate
authority was vested in the collective group or emigration to settle civil disputes and to arrest, try, and punish wrongdoers. "We
had a long meeting to settle some little difficulties between some
members of the company," an emigrant of 1850 wrote, adding that
the event was "not worth mentioning," implying that it needed
neither explanation nor justification.[8] It was never overtly suggested that the authority to try and punish was inherent in those
who arrested the culprit and who constituted the personnel of the
"court." From just where the authority was derived may not have
been clearly articulated, but there was sometimes a suggestion that
numbers strengthened legitimacy. A manslayer on the Gila "was
arrested by order of the emmigrants generally, there being several
companies on the ground."[9] This statement was made not in a private diary but in a public notice posted on the trail to explain and
justify the trial and execution of the person arrested. Part of the
justification was in the size of support. It was not just that "several companies on the ground" meant additional legitimacy
furnished by the greater number of people expressing support and
approval. More important, "several companies" meant that support
and approval for arresting the manslayer on the Gila came from
people who were strangers both to him and to his victim. It took

---

[7]Cranfill, *Journal*.
[8]Entry for 15 August 1850, Goodridge, "Mormon Diary," p. 223.
[9]Entry for 29 November 1849, Eccleston, *Overland*, p. 217.

only one or two companies to make strangers a majority of those expressing support and approval.

Emigrants aiding collective social defense not only accepted onerous responsibilities, they assumed that they had the right to perform them. One was to investigate suspected homicides—to enquire about persons who had disappeared, search for bodies, and question likely perpetrators.

Suspicions were easily and quickly aroused on the trail. A husband and wife who had been traveling toward the Pacific were seen returning back east in sole possession of the wagon and team they had been sharing with another couple. "They reported to emigrants who inquired of them the reason of their turning back that he and his wife had become discouraged and concluded they would go no further." Within a day or two the bodies of the second couple were found. Under the demanding, dangerous circumstances of life on the overland trail, one might expect that the discovery would have been the end of the investigation. It was not. Somehow the discoverers, who may have been the emigrants who questioned the husband and wife, managed to get word back down the trail and the suspected killers were arrested.[10]

In another case that year

> [t]he murderer had a young man in his employ with whom he had been quarreling all along; yesterday he made it up and became very friendly, and at night asked him to go out into the hills with him. They departed together and the elder came back by himself, after dark, having, as he afterwards confessed, murdered him while the young man was walking before him. In the morning suspicion was aroused, the man acknowledged the act, but boast-

---

[10]Eaton, *Overland*, pp. 149–50 (1852, twenty miles beyond Fort Laramie).

ed they could not find the body. Two or three companies coming up a jury was enpanneled and the man condemned.[11]

A second account asserted that the manslayer "came back to his Train from below, not getting back until dark, saying that Charley stop[p]ed at a Train Below, and said that Charley told him to tell his train that if he was not there when the Train Started in the Morning to go on, he Would come on and Catch up, but this Statement was not heeded, but Early the Next Morning, a party started to look for the Boy, and made the Man that went hunting With him go along."[12]

Also in 1852, there was a similar case which involved two men, traveling with their families in the same train, who frequently quarreled.

> They went out hunting together at night but only one came in. The other man not returning, some of the men in the train became suspicious and quizzed him about it and made him go back with them where they found the man dead, he having been shot by his companion. As trains came in they called upon the parties and explained matters to them. The final result was that the murderer was given a jury trial, found guilty, and hung between two elevated wagon tongues.[13]

There is much more to these stories than one might think at first glance: three aspects at least are worth considering. The most obvious is the readiness of ordinary people both to assist the tasks of law enforcement and to initiate action by investigating their suspicions

---

[11]Entry for 29 June 1852, Thompson, *Crossing the Plains*, p. 56.
[12]Closing entry, 1852, Thorniley, *Diary*.
[13]Ingrim, "Gold Mines," pp. 3–4.

and arresting culprits. It tells us a great deal about nineteenth-century American citizens, their understanding of law's role, and the mechanics of enforcement that had to be implemented if there was to be rule of law. Not only did they support law enforcement but they participated actively, sometimes at great inconvenience to themselves. On the Sweetwater River, again in 1852, two brothers quarreled. "[T]he Elder drew his pistol and shot him [the younger] with 3 Balls mounted his Horse and fled." After burying the deceased, the captain of the company "called for [a] volunteer force to arrest the fugitive. 3 young men armed put out and overtook him at South Pass in the mountains 125 miles distant." The writer does not say how long they were on the manslayer's trail but surely it was a trip of several days. Moreover, they did not kill the suspect. They brought him back over all those miles to the company where he was tried, found guilty, and hanged.[14]

A second aspect to be marked is the way that trains in which killings had occurred appealed to other companies to stop and participate in the investigation. One account of the Lafayette Tate killing, which was discussed above and will be considered again in the next several chapters,[15] says that when the manslayer fled his company dispatched a party to arrest him. After he was brought back, the company "sent two men in advance to request the first trains to stop and assist in the examination."[16] The reason was not that they needed more people to hang the killer. Increased participation promised greater fairness of procedure and less heat of passion: more people could mean there would be cooler heads, wider and more diverse experience, and, perhaps, sounder advice.

A third notable aspect was the probative weight accorded evidence. If they had no eyewitnesses, the emigrants wanted

---

[14]Dickinson, *Overland Journal.*
[15]Pp. 80–81, 99–100, 123; Duffin, "Miller-Tate Murder," pp. 24–26.
[16]Entry for 15 June 1852, Richardson, *Journal,* p. 64.

circumstantial facts proving guilt. According to what may be another version of the killing of the boy by his employer[17] (but which may have been a different case, as the victim is described as a "man") the company to which the suspect and victim both belonged "made the man go back" when the victim did not return. The people wanted him to "show them where he saw him last and as they was a going he confessed and said he supposed he had killed him that they got to fighting and he killed him   he said he had to do it to defend himself but they examined the man and see how he had been shot and how he had been beaten with the but[t] of the gun after he was shot." Put in slightly clearer language, it seems that the investigators had not believed the suspect when he said the victim had stayed behind. On locating the body they determined the victim had been shot from the rear and, not finding as much blood as they thought should have flowed from the wounds, concluded that he had been beaten after he was killed. Satisfied they knew what had happened, they tried the suspect and "found him guilty."[18]

In 1849 a man from Ohio was traveling with one companion on pack mules. By the time he reached the Sweetwater he was alone. "Some who had seen them on the road asked him of his friend. He answered he saw him drown in the Platte. They immediately took the rascal prisoner, previously having found the deceased pierced by a bullet. An Illinois train has charge of the prisoner."[19]

The last case needs a second look. It differed from the others that have been described. In each of those the manslayer and the victim had belonged to the same company, and members of those companies, people who knew both parties and felt some civic responsibility toward them, were the ones who took the lead inves-

---

[17]The killing occurred about the same time and in the same vicinity, but throughout this account the victim is clearly identified as a family man.

[18]Entry for 2 July 1852, Chadwick, *Travels*.

[19]Entry for 3 July 1849, Banks, *Diary*, p. 31.

tigating, arresting, and punishing the culprit. In the last case, the killing of the lone companion on the Platte River, it was strangers, not fellow members of a train, who did the arresting. This fact may not be too surprising, but it is extremely important and has not been sufficiently appreciated by some students of the overland trail. "The only law obtaining on the trail as it wound across through the plains and the Great Basin at this time," one writer has asserted, "was that exercised by the separate companies themselves by virtue of their corporate agreement drawn up to cover the journey. Since many, perhaps most, companies formally dissolved their bonds or disintegrated informally early on the journey, this restraining force was at a minimum."[20] It is true, as the writer says, that most overland companies disintegrated, but those events, serious as they may have appeared at the time, created few if any problems of social deviance. It may seem surprising, but the fact that companies fell apart had little bearing on legal behavior. Company agreements, contracts, and constitutions were not very significant as authority for enforcing criminal law on the overland trail. Companies did, of course, police their own members but, more importantly and probably just as frequently and readily, they policed strangers as well. So, too, did individuals who belonged to no companies.

When emigrants policed strangers it was usually for homicides. Aside from theft and grass burning, other antisocial behavior lacked the same compelling public interest. Besides, emigrants could not afford to stop to investigate any antisocial offense less serious than theft, grass burning, or homicide. If just one word summed up life on the overland trail it was "rush." Fear of missing out at the gold diggings or of being trapped by the Sierra snows put pressure on emigrants, so it was that much more remarkable that they would not only stop to investigate, try, and execute manslay-

---

[20]Read, "Diseases," p. 273. For what the writer quoted calls "corporate agreements," see "Governance of the Elephant."

ers, but that they would return back over the trail to track them down. And both the killer and the victim could be complete strangers to the manhunters. "[S]ome of our party went on to-day in pursuit of a murderer, who is said to have killed a man a short distance back, and took his mules," a lawyer who was also a Presbyterian minister wrote two days beyond Devil's Gate.[21] Three years afterward a man and his son were found with their throats cut. Soon emigrants encountered some "Frenchmen" and Indians with a wagon and team that could have belonged to the dead man.[22] "[T]hinking that they had murdered the man and took his team," the emigrants investigated. The French and Indians explained that they had purchased the property from an emigrant returning home. The description of this emigrant fitted a man who had been traveling with the two victims. Some volunteers "followed the man back and found him before he got a great ways and fetched him back and hung him from a tree."[23]

As soon as Lafayette Tate stabbed to death his traveling companion, "a young man by the name of Miller," he "went to Miller's wagon and took Miller's pistol and knife and started ahead on the road to California." In other words, expecting punishment, he fled. The company was small and appealed for help. "As fast as the trains came up they were stopped until there was a crowd to pick from to send after Tate. In a short time fifteen men had volunteered their services and started in pursuit of the murderer." They caught him

---

[21]Entry for 30 June 1849, Foster, "First Diary," p. 36. "Our company seized the supposed murderer." Entry for 1 July 1849, ibid. The man was hanged. Mattes, *Narratives*, p. 156. For similar pursuits, see entry for 5 September 1849, King, *Journal*, p. 60; entry for 29 June 1852, Moreland, *Diary*; entry for 30 May 1852, Bradley, *Daily Journal*; Davis, "Introduction and Notes," pp. 198–99.

[22]"I met them myself and spoke to them as having emigrants cattle and waggons and thinking I had seen them before somewhere on the road." Entry for 2 July 1852, Chadwick, *Travels*.

[23]Entry for 2 July 1852, Chadwick, *Travels*; Eaton, *Overland*, p. 151.

and brought him back for trial.[24] Ten years later, at Devil's Gate, a company was told of a killing "committed near them today. Two men quarrelled about a team, one shot the other, [and] took his team and money." Next day the company came to a place where there was good grass. "Several trains were camped here so we drove in and camped too. We are informed the murderer is camped here. By request of some men from another camp, Captain Kennedy of our train ordered out twenty men well armed to surround and take him which they did." Kennedy's company put the accused under guard while he was tried and found "guilty of willful murder." Keeping the prisoner tied up, the company then moved on about eight miles where it found good grass and water. "A large train was camped here. Captain Kennedy called their whole company together and laid the case before them. They decided that the prisoner be executed tomorrow morning."[25] He was.

Kennedy's conduct has aroused a bit of comment. One historian referred to "Kennedy's unsavory role in the affair,"[26] and he was criticized somewhat harshly "for meddling" by at least one emigrant.[27] The issue can be postponed to the final chapters where emigrants' theories justifying their acts of prosecution and punishment are considered. For purposes of this chapter it is enough to realize how decisively Kennedy reacted to a homicide in which the victim and perpetrator were strangers both to him and to his company. More to the point, even if it were argued that, by using excessive force, he determined the outcome, the telling fact for us

---

[24]Ingrim, "Gold Mines," p. 7; Eaton, *Overland*, p. 118.

[25]Entries for 6, 7 July 1862, Scott, "Across the Plains."

[26]Mattes, *Narratives*, pp. 553–54.

[27]Entry for 3 August 1862, Gould, "Journal," p. 30. This criticism may be "the one clear doubt so far found" questioning the legality of overland punishment. "Coercing the Elephant," p. 192*n*132.

remains his willingness to intervene. Even more significant, it was not unusual behavior on the overland trail. It was, rather, the norm. So, too, was the deliberate pace. There was no haste to execute. After the manslayer was found guilty of murder he was transported eight miles where a "large train" was camped. There the case was "laid" before yet another group of people. If we can make any sense out of the account, Kennedy sought the support—perhaps active but at least passive—of as many emigrants as he could contact, and he got it.

Indeed, what can be termed the "town meeting" element of overland justice was not limited to arrest, trial, and punishment. It could precede arrest. There were occasions when emigrants called meetings just to discuss whether a suspected manslayer should be apprehended—not how he should be tried or how punished, but how he should be apprehended. One case is of interest because a military officer not only participated, he had soldiers assist the civilians in making the arrest. Even the facts of the killing deserve mention because the very triviality of the cause, almost incomprehensible to us, was typical of homicides on the overland trail.

> A reckless villain, named Brown, requested a young man who acted as cook in his mess, to get him a piece of soap. The young man was at the moment bending over the fire, engaged in preparing the meal, and replied by telling him to get it himself, as he was busy. Without further provocation, as it appeared, the wretch raised his knife and stabbed him in the back, killing the young man almost instantly. The murderer fled. A meeting of emigrants was called, and General Allen, from Lewis county, Missouri, was called to the chair, when the atrocious deed was set forth, and it was determined by a series of resolutions to arrest the villain, give

him a fair trial, and if found guilty, to execute him on the spot. Major Simonton seconded the views of the emigrants. . . . In addition to a dozen athletic volunteers, who stood forth at the call, he detailed a file of soldiers to assist in the capture of the murderer.[28]

We should contemplate that scene at Green River in 1849. It tells us a great deal about the governance of nineteenth-century America. We would learn even more if we only knew the nature of the "series of resolutions to arrest the villain": what they said, and what resolutions, if any, were voted down. It would be of interest to know who voted, not the question that dominates late twentieth-century (but not nineteenth-century) thinking, that is, whether women participated, for women participated and voted in most collective decisions reached by companies on the overland trail. What is not mentioned by journal writers is whether young men under the age of twenty-one, who quite likely made up part of the volunteer party, could vote or, possibly, whether the question was left to those who volunteered to go after a culprit. But just the fact that these people thought resolutions necessary, or even worth the effort, deserves attention. Once upon a time scholars would have drawn lessons about the nineteenth-century American bent for organization and democratic action. Currently there is little interest in exploring these themes. But more was going on among those resolution writers than self-government. Out on the overland trail they were blending two nineteenth-century civil values, subordinating the national tolerance of extreme individualism to the felt need and necessity for collective social defense.

---

[28]Entry for 3 July 1849, Delano, *Life*, p. 124; Delano, *Across the Plains*, p. 52.

*Accusing the Elephant*

# 8 | CONSTITUTIONS AND TRIBUNALS

During the early years of the overland emigration, companies frequently wrote constitutions and adopted bylaws before they started out on the trail. The practice was largely discontinued after the 1850 emigration. By then most emigrants knew that few companies would remain united and rules could be made ad hoc to deal with problems as they arose.

One fact stands out when we read the judiciary sections of overland constitutions. The drafters did not create courts to try and to punish criminal offenses. They were not primarily concerned about crime committed either by traveling companies or strangers. The judicial institutions that they devised were intended to resolve disputes and maintain harmony between members of their own train by mandating adjudication in place of potentially disruptive face-to-face conflict. This purpose was especially relevant to joint-stock companies which were formed by members who purchased equal shares and owned equal rights in the company's concurrent property. It was expected that once beyond the Missouri River concurrently owned property would be divided only with difficulty, and to prevent controversy tribunals of adjudication should be established to settle questions that might arise regarding distributions and fair shares. Many traveling companies—companies organized by individual emigrants seeking companions for the overland trip—also created courts. As property was not concurrently owned, but belonged to individuals, families, messes, or partnerships,[1] traveling-company tribunals were intended more to resolve personal disputes and enforce discipline than to decide rights of

---

[1] For ownership of property on the overland trail generally, see *Law for the Elephant*.

103

concurrent ownership. "Resolved," a typical traveling company voted in 1850 before crossing the Missouri River, "That in case of any dispute arising between any members of the Company, that they shall be referred to three arbiters, one chosen by each party, and one by the two chosen, whose decision shall be final."[2]

We are not concerned with the resolution of civil disputes on the overland trail, only with the trial of antisocial offenses. There is something to be learned, however, about nineteenth-century American attitudes toward criminal prosecution by considering, in brief outline, the mechanisms overland emigrants devised to avoid violence by creating tribunals for the resolution of conflicts. Some companies, like the one just quoted, utilized arbitration. Others decreed adjudication. One company had a three-man "Committee to settle difficulties."[3] Another had "a judicial committee, to decide on all causes of complaint that might arise on the road, whether civil or criminal."[4] Although both these provisions conferred a remarkably wide jurisdiction, neither was unusual by overland standards.

Considering that separation of powers was one constitutional doctrine widely known to Americans, it is surprising how often overland companies combined executive and judicial functions in the same officers. The Muscatine–California Emigrants' Association vested in its governing "Committee on Regulations" the duty "to adjudicate all questions of dispute and to see that the rights of each emigrant are protected and enforced."[5] Another company made it "the duty of the Pilot Camp Master & Guard Master to Call a Jury to settle all questions of difference ariseing in the Company."[6]

---

[2]Resolutions of the Beloit Company, 6 May 1850, recorded in Newcomb, *Journal*, p. 30.
[3]*Frontier Guardian*, 29 May 1850, p. 2, col. 5 (Missouri and Iowa Mining Company).
[4]Entry for 11 May 1850, Langworthy, *Scenery*, p. 14.
[5]"Report on General Regulations," in Lorch, "Gold Rush," p. 315.
[6]Cranfill, *Journal* (Bylaws of an 1847 Oregon-bound company).

Even a few passenger trains had tribunals. They were companies in which members paid for their passage overland (always to California) much as if purchasing tickets on a common carrier. A passenger train traveling via the Texas route set up a "panel of *Jurors*" consisting of thirty-two members. From that panel each party to a dispute was to choose six, and the twelve jurors selected were then to "choose one more from the same body, whose duty it shall be to give the casting vote and fix the degree of punishment to all persons found guilty."[7] Here was a remarkably imaginative approach to lay adjudication, a compromise between allowing litigants to select their own arbitrators and obtaining the uniformity and continuity in judgments expected of permanent, professional tribunals, an important element when the jurisdiction included crime and punishment. A panel of thirty-two jurors may seem large, but in the small world of an overland-trail company, where every member was involved in the affairs of every other member, it gave parties an opportunity to select neutral jurors. At the same time, as membership on the panel was permanent, jurors could be expected to keep themselves informed about decisions and the criteria used in judgments. That would have made verdicts more uniform than if jurors had been taken at random from the entire company each time a dispute arose.

Some constitutions allowed defendants the selection of triers of fact. Even when standing committees were formed to try violations of company rules or antisocial offenses committed against fellow members of the company, defendants might be given the option of substituting trial by jury.[8]

The right of picking the triers of fact was part of the bylaws of a company from Illinois whose elaborate regulations are well worth

---

[7]Miles, *Journal*, p. 9.

[8]*Frontier Guardian*, 30 May 1849 (Constitution of the California Express Company, article 5). Article 5 is reprinted in "Prosecuting the Elephant," p. 331*n*25.

a detailed look. The members of this 1849 company devised a remarkable hierarchy of crimes, with delicts graded into three categories—minor offenses, assault with a deadly weapon, and homicide—and different trial standards for each category. Anticipating conditions of law enforcement as they actually existed on the trail, the Illinois constitution makers realized there was no point defining lesser offenses. They left the question of what was an offense to the vote of the entire company to be determined after the fact.

> In case [of] any complaints made to the Captain, by any member of the company, that any of the rules or regulations have been violated, or that any of the company have violated the laws of order, right and justice, which are evident to all men, it shall be his duty at the first camping place, to call a meeting of the company, and state to them the complaint that has been made, when, if the company decide, by a vote of a majority, that the offence is of that character — deserving punishment, they shall proceed to the trial of the person complained of, in the following manner. The names of all the company except the parties, the witnesses, and the mess-mates of the party complained of, shall be placed in a box, and five drawn promiscuously therefrom, which five persons shall constitute a jury to try the case. The witnesses, shall be examined under oath, by the person appointed by the Captain, and after a full and fair hearing, the jury shall decide the case by a majority, the jurors to be sworn to do justice between the two parties.[9]

---

[9]Page, *Wagons*, p. 338 (Bylaws of the Green and Jersey County Company, § 1 [1849]).

It was a wonderfully flexible jurisprudence. The violations "of order, right and justice, which are evident to all men" could be either tortious acts or criminal offenses, brought by one member against another, or by the entire company against an individual wrongdoer.

For homicide the procedure was different. The jury was increased to twelve persons, "and six unqualified challenges shall be allowed on both sides, and as many more as good reason can be shown for."[10] The verdict, of course, had to be unanimous, and "from it there shall be no appeal."[11] Why there were no appeals in homicide cases is a bit puzzling. Appeals were allowed defendants convicted of crimes not involving homicide. In those cases, "Any person feeling himself ag[g]rieved by the decision of a jury, shall have the right of appeal to the whole company, but it shall require a vote of two-thirds of the whole company to set aside the verdict of a jury."[12] Yet, when convicted of "taking the life of another" the verdict was final. It is an unexpected distinction that at first looks like one more piece of evidence that emigrants thought of homicide as belonging to a separate category from other offenses. But why no appeal? Maybe they had been anticipating that appeals "to the whole company" would be taken mostly in lesser cases of, for example, sleeping on guard duty, where the culprit would ask for sympathy from people well aware of the difficulties of staying awake after a long day of travel. The decisions would not be on the merits of the case so much as on popularity, sentiment, or oratory. Emotions tolerable for lesser offenses were out of place with homicide.

The bylaws of this Illinois company had another provision, perhaps unique in overland lawmaking. It dealt with hung juries but

---

[10]§ 4, ibid., p. 339.
[11]§ 4, ibid.
[12]§ 1, ibid., p. 338.

only in homicide cases, another indication that emigrants thought homicide belonged to a species different from all other offenses. "If the jury cannot agree, a new jury shall be empannelled from the balance of the company, and second trial be had, and so on, to a third jury, when, if the third jury cannot agree, it shall be considered as an acquittal."[13] There is no legislative history telling us why this provision applied only to homicide trials. The likely reason is that hung juries were not much of a problem in nonhomicide cases because those verdicts were by majority of an uneven number of jurors and were also less final. They could always be appealed to the company.

It is important to understand that these provisions, adopted by members of this company from Illinois, were more extensive than those found in the average overland constitution or bylaws. Except for the clauses discussed, and one mandating that the secretary of the company make a record,[14] however, they were not unique. All the constitutions shared certain basic principles and were more alike than they were different. This is hardly surprising when we consider that emigrants sought to duplicate the judicial tribunals they had known at home. Some even had provisions for a separate court of appeals,[15] probably to prevent the situation where questions of law depended on the popular vote of the entire membership of the company.

The only surprises to the judicial provisions of overland constitutions were those which attempted to avoid jury trial. It is a move that goes against the pattern of duplicating known institutions and, in the few constitutions where it occurs, the purpose is not stated. The Oregon Emigrating Company of 1843 may, when it vested all

---

[13]§ 4, ibid., p. 339.
[14]§ 5, ibid.
[15]Delano, *Life*, p. 85.

judicial authority in its executive council, have hoped to strengthen the position of its elected officers by preventing power from being diluted. After all, for the officers to discipline a man who slacked on guard duty and for a jury to overrule the penalty would undermine authority in a small company. Nine men elected to various executive posts were "to settle all disputes arising between individuals, and to try and pass sentence on all persons for any act for which they may be guilty, which is subversive of good order and military discipline."[16] That they left the authority so open-ended suggests another possible purpose. It may be that the drafters made the council the triers of fact so that the council could retain the definition of the crime.

There were other bylaws or constitutional provisions curtailing jury autonomy. An obvious tactic was to have the officers define the crime by charging the culprit with an offense, leaving only the question of whether or not the defendant committed the particular physical act, but not the culpability of the act itself, to jurors selected from the membership. Another is found in the rules of the 1846 emigration vesting adjudication with the executive committee but reserving the issue of punishment for the membership as a whole. "The committee of inspection," the bylaws provided, "shall have power to arraign any person for delinquency of duty, or for the violation of any of the rules or regulations, . . . and the punishment for such delinq[u]ency shall be decided upon by a vote of the company."[17]

Were we to believe Jesse Applegate, an emigrant of 1846 who romanticized the journey to Oregon, the provision vesting judicial authority in the executive council worked wonderfully well.

---

[16] *Frontier Experience*, p. 97.
[17] Laws of the 1846 Emigration, law 8, in Letter from George L. Curry to the St. Louis *Reveille*, 11 May 1846, reprinted in Morgan, *Second Overland*, p. 522.

> The council was a high court in the most exalted sense. . . . The offender and the aggrieved appeared before it; witnesses were examined, and the parties were heard by themselves and sometimes by counsel. The judges being thus made fully acquainted with the case, and being in no way influenced or cramped by technicalities, decided all cases according to their merits. There was but little use for lawyers before this court, for no plea was entertained which was calculated to hinder or defeat the ends of justice.[18]

Edwin Bryant, who also was in the emigration of 1846, remembered a very different court. Unlike Applegate who wrote his recollections long after crossing the continent, Bryant published his account only three years after reaching the Pacific and his memory was much fresher. "The court or arbitrators, appointed to decide disputes between parties, and to punish offenders against the peace and order of the company, does not appear to have much authority," Bryant reported. "The party condemned is certain to take an appeal to an assembly of the whole, and he is nearly as certain of an acquittal, whatever may have been his transgressions."[19]

Bryant should not be misunderstood. He exaggerated almost as much as did Applegate. There was a difference, however. Applegate idealized and may have intended doing so. Bryant was critical but did not intend it. He found fault neither with the right of appeal nor with the fact that it generally led to acquittals. Because overland emigrants were living under civic conditions "where no law prevails except their will,"[20] he believed it was just as well there

---

[18]Applegate, "Cow Column," pp. 101–102.
[19]Entry for 26 May 1846, Bryant, *Journal*, p. 60.
[20]Entry for 27 May 1846, ibid., p. 61.

were not many punishments. In fact, rather surprisingly, Bryant thought appeals to the assembled group, even if they meant certain acquittal, did not turn criminal law into political demagogy. A company's collective judgment could be trusted to make correct, even legal, decisions.

> So thoroughly, however, are our people imbued with conservative republican principles, and so accustomed are they to order and propriety of deportment, that with a fair understanding, a majority will always be found on the side of right, and opposed to disorganization. "Our glorious constitution," is their motto and their model, and they will sanction nothing in derogation of the principles of the American constitution and American justice.[21]

Bryant's words are important. He was not just another anonymous overland traveler scribbling his thoughts in the privacy of his personal journal. He wrote for publication. His book would not only encourage future emigrants to undertake the crossing to the Pacific but would become a guide carried by countless travelers, and it would be read by the officers of companies not just to discover what physical obstacles lay ahead but to learn what problems of governance might be expected and how they could be resolved. That is why what Bryant just said must be accorded more heed than the average emigrant's account. It should be remembered that the emigrations of the years after Bryant's book became available were less likely to write constitutions and create permanent tribunals of adjudication. It may be an exaggeration to suggest it, but his book could have been a cause. If we read between the lines, Bryant

---

[21]Ibid., pp. 61–62.

implies there was no need to create permanent judicial tribunals. Emigrants on the trail could establish courts of justice ad hoc whenever needed, and they would be competent and fair. Surprisingly, some lawyers agreed. Addison Crane, a former judge in Indiana who would become a California judge after crossing with the 1852 emigration, thought constitutions and bylaws a waste of time.[22]

Not all constitutions established courts. The constitution of the Charlestown, Virginia, Mining Company—a company consisting mainly of "farmers, mechanics and lawyers"[23]—was drafted in what is today's West Virginia long before its members began the trek west. It has to have been the work of an attorney, though how competent an attorney is a good question. The constitution contained an unusually large number of duties and implied offenses,[24] and a section calling for the assessment of penalties;[25] yet there was no provision for trials. The constitution did not even specify what body of officers was to mete out the punishments.[26] Even though expulsion by majority vote was authorized, and the officers were empowered to impose fines for offenses such as gambling and intoxication, there was no mention made of adjudication, argumentation, or defense.

We cannot be certain but it is quite possible that members of some companies made a conscious, deliberate decision not to create judicial tribunals except ad hoc. What other conclusion can be drawn from a constitution that mentions neither courts nor penalties yet created an executive committee both for the purpose of

---

[22]Entry for 12 May 1852, Crane, *Journal.*

[23]Mattes, *Platte River Road,* p. 33.

[24]For example, see Articles XV and XVI, Constitution of the Charlestown, Virginia, Mining Company. Potter, "Introduction," pp. 219–20.

[25]Ibid., Article XVII, p. 220.

[26]Ibid., p. 18.

"enforcing the Laws of the Company" and to see that the laws were "exercised at all Times."[27] The implication is that the drafters anticipated how most disputes would be adjudicated on the overland trail. They may have guessed that when violations occurred, or members argued over the meaning of rules, there would always be time to call a meeting; and, no matter what the constitution said, the membership would surely debate how the question should be resolved, probably creating a tribunal just for the occasion.

Provisions such as these are a warning that we should be careful where to look for evidence. The obvious sources, the constitutions and bylaws, may tell us less than we hope. Even worse, they may mislead us. The point is not that we should ignore constitutions and bylaws. In fact, we should be grateful to those overland companies that created judicial tribunals or elected judges before civil controversy arose or crime was committed. The fact that they did so when there was no immediate pressure on them to convene a court allowed them time for reflection. The rules they wrote provide some of the only evidence we have of what ordinary nineteenth-century American citizens understood of the judicial process—of jurisdiction, rules of procedure, and principles of due process. The point, rather, is that the constitutions and bylaws are not a reliable guide to how judicial matters were conducted on the overland trail. As David Langum remarked:

> [T]here is no evidence suggesting a correlation between elaborate rules or judicial machinery and an actual effective operation of pioneer [i.e., emigrant] courts. These ordinances or constitutions . . . may be of interest as guides to pioneers' philoso-

---

[27]Article II, Constitution of the California Banner Company. Entry for 7 May 1850, Paschal, "Diary," p. 10.

phies about law and social organization, [but] they do not help answer the more essential question of how, in fact, not in theory, did the overland pioneer face problems of social disorder, crime, and private conflict.[28]

Again we meet a problem encountered before. Overland diarists do not tell us enough. That a trial was conducted was sufficient information for most writers. "Tried a member for a violent assault with a Bowie-Knife, on his messmate," is all that was said by the captain of a large company governed by a joint-stock constitution.[29] There is no hint whether he convened the tribunal authorized by his constitution or created a court for the occasion. Other emigrants mention trials but do not say who rendered the verdict or what procedure was followed. Moreover, it was not unknown for an emigrant to discuss a case, to give details of both the crime and the punishment, yet not mention whether a trial had been conducted.

There are, of course, facts we do not have to be told. If a defendant's sex was not mentioned we can be sure it was male. If it had been a woman the diarist would have said so. We can be equally certain that he was not an Indian and probably not black. The writer would have at least said he was an Indian, although he might not have identified the tribe, and more than likely he would have said if a defendant was black. Also, if the nationality was not stated it is safe to assume the defendant was American or Canadian. Europeans, including English, Irish, and Scots, were identified. Moreover we can be certain that, if a defendant was tried, most people present—if asked—would have said that the trial was "fair."

---

[28]Langum, "Pioneer Justice," p. 424*n*12.
[29]Entry for 17 October 1849, Bruff, *Journals*, p. 227.

The criteria of judgment would not have been those of a criminal lawyer. They would rather have been based on the emigrants' remembrance of scenes witnessed in the local courtroom back home. Fortunately, a number of emigrants were sufficiently interested to furnish us with accounts of trials and punishment on the overland trail. There were not as many as we might wish; they are at best a random sampling, telling us more about emigrant attitudes than about rules and procedures. The quantity of evidence is not large enough to enable us to reconstruct a typical trial, yet it is more than sufficient to allow conclusions about motivations, objectives, and philosophies.

*Prosecuting the Elephant*

# 9 | TRIALS, JURORS, AND PROCEDURE

We owe even more to the act of homicide for our knowledge of overland trials than we do for our knowledge of overland crime. Homicide was the crime the emigrants recounted in the greatest detail and trials for homicides were practically the only criminal proceedings they described. Emigrants mentioned occasional prosecutions for theft[1] or for sleeping on guard duty,[2] but only rarely gave details. What we know, then, about criminal trials and criminal procedure on the Oregon and California trails comes almost exclusively from accounts of trials of defendants accused of deliberate homicide.[3]

One basic generality can be gleaned from these accounts. Whether their courts were structured in their constitutions, by their bylaws, or formed ad hoc to meet each emergency, the emigrants did not attempt to create *sui generis* institutions. Instead, they duplicated or imitated the courts and judicial procedures remembered—or half-remembered—from back home. That is a very significant fact. It tells us something of the emigrants' desire for legitimacy and how they defined "fair trials," and also why they had little difficulty agreeing on procedures.[4] If a lawyer was present, the task was that much easier. There seems to have been no reluctance to ask lawyers to take the lead. If there were two lawyers

---

[1] "[H]ere they are trying a man for stealing a horse." Entry for 1 July 1854, Reber, *Journal*, p. 49.

[2] Entry for 10 June 1841, Bidwell, *Journey*, p. 14.

[3] Langum, however, was wrong to suggest that emigrants took seriously only trials of what he calls "deliberate murder." Langum, "Pioneer Justice," p. 439.

[4] There is one case reported of a manslayer who avoided trial near Green River because the crowd could not agree on procedures. Mattes, *Narratives*, p. 214.

available, one might be elected to prosecute, the other asked to defend.[5] In nonhomicide cases prosecutors were appointed for minor as well as major offenses. Defendants seem always to have been permitted to hire a defense attorney, even a stranger passing by in another train.[6]

Undoubtedly, the most revealing feature of overland trials was the emigrants' attempt to have the triers of fact duplicate the function of the American criminal-law jury. The criminal jury was not just their model: they wanted their juries to be exactly the same. To the undiscerning eye it might appear at first glance that they had a different idea in mind. In noncapital cases the entire company were sometimes the triers of fact, deciding guilt or innocence by majority vote,[7] and it was not unknown for a homicide prosecution to be settled by vote of every emigrant present—whether witnesses, companions, or strangers.[8] Inconsistent as it may seem, a popular vote was even used on one occasion to spur a jury to action. It involved one of the few overland cases in which an eyewitness makes it clear that the homicide was blatant, inexcusable murder.

> The jeury gave an ascenting voice to the prisinars guilt but could not agree on the punishment seven being for amediate punishment and five for delivering him to the authorities of California    The company was then caled together and a vote was taken on this question and the majority of the company ware in favour of amediate punishment    The jeury again asembled and after a short consultation

[5]Sullivan, "Crossing," p, 5. Also, see Burroughs, "Reminiscences," p. 47.
[6]Delano, *Life*, p. 125; Potter, "Introduction," p. 135n7.
[7]Entry for 4 June 1859, Dutton, "Journal and Letters," p. 461.
[8]Sullivan, "Crossing," p. 5.

returned with the verdict as follows    Leanadas
Balsley arise and receive your sentance    Wee the
Jeury find you guilty of willful murder and sentence
you to death by shooting tomorrow morning at six
O'clock.[9]

The voting crowd, comprised of several separate traveling companies, totaled about one hundred. Unfortunately we do not know
what question was put to the assembly. The account says they voted
for "amediate punishment," but it seems more likely they instructed the jury to reconsider.

It might be thought that these votes did not constitute a trial
and were a drastic departure from the Anglo-American norm of
deliberative, adversarial justice. In a sense they were, but not as
much as they might have been, and the departure was not basic.
The overland emigrants were almost slavishly intent on recon-
structing American criminal process. After all, they did not do
what logic might have dictated—that is, they did not go back to
the early English pattern and entrust the verdict to those who
knew the facts. With a small population, no regular tribunals, no
police, no rules of evidence, and an uncertain supply of lawyers, it
would have made sense to have adopted the old English practice
of putting the question of guilt or innocence to people who had
been witnesses to the events. Who better could understand the circumstances of a homicide than the members of the same company
as the victim and the manslayer? They had been traveling with
them for weeks, heard their daily quarrels, and knew their frustrations, anger, and antagonisms.

Instead, overland practice was the opposite. Seeking to copy
nineteenth-century common-law trials as closely as possible, emi-

---

[9]Entry for 13 June 1852, Green, 1852 *Diary*, pp. 13–14. This homicide was mentioned above, p. 79.

grants wanted jurors who were not witnesses, who before trial did not know the circumstances of the alleged crime, and who were strangers to the defendant, the victim, and the witnesses. Indeed, although it was not considered inappropriate for very large companies to pick triers of fact from among their own membership, the preferred procedure for homicide prosecutions was to obtain jurors who did not belong to the company of the victim, the accused, or the witnesses. Legal theory on the overland trail took for granted that what were called "stranger emigrants"[10] could render a just verdict, much as if they had been in an established American court of law, by hearing evidence from witnesses, weighing arguments, and deliberating in secret. The preferred way to try a homicide accusation on the overland trail was with "a jury of men out of another train and witnesses out of our train," as one emigrant explained when describing a trial.[11] One manslayer whose case is discussed below, was tried by jurors drawn from over two hundred wagons,[12] while another panel was selected from fifty men "collected from both front and rear trains."[13] There were two purposes. One was to have strangers try the facts. The second was to reinforce the legitimacy of the process.

The search for "stranger" jurors was universal. It occurred in several emigrations and was practiced by trains that had no idea what other companies were doing. The following case was not unusual. It was, rather, more typical than not of judicial procedure on the overland trail.

> One morning, cooking breakfast, two partners quarreled. One, stooping over a skillet, was, from

---

[10]Maxwell, *Crossing the Plains*, p. 152.
[11]Entry for 15 July 1852, Chadwick, *Travels*; Eaton, *Overland*, p. 225.
[12]Entry for 6 July 1852, Verdenal, "Journal," p. 22.
[13]Burroughs, "Reminiscences," p. 47.

behind, stabbed to the heart. His slayer was immediately disarmed and his hands tied. A man [who]
had presided as Judge in Illinois, a stranger, was
forced to preside as Judge, and attorneys appointed
to prosecute and defend; a jury of twelve men, also
strangers, were empaneled; and, after argument and
charge, the defendant was found guilty and sentenced to be hung.[14]

This story, which was a recollection written some years after the
event, seems to be the only extant account of the trial. Just what is
meant by the former Illinois judge being "forced" to preside will
have to remain a mystery. A point on which the writer was clear,
and which is worth a second look, is the way he emphasized the
"stranger" element. Even years later, the gathering of strangers to try
the case remained significant in his mind. There is no doubt this
was of great importance to emigrants responsible for bringing a
manslayer to justice. We can measure their concern by considering
the trouble to which they went to obtain a "stranger" jury. A good
instance is the case just mentioned, told by an eyewitness to the
killing, of the hung jury instructed to reconsider its verdict by the
assembled crowd wanting "amediate punishment." The company
to which the victim and the manslayer had belonged "was composed of eleven men and three wagons,"[15] hardly enough to make
a jury and, besides, they were the witnesses. An ox train of thirty
members was just behind, and the first company, the one of the
slayer and victim, "concluded to await their ar[r]ival  they came up
buried the murdered man and after a short counsil took the murderer into custody."[16] The next day

---

[14]Terrell, "Overland Trip," p. 79 (1852).
[15]Entry for 31 May 1852, Green, *1852 Diary*, p. 11.
[16]Entry for 12 June 1852, ibid., p. 13.

> A council being held upon the best way of disposing of the prisoner and it being agreed upon that wee travel on about thirteen miles to a large crick (hams fork of queen river [Hams Fork of Green River]) whare we expected to overtake a large train — in doing so our object was to get more council — accordingly wee set out for that place over a verry ruff and mountainous way. Wee arrived at Hams fork about one O'clock P.M. Here wee found a large ox train from Iowa a mule train from pensylvania and some packers making in all about one hundred men.

They now were satisfied. "After dinner the trains and companys were respectfuly invited to meet and attend the tryal of Balsley for the murder of Beel."[17]

The perseverance of these emigrants is impressive. They pushed on, with the manslayer in tow, until they collected men sufficient to form a jury. The eyewitness does not say what legal theory motivated these people, but the emphasis on gathering together "about one hundred men" implies that they sought a group sufficiently large to be both disinterested and a fair representation of the emigration.

Other manslayers were apprehended at places where large enough crowds were already gathered. The company that forced the employer to go and find the body of the boy he had lured to his death simply returned to camp, called "in others from other Trains and tried the Case."[18] When a homicide occurred between two partners in a Wisconsin train, "the company concluded to drive on that day untill the excitement was over and have a trial of it tomorrow."[19]

---

[17]Entry for 13 June 1852, ibid., pp. 13–14. Also, see entry for 13 June 1852, Chadwick, *Travels*, in Eaton, *Overland*, pp. 221–22.

[18]Closing entry for 1852, Thorniley, *Diary*. See above, pp. 94–95.

[19]Entry for 14 July 1852, Chadwick, *Travels*.

The emigrants must have felt that the proceedings would be fairer to the defendant if they allowed passions to cool. When they camped half a mile from an Illinois train, it became that company's turn to be "thrown into considerable excitement." The reason was that its members were *"called upon as jurymen."*[20]

Perhaps it should be expected, but it nonetheless seems remarkable, that these isolated companies, not in communication with one another and not knowing what others were doing, established a rather standard procedure for selecting jurymen. After the killing of Miller by Tate, and the capture of Tate by volunteers who rode after him,[21] the company to which the prisoner was returned simply pulled over to the side of the trail and waited. "As fast as teams came up they were stopped until there was a big crowd. As soon as Brown's train came up with the witnesses there was judge and jury picked out of the crowd and a man on each side as lawyers."[22] In fact, it was quite a sizeable crowd. Another emigrant reported that Tate was "brought before a tribunal representative from 200 wagons in the neighborhood."[23]

Practically the same procedure had been followed three years earlier on the Gila River on the southern trail, where the emigration was so sparse wagon trains drove close together for protection. The killing had resulted from a spontaneous burst of anger, also between fellow members of a company, with the manslayer arrested by someone from a different company. "[A]t six O'clock the horn was blown, at Capt Rogers tent for the purpose of as[s]embling the Emigrating community which a general collection came from every direction. After the crowd had as[s]embled, and a few remarks

---

[20]Entry for 15 July 1852, Scott, "Oregon Journal," p. 87.
[21]Above, pp. 96, 99–100.
[22]Ingrim, "Gold Mines," pp. 7–8; Eaton, *Overland*, p. 118.
[23]Entry for 6 July 1852, Verdenal, "Journal," p. 22.

made by Maj Jno Patrick & Captain R. Rogers, the trial was gone into."[24] The jury was drawn from three different trains.[25]

The more we look at overland trials and punishment, the more there is to be wondered about. At the risk of appearing repetitious, the willingness of emigrants to stop and conduct these trials must be remarked. If we fail to give them special credit it is because we forget the conditions of trail life. One man who, as a stranger, participated in a hearing lasting an entire day wrote of the high cost. True, he admitted, jury service was a civic duty that had to be performed, but it was a sacrifice nonetheless.

> You must know it was no small matter, hundreds and hundreds of miles from anywhere, with no certain knowledge of just when you can get there, and every dollar you are worth invested in what you have with you, and in many, yes in most, instances, that year, families, women and children, that from the day they leave the borders of civilization until they reach them again are day by day exposed to suffering, danger and death, or worse. I say it is no small thing for train after train to stop and voluntarily loan themselves and their all, and in most instances possibly not for their own good either.[26]

Of course, not all emigrants were so civic-minded. A few thought jury duty too heavy a price to pay for law on the overland trail. A train of thirty-two wagons with a guard list of seventy men[27] was traveling in close proximity to a smaller company in which a man named Gadson killed a fellow emigrant. The second

---

[24]Entry for 5 September 1849, King, *Journal,* p. 60.
[25]Entry for 21 October 1849, Forsyth, "Journal," p. 87.
[26]Burroughs, "Reminiscences," p. 57 (1856).
[27]Entry for 7 September 1849, Powell, *1849 Diary,* p. 106.

company, because it "is so small that they do not like to take the responsibility of punishing him,"[28] asked the larger "to let them pick a jury from [its] train to try Gadson for the murder, but [it] declined having anything to do with the business."[29] It is not clear why the larger group did "not choose to be mixed with it in any way."[30] Delay could not have been the reason. Although the larger company did move ahead, the two trains were close together when the trial took place, for members of the larger company witnessed both the proceedings and the subsequent punishment.[31]

The objective of emigrants, traveling in different years, on different routes, in different companies with no communication with one another, to select jurors who were strangers—not acquainted with the defendant or victim, not witnesses to the homicide, and who had no knowledge prior to trial of the facts—came from their collective unconscious, their remembrance of trials in the states. If we accept what they tell us, trials were often mirror images of American criminal justice. It was as if they had a pragmatic, felt need to think their trials were like those at home. The one thing that they wanted above all else was to conduct "fair" trials, and their standard for a "fair trial" was how much it resembled criminal trials held in their county courts.[32]

Emigrants thought it important to record just how "regular" a trial had been. "[A] regular court was organized, consisting of judge, jury of twelve and two attorneys, one for prosecuting and one for defending," an eyewitness who participated in the decisions creating the tribunal wrote of one trial that led to a conviction.[33] "The trial,"

---

[28]Entry for 5 September 1849, ibid., p. 103.

[29]Entry for 4 September 1849, ibid., pp. 101–102.

[30]Entry for 5 September 1849, ibid., p. 103.

[31]Entries for 7 and 8 September 1849, ibid., p. 106.

[32]Another standard for a "fair trial"—a term frequently used by those few emigrants who encountered criminal proceedings—was that "the Jury was smart intelligent men." Entry for 15 July 1852, Chadwick, *Travels.*

[33]Burroughs, "Reminiscences," p. 47.

another emigrant wrote of a different case, "had been as orderly and impartial as the proceedings in any court established by constitutional authority. All those concerned in it realized that they were performing a duty of grave importance. There was nothing of vindictiveness, nothing of rashness."[34] We do not have to believe that these descriptions are accurate to believe the writers thought they were true. They were reporting fairness, decorum, and regularity because fairness, decorum, and regularity were important to them. Just consider this account of a trial for homicide written by a man who was not present. The very fact that it is hearsay is important because it indicates the standard of procedural competency one emigrant believed could be obtained on the overland trail. More significantly, it reveals the level of objective fairness his informants wanted him to believe they had followed.

> The company chose a judge to preside over the trial, and a sheriff, who empaneled a trial jury of twelve men, who heard all the evidence, after which the judge charged the jury. The jury retired a short distance from camp, under the charge of the sheriff chosen by the company for the emergency, for their deliberation. In about twenty minutes they returned and informed the court that they had decided on a verdict. The foreman then handed their written verdict to the court, which read as follows: 'We, the jury, do find the defendant guilty of murder in the first degree as charged.' Signed by all the jurors. The court immediately passed sentenced on the defendant, to be hanged by the neck until dead, dead, dead, and may God have mercy on your soul.[35]

---

[34]Maxwell, *Crossing the Plains*, p. 158.
[35]Entry for 5 July 1852, Conyers, "1852 Diary," p. 459; Eaton, *Overland*, p. 171.

These words are worth a second reading. Even if the emigrants who described this trial to the writer exaggerated or misrepresented some facts, it would not matter. Just the accomplishment of being out somewhere amid all the perils of the overland trail and being able to recite this half-remembered form of words from this half-understood process is remarkable. Everything is included, all the touches needed to persuade the laity that the trial had been just like those at home. The judge's instructions, the jury retiring under the charge of the sheriff, deliberations protected from outside influence, the written verdict, the expressions "We the jury" and "to be hanged by the neck," the signing of the verdict, and the invocation of God's mercy, all helped to standardize, regularize, and legitimatize a "fair trial." And this account was not written with the intention of convincing any other person of the legitimacy of the process. It is an entry in a private diary made by an emigrant to record what he had been told that day.

One procedural step beneficial to the defendant was overlooked. As the account goes on to relate that "two graves were dug, one for the murdered man, the other for the murderer," and both bodies were buried together,[36] it is evident the accused had little time to prepare a defense. Trials were not delayed more than seventy-two hours on the overland trail. Participants knew they hurried judgment. "Last night there was a man kill[ed] or shot by one of his own men," an observer wrote in 1853. "[T]he man was arrested tried and [sentenced] and hund [*sic*] all within 12 hours   it was a short time for him to have his neck streached."[37]

When trials were delayed, it was usually for reasons the emigrants would have classified as "judicial fairness." As we have seen, defendants were sometimes transported for two days while their

---

[36]Ibid.
[37]Entry for 14 May 1853, Compton, *Diary*.

captors looked for jurors, and an emigrant was quoted earlier in this chapter who said his company was waiting "to have a trial tomorrow after the excitement is over." At least one company had a constitutional prohibition against forcing trial "within three days,"[38] although we have no indication if the rule was ever applied or even if it could have worked in practice.

Important as haste was to the emigrants, their definition of "fair trial" required some delays and they usually managed to be reasonable. Even the one prosecution of "white Indians" of which we have sufficient details avoided summary judgment. The jury, after receiving the familiar warning that the accused be tried only by the evidence heard from witnesses in open court, was allowed ample time for deliberation. The trial, for cattle stealing, had

> consumed the entire day until dark, and the Jury were given 'til next morning to bring in their verdict. Of course, they returned to their respective camps to sleep, the judge charging them to discuss the matter with no one and to return in the morning, get together and make up their verdict.[39]

In one important respect, however, defendants on the overland trail received trials different from those they would have had at home. They benefited from few of the rules for the reception of evidence or for the exclusion of hearsay and opinion testimony. We have to guess at this since there is little supporting evidence, as we have almost no accounts of trials on the overland trail. But it cannot be doubted. We do have one report which indicates that, for one trial at least, anything a witness felt like saying was admitted as testimony. This account is not clear, but, from what is said, it

---

[38]Bylaws of the Oregon Emigrating Company Constitution, 5 May 1845, in "Savannah Company Journal." See also Lockley, "Migration of 1845," pp. 353, 372.
[39]Burroughs, "Reminiscences," p. 47.

appears that the witness was called and required to tell his story, which he did, uninterrupted. The defendant was Balsley, whose trial for killing Beal has been twice referred to in this chapter.[40] The reporter was not a witness to the slaying. He was, rather, a member of a stranger company that had come along after the homicide had been committed. Although his train provided five of the jurors, he did not participate in the trial. He did, however, attend and his diary entry for that day may be the only extant account of a witness's testimony in an overland trial.

There were five witnesses "sworn by the uplifted hand," but the reporter mentioned and discussed only one of them. This witness's name was David Dye and he had come west with both the manslayer and the victim. A member of their mess, Dye apparently had been paying his way overland by working for Balsley. So too was another young man, Stephen, who had been hired at St. Joseph. Oddly enough, although Dye was the main witness against him, Balsley told the jury "that what ever David said was the truth." Dye testified that

> he knew the prisoner for about 5 years and that his people were of the best in the state of Ken   That when he first knew the prisoner he was considered as fine a young man as there was in the county of Boon Ken. and that he went in the first society but that of late years he heard that he was in the habit of associating with the lowest as well as the highest and in truth he did look like a man that could grace the highest or disgrace to lowest circle   He said he joined Beal and Beausly at home in Boon co Ken and was with them untill Beal was shot   That he never heard them have any angry words but that he thought they were not friendly towards one another

---

[40]See above, pp. 118–19, 121–22.

He said he thought Beal was to bear half the expenses to Cal. but that he had no money and always when he wanted any he got it from Beausly. The morning that Beal was shot the company they had joined concluded not to start for the day untill 10 oclock AM. Beausly did not like the arrangement and hitched up his two mules and asked Beal if he was going along with him, he said, he was not, "Very well," says Beausly, "You can do just as you please I do not wish to controle you or your property" and he left As he was about to leave he turns to Beal and says to him "Major you had better tye your mules or they will follow me" When he had left the camp for a short distance Beal followed him and told him there was a pair of lines in the wagon belonging to him When Beausly got them and handed them to Beal. . . .

When Beausly had left Beal put his mules in with another man's[41] and about 10 oclock they followed A short time after noon they passed Beausly who was grazing his mules Beausly than says to D Dye "I wonder if they are going to leave us" They then hurried and harnessed up a[nd] took after Beal When they were a short distance behind[,] Beausly asked Stephen to hand him his double barrel shot gun (which he was in the habit of taking every day & going ahead to kill game) Stephen handed it to him and he went on after Beals wagon. When he road up to Beausly and says to him "Major are you

---

[41]"Beel applied to Mr. Gray my partner for conveyance to California wee took him into our wagon." Entry for 12 June 1852, Green, *1852 Diary*, p. 13.

going to leave me in this manner" Beal answered
"Yes Sir, I am" The words were no sooner out of
his mouth than Beausly raised his gun and shot him
the ball or load passing through his left breast and
comeing out at his back Beal was not more than 12
feet distant when [Balsley] fired and ran about 12
steps after when he fell He died almost immediately this happened on the 12th[42] Beausly did not
offer to leave but laid a claim on the mules which
Beal had saying they were his and that he could
prove them to be so in the course of half an hour
the Telegraph train came up to where Beal was shot
and took Beausly prisoner.[43]

There was a good deal of speculation in this evidence, and also
a bit of hearsay testimony. By what seems to be his own statement,
Dye had only "heard" that Balsley had taken up with "the lowest
society," and although he did not seem to know much about the
business arrangement between Balsley and Beal he readily offered
his opinion about what he "thought" it was. It was probably all
good evidence to the court, as well as relevant, as the jury may
have wanted to know what kind of a man Balsley was and it is
likely that Balsley had claimed he shot Beal because he was running off with the mules. According to Dye, Balsley had told Beal
that the animals were "<u>your mules</u>" and later, after shooting him,
said they were his. It is evident Dye did not know who was the
owner, but that fact did not matter to the jurors. Balsley could not
justify his cold-blooded slaying of Beal by claiming he was defending his right to property.

---

[42]"Balsley rode up to my wagon and shot Beel in the left breast cosing (causing)
instant Death." Ibid.

[43]Entry for 13 June 1852, McKieran, *Diary*.

These issues of relevancy, of opinion evidence, and of speculative testimony probably were of no more concern to jurors trying Balsley than they would have been to most other emigrants. Those emigrants who have left us their thoughts had little patience for legal distinctions. Had Dye's hearsay and guesses been called to their attention, they would have dismissed any objections as "technicalities," tricks lawyers used to confuse trials, hide the truth, and defeat justice. Even the writer quoted a few pages ago praising a trial "as orderly and impartial as the proceedings in any court" conceded that in some respects that process had not been a perfect copy of the model being followed. "It was without 'due process,'" he admitted, "and it was swift; a proceeding without the delays commonly due to technicalities observed in a legal tribunal; but it was justice conscientiously administered."[44] We may safely guess that most emigrants, sharing the general American disdain for the common-law canons of relevancy, competency, and procedure, would have said that overland trials, in this one respect, were an improvement on those at home. "The tedious, tardy, and often doubtful manner of administering what is termed justice in the States," one wrote, "has but few admirers or advocates on the plains."[45]

It really did not matter if emigrants were intolerant of common-law procedure. Even had they wished, they could not have practiced it in most of their overland criminal trials. They would have needed at least three competent trial lawyers—to serve as judge, prosecutor, and defense attorney—lawyers who had committed a reasonable part of the rules of evidence to memory. And even the best lawyers might have disagreed on rules of evidence if they came from different states. The niceties of criminal procedure were not intended to be taken onto the overland trail.

---

[44]Maxwell, *Crossing the Plains*, pp. 158–59.
[45]Mattes, *Narratives*, p. 548 (quoting R. H. Hewitt, 1862).

# 10

*Defending the Elephant*

# JUSTIFICATION AND DEFENSE

The evidence which has survived is one-sided. Overland diarists thought it right that wrongdoers be tried and punished on the overland trail, and reported the strengths, not the failings, of trials. They said that trials were regular and conducted with decorum because the procedure looked familiar to them, and familiarity was their test for regularity and decorum. When judges strayed from the common-law model and admitted opinion, irrelevant, and perhaps even prejudicial, testimony, they did not criticize in their diaries because they did not realize what had happened. They did not know there were rules of evidence and, if told there were rules, would not have thought them relevant to the overland trail. There also are few accounts of miscarriage of justice, although diarists often tell us so little there is no way to be sure. There may have been a summary execution or two, where the evidence was overwhelming and eyewitnesses to a homicide were also the executioners. Despite what extant journals tell us, there must have been trials that in spirit and outcome were closer to lynching than to common-law proceedings. Also, there was surely a good amount of diversion, even entertainment, obtained from trials, especially from noncapital cases involving offenses such as sleeping on guard duty or violating the rules of march.[1]

Alonzo Delano, who like Edwin Bryant wrote his diary for commercial publication, told of a homicide trial that did not measure up to the standards usually reported. It is an improbable story,

---

[1]One legal historian has charged that a good deal of "lightheartedness" prevailed at criminal trials, but the evidence can be interpreted in other ways. Langum, "Pioneer Justice," p. 431.

and Delano may have gotten it wrong or embellished the facts a bit to make his book more interesting, but it is the only detailed account we have.

> An emigrant named Williams, from Plymouth, Marshall county, Indiana, had taken a stranger into his employ at St. Joseph, who was anxious to get to California. It proved, after they got beyond the limits of law and order, that this man was a perfect desperado. . . . Some difficulty occurred between him and Mr. Williams, on account of the latter reproaching him for being remiss in his duty, when he threatened to take Mr. Williams' life, . . . subsequently it appeared that he was determined to put his threat into execution, and Williams, from the advice of his friends, kept out of the way as much as possible, and at night slept either out of the camp, or where his enemy could not commit the deed. The man . . . continued his threats in such a manner, and sought so palpably to carry them into effect, that Williams, who was a quiet and peaceable man, came to the conclusion that there was no safety for himself but to anticipate his antagonist. At this time, the man was detailed as one of the night-guard, and Williams was to relieve him. The hour of relief came, when, on approaching Williams, the latter took his pistol and shot him down. The man lived two days, and confessed that it was his intention to have killed Williams, and that he should have done so, if he had had an opportunity. In the morning, Williams went to several trains and offered to give himself up for trial, but upon a just representation of the facts by his

company, he was honorably acquited, on the ground of self-defence, where a judicial investigation could not be had.[2]

The homicide had been perpetrated at Devil's Gate on the Sweetwater River. Ten days later, at Green River, a particularly brutal killing occurred, the manslayer fled, and companies in the vicinity sent volunteers on his trail to arrest him. The volunteers did not overtake the killer but they did come upon Williams. "[T]hinking that some example of justice was necessary, they intimated that his presence was required to stand trial before a Green River jury, and he willingly returned." Williams's company refused to go back with him, leaving him without witnesses, a fact, Delano says, which persuaded him to retain a defense attorney. "At the commencement, as much order reigned as in any lawful tribunal of the States. But it was the 4th of July, and the officers and lawyers had been celebrating it to the full, and a spirit other than that of '76 was apparent."[3]

The officers were members of the Army's regiment of mounted riflemen bound for Fort Hall, and among the lawyers was Williams's defense counsel. He,

> in a somewhat lengthy and occasionally flighty speech, denied the right of the court to act in the case at all. This, as a matter of law, was true enough, but his remark touched the pride of the old commandant [the man chosen to preside as "chief justice"], who gave a short, pithy and *spirited* contradiction to some of the learned counsel's remarks. This elicited a *spirited* reply. . . . From taking up words, they finally proceeded to take up stools and

---

[2]Entry for 23 June 1849, Delano, *Life*, pp. 100–101.
[3]Entry for 4 July 1849, ibid., pp. 125–26.

other belligerent attitudes. Blows, in short, began to be exchanged, the cause of which would have puzzled a *"Philadelphia lawyer"* to determine, when the emigrants interfered to prevent a further ebullition of patriotic feeling, and words were recalled, hands shaken, a general amnesty proclaimed.[4]

The defendant was forgotten. "[S]eeing that his affair had merged into something wholly irrelevant, with a sort of tacit consent, [he] withdrew, for his innocence was generally understood, and no attempt was made to detain him."[5]

Delano's story is important in the literature of crime and prosecution on the overland trail. Termed "[t]he nadir of judicial solemnity for overland parties," it is the trial exhibited to prove that emigrant justice was as likely to be staged for comic relief as to determine guilt for criminal actions.[6] It should not be taken so seriously. Delano not only wrote with an eye on entertaining his reader, he was very sick that day. He did not get up until four in the afternoon and may not even have seen the trial. If we rely on his account alone, Williams should have been acquitted and at least some of the people involved in his trial knew it. Although Delano's account is not clear, he implied that back at Devil's Gate where the homicide occurred Williams had received some sort of a hearing, for "upon a just representation of the fact by his company, he was honorably acquited."[7] Most likely, therefore, his lawyer questioned "the right of the court to act" not, as Delano assumed, because the trial was not authorized by act of Congress

---

[4]Ibid., p. 126.
[5]Ibid., pp. 126–27.
[6]Langum, "Pioneer Justice," p. 431.
[7]See above, text to note 2.

but on grounds of double jeopardy.[8] Moreover, as Delano says, "his innocence was generally understood." What Delano had not known, as the accused was among strangers and separated from his own company, was that "there were witnesses enough in the crowd to have justified" his killing of his "enemy."[9] Their story probably became known as the trial progressed, contributing to the arguments and the breakdown of order. It is not irrelevant to the historical importance attributed to the proceedings to note that at least three people who were there did not bother to mention the trial in their diaries.[10]

There is, however, another side. The pursuers who had arrested Williams and went to the trouble of bringing him back to the Green River for prosecution must have thought the man had done something deserving of trial and probably punishment. Also, two of the emigrants who served as jurors believed there had been a miscarriage of justice. One blamed the army officers for not taking the lead and conducting "a fair investigation of the case." This juror agreed with Delano that "the court broke up in a rowe" and he was annoyed by the outcome, claiming that many others were as well. "There is a general expression of disapprobation amongst the people at the result," he wrote, "and in this case we believe we see a fair sample of the protection that we may expect of lives and property during our residence in California."[11] It is not clear what he was complaining about—that a "murderer" had gone free or that the army had not lived up to his expectations. The second juror described the trial much as Delano did, saying that the army major

---

[8]An eyewitness, who also served as a juror, reported that the lawyer "opened by his denying that the emigrants had the right to try him." Morgan, "Green River Ferries," p. 182 (quoting Springfield *Illinois Journal*, 12 December 1849).

[9]Entry for 4 July 1849, Delano, *Life*, pp. 125–27.

[10]Potter, "Introduction," p. 135*n*7.

[11]Entry for 4 July 1849, Ramsay, "Diary," p. 452.

and the defense counsel threatened one another "with an arrest" and complaining of the military, "Thus it is that these officers and men protect the interests of the emigrant by getting drunk."[12]

A clearer case of a miscarriage of justice occurred in 1853, at Council Bluffs, east of the Missouri River. A young, wealthy emigrant from Columbus, Ohio was found murdered. Suspicion fixed on an even younger man with whom he was traveling:[13] first, because he told an improbable story of being attacked by Indians; and second, because a horse had been stolen that night and the owner, looking for it, recovered it near the site of the homicide. It had, people said, been tied there so the killer could flee. Deprived of his means of escape, the suspect was immediately seized by the crowd.[14]

"Some wanted to take justice into their own hands and execute him," a historian has observed. Instead, "law and order prevailed, and the accused stood trial."[15] But did "law and order" prevail? Henry Allyn was an eyewitness. He was also a pious, religious man, as was his companion "James" who was a preacher.[16] They had arrived in Council Bluffs three days before the homicide and were waiting to cross the river.[17] It is revealing that, despite their religious convictions, neither of them expressed any reservations about either the legal or moral right of the crowd to prosecute and punish the accused. And despite being transients "James," the preacher,

---

[12]Morgan, "Green River Ferries," p. 182 (quoting B. R. Biddle in Springfield *Illinois Journal*, 12 December 1849).

[13]Apparently hired by the dead man "to drive cattle." Entry for 14 May 1853, Belshaw, "Diary Kept," p. 219.

[14]Entry for 14 May 1853, Allyn, "Journal," p. 386.

[15]Castle, "Belshaw Journey," p. 223.

[16]"The neighbors assemble here for worship. James preaches from Job. A class meeting follows, in which some speak very feelingly and could not refrain from praising God aloud." Entry for 10 April 1853, Allyn, "Journal," p. 374.

[17]Entry for 10 May 1853, ibid., p. 384.

served on the jury and Allyn, who wrote the most detailed account
of what happened, participated in the proceedings.

> A jury was summoned, partly of citizens and emi-
> grants. James was on the jury. The jury was
> unanimous in their verdict of guilt. He was delivered
> up to the emigrants, to take him on to California, or
> to execute him on the spot. A resolution was offered
> to keep him till 10 A.M. on Monday,[18] in order to
> make his peace with God, which I voted for with all
> my heart. But the resolution was lost and two hours
> was given him and he was hung on the limb of a
> basswood tree that stood about 12 yards from the
> scene of the murder. . . . The Methodist preacher
> who is stationed here, waited on him, to whom he
> confessed he was knowing of the circumstances, but
> did not have a hand in it.[19]

There were about five thousand emigrants camped within two
or three miles of the town of Council Bluffs when the trial and
execution occurred, and it seems that just about all of them
approved of the proceedings. "Judge Lynch is a hard faced old fellow," an emigrant witnessing his first hanging observed, "but I
guess his judgment is generally good and I would rather trust him
than any Judge, sitting in any Civil Court. In the Case here it was
certainly a richeous decision as the Culprit had been guilty of a
most brutal murder."[20] Just how "richeous" is a question that could

---

[18]This was Saturday.

[19]Entry for 14 May 1853, Allyn, "Journal," p. 386. Another emigrant who was
there but did not participate in the trial wrote that the convicted man "had his trial and
was hung the next day  he was swung off of a mule under the gallase  he killed the man
for about 150 dollars." Entry for 15 May 1853, Belshaw, "Journey," p. 5.

[20]Cowden, *Diary*, pp. 3–4.

be debated. The procedure, although not completely unprecedented, was quite bizarre when compared to other overland criminal trials. The jury may have been unanimous in their verdict, but why was the convicted man "delivered up to the emigrants, to take him on to California, or to execute him on the spot"? It appears the jurors were relinquishing their responsibility by appealing for a popular vote.

More serious questions can be raised about the venue of the trial and the execution. They did not take place out on the overland trail far from any organized police authority, duly appointed judges, or established courts of law. They occurred within the jurisdiction of Iowa which had been organized as a territory fifteen years before and had been a state for seven years. Moreover, the place of execution was populated enough to support a "Methodist preacher." It had been settled as Kanesville by Mormons moving west in 1846 and was incorporated as Council Bluffs the same year as the execution. The mere fact that the emigration was crossing the river and would soon be far away was no excuse. There had been no witness to the killing and the evidence was all circumstantial. Since the jury, as Allyn said, was part "citizens" and part emigrants there were local people, if not county officials, who could have held the suspect in custody and testified to the homicide, the story of the horse, and the suspicion of robbery.[21]

The Council Bluffs hanging was an anomaly in the history of justice on the overland trail. The killing seems to have aroused the interest of just too many people. The large, excited crowd rushed the defendant to trial without giving him the opportunity to develop a defense[22] and then rushed to execution, perhaps to prevent

---

[21]In fact, another emigrant reported that, "the officers delivered him to the emigrants," but what she means is not clear. Entry for 14 May 1853, Belshaw, "Diary Kept," p. 219.

[22]It is not reported if he had a defense attorney. Most likely, he did.

Iowa officials from taking custody. The proceedings do not fit the overland pattern. It has too much the taste of passion, retribution, and even vindictiveness. If any fact stands out from the cases reported in overland diaries and letters it is that emigrants did not seek vengeance; they did not desire to convict and punish an individual for an act that would not have been considered criminal back home. Moreover, they wanted evidence of guilt and the opportunity for accused persons to be allowed to defend themselves. Most telling is the fact that a surprising percentage of defendants were exonerated at their trials.

We may marvel, but accusation did not mean automatic conviction. Unfortunately, however, we are not always given an explanation why a jury failed to convict. Diaries simply note that a defendant was "not found guilty,"[23] or that he was "acquitted."[24] Sometimes we are told that the accuseds were "honorably acquitted"[25] or "equitted honorably."[26] In at least one case even a "white Indian" was exonerated. This was the most extensively reported trial of white cattle rustlers, in which seven men were charged and six were convicted and sentenced to death. The seventh was acquitted on the testimony of the condemned men, even though one was his older brother who might have been suspected of partiality.[27] It was believed he had been coerced into joining the gang and had acted without either intent or free will.[28]

-----

[23]For example, entry for 27 June 1852, Davis, "Diary of 1852," p. 374.

[24]Mattes, *Narratives*, p. 305.

[25]For example, above, p. 63; entry for 4 July 1849, Wood, *Diaries*. A note added to a diary at a later time reported of a defendant who had been "honorably acquitted": "This man was afterward hung by Vigalence Committee in California." Entry for 1 July 1849, Parke, *Notes*; Davis, "Introduction and Notes," p. 199n35.

[26]Mattes, *Narratives*, p. 170 (1849).

[27]Burroughs, "Reminiscences," pp. 48–49.

[28]Ibid., pp. 49–50.

A somewhat common explanation by overland writers for acquittal was "justification"—a homicide, it would be said, had been "justified."[29] A diarist who recorded the killing near Fort Kearny, where a man's head had been split open by an axe when he was trying to climb into bed with the manslayer's wife, said that "[a] court of enquiry pronounced it justifyable homicide."[30] A captain of a passenger train who seized a man he thought a murderer was told the man had been "justified in doing it."[31]

As far as can be determined, "justification" meant the defendant had convinced the triers of fact that he had acted either in self-defense or from sufficient provocation. Self-defense was probably the one ground for exonerating a manslayer known to every emigrant but it is impossible to say how it was defined on the overland trail. There are simply too few explanations of verdicts. To understand how the doctrine of justification was applied on the overland trail consider three representative fact situations. In the first, two men, Frasier and Hosstetter, had been quarreling. "You may consider yourself lucky if you ever see Montana," Frasier warned the other. "It was getting dark, and Frasier stood with one hand on a wheel as he talked. He then got into the wagon and out again, with something in his hand, which Hosstetter thought was a revolver in the gathering darkness." Hosstetter fired two shots killing Frasier who had no gun but a hatchet which he had fetched to straighten a tire on the wheel. "The men from these four trains elected judge, jury, prosecuting attorney and lawyer for the defense, and have tried Hosstetter for murder. The jury brought in a verdict of 'Not guilty.' He shot in self-defense, as Frasier had threatened to

---

[29]Entry of 10 September 1849, Doyle, *Journals and Letters.*
[30]Entry for 23 May 1849, Steuben, *Journals.*
[31]Entry for 5 August 1852, Sharp, *Travel Diary.* Or was told "that the man was justified in shooting the fellow." Entry for 5 August 1852, "Diary of Robert Lee Sharp," p. 42.

kill him."[32] If that explanation is true it would make self-defense in this case a much broader category than it was at common law, although, of course, a jury anywhere might have considered Frasier's threat a reason why Hosstetter believed he had a weapon.

Abigail Scott Duniway wrote the longest account of a plea of self-defense. She was not an eyewitness but, as the men of her train furnished all the jurors in the case, she surely had every opportunity to learn the facts. As she understood them, they were in one respect the opposite of those in the last case. This time it was the manslayer, not the victim, who made the death threat.

> One Daniel Olmstead was taking five men across the plains, and it appears that they had not lived very agreeably together as it was proved in the trial which came off to day that the five had boasted that they had their boss under their thumb and intended to keep him there. It was proved that Olmstead went out in the morning to watch his cattle telling Sherman Dunmore . . . to make a fire and put on the teakettle so they could have some breakfast,; When he returned at breakfast time . . . he asked where his breakfast was  Dunmore replied that if he wanted any he might cook it himself.; This was the result of much abusive language on both sides; however Olmstead prepared his breakfast himself, Dunmore threatening in the most abusive manner to whip him Olmstead calmly replied that if he did he would not live long to brag about it  Upon this

---

[32]Entry for 5 August 1865, Herndon, *Crossing the Plains*, pp. 195–96, 199–200. Two days later soldiers had taken Hosstetter into custody "and I suppose the witnesses came too." Entry for 7 August 1865, ibid., p. 205.

> he left him and went into the tent and commenced eating his breakfast, using for the purpose a small sized butcher knife; Dunmore followed him and jumping upon him commenced beating him and endeavored to kick him in the face with his boots Olmste[a]d called upon the bystanders to take him off saying at the same time he had a k[n]ife; As no one interfered he stabbed him in the lower part of the chest. . . . [Dunmore] fell and in twenty minutes was a corpse.:, The jury after an impartial investigation of the tragical affair brought in a verdict to this effect; That the wound made by the knife of Olmsted caused the death of the said Dunmore and the same was inflicted by the aforesaid Olmstead in self defense.[33]

Writing to her grandfather three days later, Duniway asserted that "It was clearly proven that he had killed him in self defense."[34] An eyewitness to the killing, a member of the company to which the manslayer and victim belonged, said that "the Jury dismissed him as he was fighting in his own defence."[35]

Perhaps the jurors, when weighing the facts, took into consideration the social circumstances of life on the overland trail, the frustrations, the petty annoyances, the sudden bursts of anger. That probably is what happened in our third illustration, a case where the jury "justified" the defendant,[36] also apparently ruling that he had acted in self-defense. The victim was an Englishman named

---

[33]Entry for 15 July 1852, Scott, "Oregon Journal," pp. 87–88.
[34]Letter from Abigail Jane Scott to Grandfather, 18 July 1852, Scott, "Letters," p. 153.
[35]Entry for 15 July 1852, Chadwick, *Diary*; Eaton, *Overland*, p. 225.
[36]Entry for 10 September 1849, Doyle, *Journals and Letters*.

Bently and the manslayer was a physician named Shields. They were messmates, owning in partnership a wagon and team which they drove as far as Mud Lake on Lassen's cutoff in today's California

> when Shields & Bently quarrelled which I learned had almost be[e]n daily since they left St Jo    but here Shields wanted to divide their provisions and team and said he would join another train    but B refused so S went to another train and told his circumstances which he said was gloomy if he could not get aid as B was a large stout man and had threatened to whip him to death if he took a pound of provisions or any thing that belonged to the co[partnership]   three or four men instantly volunteered their services and said they would see him righted   so they all went to his waggon when Bently was off looking after the cattle   so S got in the waggon and began to divide the provisions when Bently came up and said he would thrash him to death but as B approached the waggon S commanded him to stop which he did not do so S shot at him   the ball took affect in the left side of his breast but did not disable him from the attact so shields shot him again this took affect in his forehead   the ball lodging in his brain   this last shot brought him down.[37]

To "justify" this killing the jurors had to have been thinking of Shields's frustrations and the hardships of trail life. For the last two months they all had been experiencing similar vexations and some of the jurors may well have seen other men break under the strain.

---

[37]Entry for 9 September 1849, Castleman, *Diary*.

How else was the shooting "justified"? Shields was the one with the physical support of men who had agreed to protect him. He could have gotten his property and preserved his life without shooting Bently. He had no justification killing him—except on the overland trail where the pressures and stress of life seem to have been mitigating factors that "justified" the homicide.

Another legal concept that, like justification or self-defense, was generally defined more broadly on the overland trail than at common law was "provocation." A case in which it appears to have been a factor occurred at Shinn's Ferry on the Platte River during a relatively late emigration, that of 1862. This was a time when there was not only a ferry across the Platte but also "ranches" along its banks, a combination of emigrant trading posts and roadhouses.[38]

> An emmigrant with some loose stock had crossed in his turn, but was unable to get all of his stock on the ferry, being compelled to leave one cow. So he returned to get his cow. It so happened that a man who conducted a ranch somewhere on the South side of the Platte was registered for that trip. He was loaded with supplies for his ranch, principally liquors, and in all probability was somewhat under the influence of his stock in trade at the time. He had no loose stock and there was plenty of room on the ferry for the emmigrant's cow; so he led her on the boat. The ranchman told him he could not take the cow across on that trip and ordered him off the boat. The emmigrant paid no attention and stood holding the rope by which he led the cow. The ranchman rushed at him and knocked him down.

[38]Mattes, *Platte River Road*, pp. 46, 129, 151–52, 270–80.

> Mr. Emmigrant lying on the bottom of the boat pulled his pistol and shot the ranchman directly through the heart.[39]

Halting service, the ferryman pressed all willing emigrants into a court. It seems that only one issue—"justification"—was presented to the jury. "The killing was either justified or not justified. If justified the emmigrant was entitled to be cleared. If not he should be punished." Every man present was permitted to serve as a juror, lawyers participated on both sides of the trial, and about half a dozen eyewitnesses testified. "All those believing the prisoner guilty of murder will step to the East of the road," the judge instructed. "And all those believing him not guilty will step to the West side." Everyone went west. "The verdict is Not Guilty, and the prisoner is free to go his way," the judge announced.[40]

There is no direct explanation why the emigrants voted as they did, but an eyewitness has left us a hint. "The emmigrant would have been cleared by a regularly organized court," he explained. "Lynch law metes out justice under such circumstances. But many a man has been lynched whose provocation was as great as in this instance."[41] The suggestion is that the verdict turned on provocation, although there could have been as many definitions of "sufficient provocation" as there were emigrants voting.

Overland emigrants wanted to make criminal trials as close as possible to those of American courts. Whether they succeeded depends on what they hoped to duplicate. If they wanted prosecutions to be like those at home, then one criterion was how defendants won acquittal. If by proving their own innocence, we are told something, for it shows that their trials, at least, were not

---

[39]Sullivan, "Crossing," pp. 4–5.
[40]Ibid., p. 5.
[41]Ibid., pp. 5–6.

lynchings. The jurors in their cases listened to the evidence and were persuaded by the facts and the arguments of the defense. A much stronger argument for showing that overland trials could match the ideal of trials in the states would be that defendants were released, not because they had proved their innocence but because the prosecution failed to carry the onus of proof. That also happened. Overland juries set prisoners free when persuaded no case had been made against them. "I heard today," a forty-niner wrote in his diary, "that the man who had his trial near the South Pass, for murder, has been aquitted. No positive proof being adduced at the trial, and he is wending his way on to California with the rest of us."[42] In 1859 a Mormon was apprehended near where the overland trail entered today's State of Nevada. He was accused of shooting a Frenchman in the back and stealing his pony. "The Emigrants were going to Hang the young man but the old Frenchman Refused to Swear positively to his Identity this morning, but he is undoubtedly guilty." The accused was released even though feelings were running high because of a recent armed conflict involving Mormons.[43]

One of the more interesting cases which was determined only by a sufficiency of proof arose from a particularly brutal murder. A woman and child were killed by a gang of "white Indians." A man named Tooly was arrested somewhere near the Sink of Humboldt. There was no question he was a member of the gang, and at the trial the husband and father of the two homicide victims identified him as one of the men who had attacked his wagon. "Still," if we are willing to believe the extant account of the trial written more than fifty years after the event, "the evidence was not deemed sufficiently pos-

---

[42]Entry for 10 July 1849, Mann, "Portion," p. 7; Davis, "Introduction and Notes," p. 199.

[43]Entry for 13 July 1859, Wilkinson, *Journal.*

itive or complete, the identity being in some doubt. The jury would not convict without conclusive proof. With the view of procuring further evidence, the judge ordered that the person of the prisoner be searched." The wagon attacked had been robbed of a box containing $1500 in British gold coins. Some of those coins were found hidden in Tooly's buckskin belt. All doubt was resolved. Tooly was found guilty and shot while trying to escape.[44]

There were occasions when the niceties of due process appear to have been carried to extremes. Stranger emigrants sometimes insisted that an individual should have a hearing before they delivered him back to the company that was charging him with wrongdoing. In one case two brothers had joined a company somewhere on the overland trail. "They had been with us but a few days before one had taken their team and left his brother behind. Two of our company went forward in pursuit, and caught up with a train which he had joined, demanding his return. The company refused to let him go without a trial of the case between the brothers which resulted in both returning to our train."[45]

There is a counterargument—that emigrants did not give heed to due process.[46] At least one situation has been reported where the killer of a messmate "was hung to a tree by the indignant emigrants," a case in which there was apparently "no semblance of a trial."[47] If so, it was a lynching pure and simple, an event so rarely reported on the overland trail it can be called an aberration. There were also crimes, even homicides, in which there were no arrests or any effort to bring the culprit to justice.[48] These instances deserve

---

[44]Maxwell, *Crossing the Plains*, pp. 153, 155–57. For other acquittals due to the evidence, see Mattes, *Narratives*, pp. 226, 353.

[45]Rowe, "Ho For California," p. 5 (1853).

[46]Langum, "Pioneer Justice."

[47]Mattes, *Platte River Road*, p. 79.

[48]Entry for 15 November 1849, Bruff, *Journals*, p. 640; Mattes, *Narratives*, p. 537.

a closer look if we are to reach conclusions about the quality of criminal adjudication on the overland trail. It must be understood, however, that for some of the reported cases where prosecutions either did not occur or were dropped no explanation for the outcome is provided.[49]

It does seem that there was one time that a criminal proceeding for theft was dropped because the prosecutors, "fearing there would be revolvers used, withdrew the suit."[50] Even without direct evidence, we may suspect other prosecutions were not brought forward for similar reasons. Usually, when we have explanations for why cases were not pursued it is for the same reasons, such as insufficient evidence, that cases might not be pursued in eastern courts. Along the Humboldt River in 1849, for example, an owner of a mule pursued a man he believed had stolen the animal. Finding the man "on the Mule," the owner recovered his property "but had to let him go as he had no way of" establishing the man's guilt.[51] On a very few occasions prosecutions were considered but not conducted because either the alleged offense had not yet been made criminal by the company's legislative process, or because the majority was persuaded that threats alone were insufficient cause for prosecuting and held that there could be no crime committed without an overt action.[52]

Some cases were resolved without holding a trial. When trouble arose in a company there might be a general consensus to take action but, as the members became familiar with the facts, opinions might change and a different consensus emerge.

---

[49]In one instance a manslayer "was a bout to be Tride [*sic*] for his life" but "was Releast" with no explanation given. Entry for 30 June 1849, Robinson, *Journey*, p. 14.

[50]Entry for 4 August 1864, Brundage, "Diary," p. 11.

[51]Entry for 18 July 1849, Nixon, *Journal*.

[52]See Hastings, *Emigrant Guide*, p. 6.

The usual quiet of our camp was disturbed this evening by a quarrel between two men from Michigan. One whom we only knew by the name of Uncle Ben . . . had refused to go for a bucket of water when asked by his partner, Buchanan, whereupon the latter sought to enforce his request at the point of a long knife, which he brought almost within scalping distance of Uncle's head. Ben deftly warded off the blow and sought refuge in flight, whereupon Buchanan sagely allowed his temper to cool and went for the water himself. The occurrence caused great excitement in camp, and was on all sides referred to as shameful, brutal and unprovoked. Uncle Ben was about fifty, and his companion scarce thirty years old, and this fact further weighed against the younger man. Some talked of expelling Buchanan immediately from the company, but he had one friend, and it seemed but only one, and he, against the universal and indignant cry of the multitude, stood up manfully in his defense. His defender was Mr. Washington, and in the end it was found that Buck . . . was not so great a sinner, that Uncle Ben was not so deserving of sympathy, and that Mr. Washington's courage had a firm basis of right. The plain truth at length became known; Ben was a very lazy old dog, and had constantly imposed on his younger partner by shirking all work whenever he could. Buchanan's patience had been so often tried, his temper, unfortunately, for the once had gotten the better of him.[53]

---

[53]Entry for 8 June 1849, Johnson, *Overland,* pp. 92–93.

Buchanan was not expelled, was apparently not even put on trial in any formal sense, although in another sense the company did try him. The members of the company understood all too well what he had gone through. As the writer said, "Buchanan's patience had been so often tried" that the equities of the case were on his side.

Equities could be the deciding factor on the overland trail. In 1849, one day's travel beyond Fort Laramie, "a stranger by the name of Blodgett" appealed to a company for help. The men whom he had fitted out had that morning left him, taking his animals, wagons, and provisions. "[S]everal of our party agreed to ride on and overtake them. After riding nine miles, about, they found that a woman Colonel Blodgett had fallen in love with and taken along, was the cause of their leaving him. . . . Finding out the cause of their leaving him, some of the men turned back, and others followed, without reclaiming Blodgett's property."[54] In another case, in 1852, a trial for theft was conducted. The defendant was guilty, but the triers of fact found the equities so much in his favor that they not only freed him but passed the hat so he would not have to steal again.

> [W]here we nooned today quite a Number of Men holding a Counsel [*sic*] over a youth that had Stolen a Horse from the Train that he formally belonged to.  by having a Difficulty in Said Train he was turned off and made [to] leave the Train so he helped himself to a horse belonging to the Train and Started ahead on the Journey on his own hook but was followed and Caught   the Men that tried the young man belonged to trains here whare he was Caught   they Considered his Case and Not

---

[54]Entry for 25 July 1849, Hutchings, *Journal*, p. 130.

> only set him at Liberty and also collected him some
> Money among the crowd Where the Counsel was
> held so the young man as some of our Boys termed
> it went on his way Rejoicing.[55]

We can only guess at motives, but it seems that the jurors found that the defendant had been treated too harshly by his company. He may have deserved to be expelled but not to be left on the trail without any transportation. Perhaps too they found he had some equitable claim to the horse even if he did not have a legal claim. Because of their respect for rights to property,[56] most of the emigrants would have ordered the horse returned to its legal owners. Yet many people, like these, could separate the two issues: the rights of the owner to property and the "guilt" of the converter.

Another reason why the impression has been created that the emigrants did not take the criminal process seriously is the way some students of the overland trail have interpreted cases. One historian, for example, discussed a company that took the southern route in 1849. On reaching Socorro, New Mexico, "two of the emigrants, Walter Beard and Byron B. Lee, quarreled over a kettle of beans, or some other trivial matter," he wrote. "Beard was the aggressor, but Lee, the smaller of the two men, had a knife in his hand when the fight started and stabbed Beard in three places, so that he died the next day. The other members of the company apparently ignored the incident."[57] The implication is obvious, that there was no interest in punishing the homicide and the manslayer got away with "murder." But much depends upon what the historian meant when he said "Beard was the aggressor" and the larger. Did Beard have a history of aggression and how aggressive was he

---

[55]Entry for 12 June 1852, Thorniley, *Diary*.
[56]For a study of their respect for property rights, see *Law for the Elephant*.
[57]Cleland, *Rushing*, p. 25. See also Cleland, "From Louisiana," p. 25.

during the fight (the fact he took three knife wounds may show he had not retreated)? And how much larger was he? The company probably had good reason to do nothing if the members concluded that Lee acted in self-defense.

Another student of the overland trail recounts how fights sometimes degenerated into homicides. "When there was a survivor of one of these lethal duels, it was a tossup whether he would get off scot-free or suffer a penalty," this writer contended. "In 1852 [Gilbert] Cole witnessed the deliberate murder of a wagon-owner by a man he had befriended. In this case the murderer was surrounded by friends, and there was no prosecution."[58] To make his point the writer has relied on a surprisingly weak case. Cole's account has already been quoted—the physician who, "armed with a neckyoke," chased "the hired man around the wagon, and both running as fast as they could," until the hired man pulled out his pistol and shot his employer.[59] It takes a very liberal stretching of the facts to call this homicide "deliberate murder." Had the matter been put on trial in any common-law court room the judge would have granted the defendant's motion to instruct the jury that it could find that the doctor was armed with a "deadly weapon." Whether the hired man should have continued to retreat or was justified in using the force that he did was part of the general question that would have been left to the jury.

It stretches the limits of interpretation of historical fact to claim there was no prosecution because "the murderer was surrounded by friends." Our only evidence about what happened is provided by Cole's account and Cole did not say the manslayer went free because he "was surrounded by friends." He said, rather, "[f]rom

---

[58]Mattes, *Platte River Road*, p. 79.
[59]Cole, *Early Days*, p. 48. See above, pp. 30n15, 46.

expressions all around in both trains, the hired man seemed to have the most friends."[60] He was not talking about friendship but about judgment. The people of the two encamped companies—Cole's company, whose members were strangers to the manslayer, and the company to which the manslayer and his victim had belonged— knew the facts of the killing and had been discussing the merits. A consensus had emerged that the man had acted in self-defense— that he was not what the writer calls him, a "murderer." He might well have received that same verdict in an American court of law.

---

[60]Cole, *Early Days*, pp. 48–49.

# 11 EXECUTION OF PUNISHMENT

It is a challenge to classify punishment on the overland trail by the standard criterion of western penology. After all, the emigrants traveling the road to the Pacific Ocean do not belong in the familiar categories to which we generally assign   those who, on their own initiative, undertake to impose sanctions upon people who, they have determined, have violated social, political, or racial norms. They were neither vigilantes nor regulators acting outside established law, for there was no sovereign command on the overland trail. They were not anonymous lynch-mobs enacting vengeance upon individuals who had transgressed some criterion of behavior offensive to part of the community. Truly, it is not necessary to fit them into a descriptive niche. As with their definition of crimes and with the standards of "fair" trial, records of their punishments provide us with evidence of the concepts and behavior of ordinary Americans meting out what they thought was "justice." The penalties they imposed and the harshness of their sanctions tell us as much as we are ever likely to learn of how average nineteenth-century middle-class citizens theorized the measure and justification for punishing social sins.

One fact is clear. Just as emigrants believed that they had a right and a duty to arrest suspected wrongdoers and to determine their guilt by subjecting them to a trial judged by their peers, so they also believed that they had the right to impose a sanction upon those convicted and that it was their civic duty to punish certain "criminal" acts. Recall a case alluded to in the last chapter. A man from an Ohio party, missing a mule, went in pursuit of it. He recovered the animal but had no proof that the man in whose possession it was found had stolen it. As a result, a physician wrote, the members of the Ohio company "had to let him go" and "consequently he escaped punishment."[1]

The physician's exact words are important. They are representative of beliefs often stated by overland emigrants. He did not mention the one thing that a legal theorist might have emphasized: the thin legal line on the overland trail between stealing a mule and requisitioning a stray or abandoned animal.[2] Instead, he commented that the man found with the mule had "escaped punishment." The point to be underlined is not that he thought the suspect should have been punished, but that he stated unequivocally the right of the emigrants to punish him had there been sufficient evidence of guilt.

The right of emigrants on the overland emigration to punish antisocial actions was seldom doubted by the diarists and letter-writers who have left us their ideas. To see the claim to authority to punish expressed, however, it is best to look at the early years of overland travel when most companies, before even starting on the overland trail, described their right to inflict sanctions upon their own members. While still east of the Missouri River, they drafted constitutions stating what actions would be criminal and defining the penalty to be imposed following conviction. In effect, they constitutionalized the authority to punish. There is no need to enumerate these organic company laws since they have been considered elsewhere.[3] Their penal aspects are what concern us, so it should be sufficient to consider a representative constitution and ask what the emigrants had in mind. Our example is the Oregon Society, an overland group of family wagons that was organized into a traveling company in western Missouri during the spring of 1845.

---

[1]Entry for 18 July 1849, Nixon, *Journal.*

[2]*Law for the Elephant*, pp. 265–74, 281–84.

[3]For a discussion of the purpose and content of overland constitutions, see "Governance of the Elephant."

The wagon owners and others allowed to vote adopted a constitution and enacted a code of bylaws establishing specific penalties for the violation of certain proscribed actions.

The bylaws of the Oregon Society deserve our attention for at least three reasons. First, they provide unmatched evidence of what Oregon-bound emigrants thought would be the most serious incidents of peccant behavior on the overland trail. It should be kept in mind that the Oregon emigrations largely consisted of families and therefore had less reason to anticipate criminality than did the younger, more diverse California emigration of the Gold Rush and later years. Second, the bylaws provide an indication of what punishments ordinary Americans at mid-nineteenth century thought fit some crimes. And finally, these bylaws (along with other overland constitutions and codes) are a unique phenomenon: criminal penalties voted by people who not only knew they might be imposed upon themselves, but appreciated that they might be called upon to execute the punishments upon fellow members of their company.

Six specific criminal actions were identified, for which five sanctions were mandated.

> Anyone guilty of wilful murder shall be punished by death and shall not be forced into trial before three days.
>
> Anyone guilty of manslaughter shall be delivered to the authorities in Oregon.
>
> Any one guilty of Rape or attempt at it shall receive thirty nine lashes for three successive days —
>
> Any one guilty of open adultery, or fornication shall receive 39 lashes on their bare back.
>
> Any one guilty of Larceny shall be fined double the amount, and receive 39 lashes on his bare back.
>
> Any one guilty of indecent language shall be fined at the discretion of the Ex[ecutive] Counsel.[4]

---

[4]Bylaws, Oregon Society, printed in Lockley, "Migration of 1845," p. 377.

There are several aspects of the Oregon Society bylaws to think about. The first is a technical point that undoubtedly did not occur to the emigrants of 1845. The men who drafted these bylaws were more precise specifying punishments than spelling out the meaning of terms. The words "murder" and "manslaughter" are not defined, and their interpretation could have caused divisive disputes had anyone been charged with either offense. A defendant accused of the crime of adultery could have argued about the word "open" in "open adultery," admitting to the act of adultery but denying that it had been "open." Using the same line of argument, an individual convicted of rape would have contended the penalty was too vague. It was unclear whether "thirty-nine lashes for three successive days" meant a total of thirty-nine lashes—that is, thirteen a day—or one hundred and seventeen. The provision, therefore, could not be applied in his case and would have to be redrafted if the company wanted to punish rape in the future.

We do not know what difficulties sloppy language caused the Oregon Society's officers enforcing these bylaws. There is no evidence. We must limit our enquiry to the known and the knowable. These bylaws do not tell us under what conditions overland punishments were imposed, only what the emigrants thought were appropriate penalties for the antisocial actions they anticipated might be committed on the Oregon trail.

There is another aspect of the Oregon Society bylaws to consider—the emigrants' expectation that, when others were convicted of crime, they, as individuals or as a group, would have the grit to inflict corporal and, if required, even capital punishment. This fact is underscored not only by the penalty for murder, but by the penalty for manslaughter. The drafters of the Oregon Society bylaws apparently expected they would have the will, as well as the ability, to hold a person accused[5] of manslaughter for "the authorities in Oregon." Yet for crimes other than manslaughter they planned to impose punishment by their own authority, even the supreme penalty for "murder."

A third aspect of the Oregon Society bylaws worth reflection is the way fixed penalties were prescribed for each offense. It is somewhat surprising, for it would have been reasonable to think that emigrants would have followed a less authoritative model. If there had been no enactment mandating a specific punishment, the easiest practice out on the trail would surely have been to adopt a sliding scale, to give the culprit a scolding and to threaten greater pain for recidivism. A man in another emigration, convicted of fighting, received an "adminision" from the captain of his company and the promise of "punishment for the next offence."[6]

To increase the penalty each time an individual repeated a misdemeanor was a theory of penology that appears particularly suited to the overland trail. Emigrants adopted it less often than would be thought, although it did sometimes occur in written laws, not just when there was no punishment legislated prior to the offense. One 1849 company, for example, made gambling an offense "for which the parties shall be tried, and on conviction, shall be required to do guard duty, one day, for the first offence, two days for the second, three days for the third, four days for the fourth, and in the same ratio for each additional offence."[7]

There was another model that would have made good sense on the overland trail. It is the one mentioned in the discussion of jury trials, which would let those most familiar with the facts of an

---

[5]Whether the issue of guilt was to be adjudicated on the trail was also left unclear, but the person to be delivered is described as "guilty."

[6]Entry for 3 June 1849, Shombre, *Diary*.

[7]Bylaws of the Green and Jersey County Company, § 6, printed in Page, *Wagons*, p. 339.

offense fix the penalty. Members of the wrongdoer's company, traveling in close proximity with both him and the victim, having experience dealing with both of them, and evaluating both their characters, would know of mitigating or special circumstances such as provocation and bad temper. Theoretically, appropriate punishment might have been left to the discretion of those familiar with these facts—to designated officers or the vote of the entire company. That possibility makes the Oregon Society's crime of indecent language worth a second look. The bylaws left punishment to the executive council, allowing its members to take into consideration factors such as the general annoyance of indecent language, who was annoyed, the insensitivity shown toward others, the harmony of the company, and recidivism.

There was one offense with a discretionary punishment, which, for some reason not readily apparent, the drafters included in the constitution rather than the bylaws of the Oregon Society. "Any man," it provided, "going to sleep on duty or deserting his post without leave The executive Council shall determine the fine or punishment."[8] The wonder is not that this sanction was discretionary. It made sense to have culpability turn on circumstances such as the presence of hostile Indians, the likelihood buffalo might stampede the cattle, the fact wolves were in the vicinity, and the relative importance of the "post" deserted. The wonder is that this was the only discretionary punishment not limited to a monetary fine. And if we were to wonder further and ask what the penalty might be, the minutes of the Oregon Society record that "David Carson paid a fine into the Treasury of 50 cents for not standing guard."[9] Perhaps the fact that it was the only discretionary sanction that

---

[8]Article 5, Oregon Society Constitution, printed in Lockley, "Migration of 1845," p. 372.

[9]Entry for 20 May 1845, Minutes of the Oregon Society, printed in ibid., p. 377.

included the possibility of physical punishment explains why it was placed in the constitution rather than in the bylaws.

Next year at least one of the companies in the Oregon emigration extended discretionary punishment to other crimes. Even more, it took the decision away from the elected council, providing instead that punishment be "decided upon by a vote of the company."[10] Perhaps it is unwise even to guess at the theory of penology which motivated this change of procedure. It could have been constitutional—the rise of popular sovereignty or the democratic instincts said to have then dominated frontier decisions. Or it could have been penal—a reluctance to leave punishment to the generally more lenient discretion of elected officials. There is a hint, but only a hint, from the year before to support this suggestion. Even before starting out on the trail, the Oregon Society of 1845 had abolished the executive council and vested its "power" on the company as a whole. It is reasonable to suppose that this "power" included the discretionary sentencing of physical punishment for going to sleep on duty or deserting a "post."[11]

Some overland companies exercised discretionary punishment by vesting the power in juries. One constitution defined several crimes and provided for their trial and punishment. Recognizing, however, that potential offenses were not covered, it gave to the jury power to designate penalties. "When any offence is com[m]itted, requiring punishment, and a punishment is not named for such offence, in our By-Laws, it shall be the duty of the jury, in such case, to name in their verdict what the punishment shall be, and how and when inflicted."[12] For companies without constitutions or

---

[10]No. 8, "Laws of the 1846 Emigration," in letter from George L. Curry to the St. Louis *Reveille*, 11 May 1846, in Morgan, *Second Overland*, p. 522.

[11]Entry for 24 May 1845, Minutes of the Oregon Society, in Lockley, "Migration of 1845," pp. 376–77.

[12]Bylaws of the Green and Jersey County Company, § 1, Page, *Wagons*, p. 338.

bylaws this was the process of necessity. They created ad hoc courts as needed, drafting judges, sheriffs, and jurors from among themselves or "stranger" emigrants. Punishment in such cases had to be discretionary, determined by the jury,[13] the judge,[14] or by popular vote after a jury of twelve had convicted.

The general pattern is not surprising. The process of punishment often followed the process of trial. When the definition of the crime as well as an individual's guilt was entrusted to an institution such as the executive council or the jury, the scope of punishment was also. There is a second comparison. As with the conduct of criminal trials, overland emigrants attempted to duplicate those standards for imposing punishments with which they had been familiar at home. They departed from remembered criteria of judgment in only one notable instance, permitting an option that, for American criminal law at least, seems peculiar to the overland trail: they allowed an accused or convicted man a choice of punishments. It was an odd practice for which there is no explanation unless it was due to a reluctance to execute capital punishment.

While a train was in the vicinity of Bear River, two members had a quarrel. One of the men shot and killed the other. Next morning, the manslayer was tried by a jury, found guilty of murder, and sentenced to be shot or expelled. Two mules, arms, and supplies were offered to him, and he was told to choose: leave the train or be shot. "He replied, that he was a Kentuckian, and would rather die an honourable death than run." The condemned man "was accordingly taken out, and seven rifle-balls lodged in his breast — he giving the signal to his executioners to fire."[15] We may think the story farfetched but it was not unique. Four years earlier an emigrant had been accused of deliberate homicide. His compa-

---

[13]For example, entry for 7 September 1849, Powell, *1849 Diary.*
[14]For example, Burroughs, "Reminiscences," p. 48.
[15][Huntley,] *California* 2: 69–70 (1856).

ny "call[e]d a metting of 100 men   they offered to let him go if he would clear out   he refused to do [so] said he was glad he had killed him   they then ordered him to be shot."[16] Later that same year, hundreds of miles farther west, following "some sharp words," a man shot his partner dead. "The train stop[p]ed & chose a jury, & the verdict was as follows, First he could have a chance to leave the train unmolested if he would do it before six o'clock the next morning, & if he would not, he would be shot." "He told them he would not leave, & they told him if he had any business to arrange, he had better do it, & write his family if he wished to." At six o'clock he was executed.[17]

Had any of these men elected expulsion, it is possible that some of the emigrants who had voted to give them the choice would have had second thoughts. That happened when Elisha Brown, who killed a German at the Green River ferry, chose life over death. The homicide has been discussed before, an example of a spontaneous killing. "Brown had asked the German to hand him some soap and on being refused said he would make him and drawing his knife killed him immediately."[18] Brown was arrested and held overnight. Next morning the emigrants gave "him his Choice Either to have a Jury Trial or Let the Guard Take him out one mile[19] from the Incampment and all those who Choosed to do anything they see fit,"[20] which meant that "any one might shoot him that chose to."[21] The idea may have been that rejecting trial and electing expulsion amounted to confessing guilt. He was given two hours in which "to

---

[16]Entry for 16 May 1852, Short, "Diary."

[17]Entry for 5 July 1852, Bradley, *Daily Journal.* For another given the option and said to have been shot, see Eaton, *Overland,* pp. 223–24.

[18]Entry for 30 June 1849, Buffum, *Diary.*

[19]Another source says 100 yards. Ibid.

[20]Entry for 30 June 1849, Stitzel, *Diary,* p. 147.

[21]Entry for 30 June 1849, Buffum, *Diary.*

prepare"[22] or "to reflect,"[23] during which time "he was partly Engaged In Writeing his will."[24] When the period of grace expired, "Mr Brown made choice to Let the Guard take him out,"[25] "but some objecting to his choosing this mode lest he should escape, demanded that he should have a trial at once."[26]

It apparently had been expected that Brown, if set free, might be shot. When he elected expulsion it was realized "that in this way there would be Nothing [done] with him that No one would take the responsibility to molest him."[27] A meeting was called, a vote taken, and it was unanimously resolved to place Brown on trial. "A sheriff was appointed but no one would act as judge, or jury as we were now in Oregon territory."[28] Someone must have raised jurisdictional issues, for it was 1849 and Oregon had an organized government. "[T]hey tried for about 2 hours & but one man could they get to sit as Juror."[29] The reason for the impasse is not stated. The jurisdictional question may have troubled too many. Then again the crowd could have been impatient to get started. Already more than four hours of travel time had been lost. Besides, Brown was not as cooperative as the Kentuckian who had elected to die at Bear River. "He said he would not stand trial but would go to Oregon and take his trial or if he got to the states would deliver himself up to the proper tribunal. It being difficult to conduct a prisoner to Oregon or Fort Hall, he was set at liberty and his things thrown out of the waggons."[30]

---

[22]Ibid.
[23]Entry for 30 June 1849, Stitzel, *Diary*, p. 147.
[24]Ibid.
[25]Ibid.
[26]Entry for 30 June 1849, Buffum, *Diary*.
[27]Entry for 30 June 1849, Stitzel, *Diary*, pp. 147–48.
[28]Entry for 30 June 1849, Buffum, *Diary*.
[29]Entry for 30 June 1849, Stitzel, *Diary*, pp. 148–49.
[30]Entry for 30 June 1849, Buffum, *Diary*.

These emigrants appear indecisive but it is probably more accurate to think them unable to agree on procedure. They were correct in one regard. They had a trip of about a month and a half ahead of them before reaching the settlements in Oregon and transporting a prisoner was just not practical. A month later, as has already been mentioned, the army released two men after deciding there was no point bringing them on.[31] Only when near the settlements—on Lassen's cutoff in California, for example—could emigrants think of holding a wrongdoer for the remainder of the trip.[32]

The variety of punishments imposed by emigrants on the overland trail was not extensive. In truth, there were few choices available. Despite what the Oregon Society bylaws provided, flagellation was not one. Even though every company was well supplied with bullwhips, flogging was so rare that when encountered in diaries it stands out as inusitate, uncharacteristic of legal conduct on the overland trail. Indeed, only special circumstances seem to have motivated punishment by whipping: betrayal of friendship, or a homicide that did not quite fit the emigrants' definition of capital crime.

> A man was detected with $194 in gold coin, which he had cut from his companions pocket & made off with it. He stole too from his friend & benefactor, who had kept him for three months during a spell of sickness, & had then fitted him out for California. He was brought back to the encampment, where he was stripped of all his clothes except under shirt & drawers, ropes were lashed to each hand and foot, he was then stretched upon the ground and whipped with a black leather waggon

---

[31]Entry for 20 July 1849, Banks, *Diary*, pp. 45–46; above, p. 65.
[32]For example, Mattes, *Narratives*, p. 165.

whip. He was whipped most unmercifully; each lash he cried aloud & implored his tormenters to desist and send him to state's prison.[33]

This incident stands out for its brutality. It occurred on the west bank of the Missouri River, just across from the town of St. Joseph where, as the accused apparently was saying, it should have been possible to have turned him over to representatives of federal or state law agencies. The conclusion that the man was whipped because of the extremely antisocial nature of his crime may be wrong. Not to be overlooked is the fact the wounds were so severe they guaranteed he had to turn back and would not again be seen that year on the overland trail.

Indeed, one reason whipping was not a feasible punishment on the overland trail is that it left the victim physically weakened and, perhaps, even disabled. A company that flogged one of its own members might have to nurse the man, carry him in a wagon, and do his chores. At Thomas Fork of Bear River horse thieves were tied to a wagon wheel and whipped.[34] It seems safe to assume they were strangers. After Lafayette Tate was tried and hanged for murder, "his brother said he would be the death of every one of the jury." That threat could not be tolerated, and "he was tied up to one of the trees and whip[p]ed."[35] After that he behaved.

The only other known case of flogging took place far out on the southern branch of the overland trail, somewhere in today's New Mexico. Two trains were traveling in close proximity to each other, a nephew traveling with one, his aunt and uncle with the second. The nephew was stabbed to death by a member of his company and the killer was arrested. Feelings ran high against the

---

[33]Entry for 2 May 1850, McBride, *Diary*.

[34]Mattes, *Narratives*, p. 296. For an account in a very unreliable reminiscence, see entry for 31 July 1865, McDonald, "A Story," p. 73 ("stealing a pair of shoes").

[35]Barry, "Notes to Clark," p. 255*n*36.

prisoner who was said to be "very indifferent" to the sufferings of his victim and who had "a bad countenance, in fact, is a truculent, ill looking fellow."[36] The account of the circumstances that circulated among the members of both trains indicated that he was guilty of a cold-blooded murder. A jury was empaneled from a third company, the man put on trial, and testimony taken which "modified the affair some. . . . [I]t was, however, still sufficiently attrocious to have subjected him in any state in the union, I think, to the Penitentiary for life."[37] It was perhaps for that reason the jury spared the defendant's life, but a problem remained. Although the man might not have been guilty of a capital offense, he had not met the overland-trail burden of "justifying" the homicide. He was guilty of some crime which was somewhat analogous to common-law manslaughter.

Unable to execute the defendant, and unwilling that no sentence be imposed, "[t]he jury sentenced him to have 50 lashes and to be expelled from the train." Some emigrants thought the punishment lenient, but if any alternative was proposed it is not reported.[38] It is apparent that the punishment of flagellation was a compromise.

The penalty probably most commonly imposed on the overland trail would not have been a suitable punishment for either murder or manslaughter. It was the assignment of extra guard duty, generally invoked for infraction of the rules,[39] though one company employed it to punish such delicts as "delinquency" and battery.[40] Guard duty was a very unpleasant task and for many

---

[36]Entry for 3 September 1849, Powell, *1849 Diary*, p. 100.

[37]Entry for 7 September, 1849, ibid., p. 106.

[38]Ibid.

[39]For example, failure to serve on guard as ordered. Leeper, *Argonauts*, p. 20.

[40]Read and Gaines, "Introduction" to Bruff, *Journals*, p. 469n108 (delinquency); entry for 9 July 1849, Bruff, *Journals*, p. 36, and Read and Gaines, "Introduction," p. 485n50.

companies it was the only penalty used to coerce internal discipline. For some reason, another very objectionable task, driving the most rearward wagon in a train and spending the day in a cloud of dust and dirt, was never mentioned as a penalty.

Military field punishments were also not mentioned. Francis Parkman, who ventured out onto the Oregon trail in 1846 as far as Fort Laramie, said that "[b]y the wholesome law of the prairie, he who falls asleep on guard is condemned to walk all day, leading his horse by the bridle."[41] If this were so, diarists did not think it important enough to report. Army penalties, like tying a man to the wheel of a wagon or putting him on short rations, seem never to have been practiced on the overland trail.[42] One reason was the fluidity of organization. Those who violated company rules might accept corporal punishment only if they had a strong desire to remain company members. But the prospect of physical pain made membership less attractive, and rather than endure it an emigrant might well have walked out. In fact, the ease with which a person could withdraw from a company made corporal punishment almost impossible to impose. A man who accepted even the penalty of extra guard duty obviously wanted to remain a member of his mess or company or he could easily have refused to serve. The major exception was during the early emigrations when the trail was sparsely traveled, there were no other trains to take you in, and most people traveled in family groups. In 1844, "a young man was ordered staked out as a punishment for making a threat to shoot another with whom he had quarrelled." He had to submit. He was with his family and his father had posted the money for his bail.[43]

---

[41] Parkman, *Oregon Trail*, p. 119

[42] One exception—tied to a wagon and forced to walk all day—occurred on the trail to Montana, not the trail to the Pacific. "Coercing the Elephant," p. 179*n*76.

[43] Minto, "Oregon Trail," p. 136; Rumer, *Wagon Trains*, p. 217.

# 12 | PUNISHMENT OF EXPULSION

Some overland travelers encountered punishment so seldom—or never at all—that they did not appreciate the range of available sanctions: banishment, whipping, stakeout, admonition, and death. A man on the way to Oregon in 1849 even supposed that only one type of sanction was possible. He was writing of a quarrel that had occurred between two family men. "The women joined in, one of which drew a knife," he wrote. "It however resulted in the expulsion of one family from the company." Expulsion, he believed, was "the only mode of punishment . . . practiced on the road."[1]

The Oregon emigrant was wrong. Expulsion was not the only overland sanction. It is possible, however, that, with the exception of extra guard duty, it was the most common punishment meted out on the overland trail. We should, perhaps, not be surprised that expulsion was the common penalty. It was easily administered and surely seemed easy to enforce. Probably more importantly, it was easily agreed to. Expulsion not only was free of the awesome consequences of the death penalty or whipping but, after a fight or a theft upsetting the harmony of a company and causing social uneasiness, it simply made good sense.

One morning ten days beyond Fort Kearny, a company of forty-niners was

> thrown into great consternation by the discharging
> of a gun, as we are in danger of attack from Indians,
> but it proved to be a gun in the hands of a

---

[1] Entry for 28 May 1847, Rayner, *Journal.*

> Kentuckian, the load taking effect in the right side of Mr. Bush. At the same place Bush and he had fought on the previous evening, about a trivial matter, and after the fight was over Bush went into the tent and kicked his opponent in the mouth as he was resting on the ground. The Kentuckian got up and getting his gun, shot Bush, the ball entered and passed through the tendon.

Bush did not die. "At a meeting of the Company it was decided that the Kentuckian should be driven out of the Company. Accordingly he left after night with two mules."[2]

On the same day in a different company there was another shooting. Two men, Tibbetts and Beach, had fought the evening before, and in the morning Beach was preparing his breakfast "& was standing with his back towards Tibbetts, when the latter came out of his tent approached within ten feet of the former & fired at Beach. . . . The Ball entered about 1½ inch from the back bone & passed out at the point of the ribs inflicting a very Dangerous & Severe wound." Again the victim was not killed.

> [I]n the evening we took the vote of the company as what should be done with Tibitts. When he was voted out of the Company by a majority. I being the only Kentuckian who voted for his being punished. I desired that we should have taken him to Laramie & sent back to the States for trial or otherwise de[a]lt with. . . . We started him off on the instant telling him to take his two mules & pack which was no punishment at all.[3]

---

[2]Entry for 20 June 1849, [Brown,] *Memoirs*, p. 11; Brown, "Gold Seeker," p. 138.
[3]Letter to Henry Lyne, 30 June 1849, Lyne, *Letters*.

The company was nine or ten days' travel away from Fort Laramie so it would have been possible to have arrested Tibbetts and delivered him to the military. Perhaps those voting for expulsion knew that it would have been futile to have taken him to Laramie. More likely they wanted to be rid of a troublemaker and so ordered him out.

Fighting was grounds for expulsion. "Some of our company had a regular fight today," an emigrant of 1852 wrote. "One or two was knocked down but no injury done, only they are all obliged to leave our company."[4] It was not the usual rule, however. Fighting was so common on the overland trail that unless it endangered a company's social harmony it had to be ignored. Even when fighters were expelled, wrongdoing was more likely to be the determining factor, not which party used deadly force. In 1849 a man got into a fight with two fellow members of his company trying to rob him. He shot both of them. They were expelled from the company, not him.[5] They were the ones, not him, who had threatened social disharmony by attempting robbery.

Expulsion was also meted out for a wide variety of other wrongs ranging from "dangerously" wounding a fellow company member[6] and stealing property,[7] including horses,[8] to disrespect for elected authority.[9] Of course, in some cases it was not necessary to banish anyone. The wrongdoer, knowing he could not remain, withdrew

---

[4]Entry for 26 June 1852, Adams, "Diary," p. 296; Adams, "Journal to Oregon," p. 11; Adams and Blank, "Diary," p. 268.

[5]Davis, "Introduction and Notes," p. 151*n*127.

[6]Besides the two cases just discussed in the text, see entry for 5 November 1849, Bruff, *Journals*, p. 259 (same case as Read and Gaines, "Introduction," pp. 619–20*n*205); Mattes, *Platte River Road*, p. 81.

[7]Entries for 10, 11 August 1857, Menefee, "Travels," p. 10.

[8]Mattes, *Platte River Road*, p. 77.

[9]Entries of 29, 30 May 1849, Pritchard, *Diary*, pp. 75, 77. Also, in 1849, an emigrant was expelled for "slandering the company." "Prosecuting the Elephant," p. 338.

voluntarily.[10] Two members of a Kentucky company were eating when "[s]ome unpleasant woords [*sic*] passed whereupon Hodges Struck Hamline & Knocked him down — and was beating him sevearly." The fight was stopped by others in the company, one of whom got cut by Hodges's bowie knife. "Hodges withdrew from the mess next morning — & we left him on the road side with his Mules & good[s] & chattels — and what became of him I Know not."[11]

There was a time early in the history of the overland trail when emigrants codified expellable crimes. One of the companies whose constitutions were discussed in an earlier chapter, for example, had a provision in its bylaws spelling out causes and standards for expulsion. Just to draw a deadly weapon or to threaten the life of a fellow member were grounds for expulsion.

> § 2. In case any member alleges to the Captain, that he believes his life, or those of his comrades, to be in danger from any other member, or complains that any member has drawn any deadly weapon on another, except in self-defence, or has threatened the life of another, it shall be the duty of the Captain to bring such person, complained of, to trial in the same manner, as is provided in section first of these By-Laws, and if the jury shall unanimously decide that it is unsafe that he shall continue with us, he shall be expelled.[12]

---

[10]The situation could be reversed. In one case a dispute arose between two members of a company. One hit the other with the butt of his whipstock. The man struck retreated and it was he, not the one who used the weapon, who "separated from the Company resolved to finish his Journey alone." Entry for 11 August 1852, Gee, *Journal.*

[11]Entry for 23 May 1849, Pritchard, *Diary,* pp. 68–69.

[12]Bylaws of the Green and Jersey County Company, Page, *Wagons,* pp. 338–39. For "section first," see above, p. 106.

The question put to the jury reveals a great deal about the purpose of expulsion on the overland trail. It was not "guilt" or "justification" as in most other trials we have seen. It was, rather, whether "it is unsafe that he shall continue with us." The felt social need to defend the group's collective safety was the paramount concern.

It is quite likely that a jury empaneled to decide the question whether "it is unsafe that he shall continue with us," would have been interpreted the word "unsafe" much more broadly than might have been intended by the provision's drafters. Companies were not long on the plains before they discovered the absolute necessity of social harmony and learned that dissension and troublesome companions retarded progress. That was why antisocial behavior could be enough for expulsion on the overland trail. Persistent antisocial conduct could destroy a company. "[W]e found two bad fellows, held a Court Marshal, and drove them off," a forty-niner wrote his wife, assuming there was no need to explain the matter further. The fact that they had been "bad fellows" said enough.[13]

It is premature to discuss the purpose of expulsion at this point. The topic is better considered when theories of overland punishment are examined and the sanction of banishment can be evaluated from the perspective of its purpose—social harmony—rather than the perspective of punishment or retribution. It is sufficient for present purposes to explore some of its mechanical aspects. In that regard it is worth repeating that expulsion was the penalty most often leveled on offenses that were more serious than those punished by extra guard duty. An important reason why companies could apply the sanction practically at will was that after 1848 an expelled man was seldom exposed to danger. It was not dif-

---

[13]Letter of 9 July 1849, Eastland, *Letters*. In one case, a company bully was not expelled but "banished to Coventry by us all." The treatment, with accompanying warnings, about his social behavior, had their effect. "I don't expect any more trouble from him." Entry for 28 July 1849, Middleton, "Across the Plains," p. 45.

ficult for the able-bodied and young to find a place in another train. If they were unable to do so, because of bad reputation or some other cause, the expellee could usually travel in sight of other emigrants. He did not have to make the trip alone. Such was certainly true for the well-populated California trail during the Gold Rush, when expulsions were relatively frequent. They were imposed not only for such serious matters as theft but minor infractions such as "insubordination."[14] What may be more surprising is that expulsions also occurred, even apparently for quarreling,[15] on the Oregon trail before 1849 and on the very sparsely traveled southern, or Gila River, trail.

A company traveling down the Gila in 1849 included a rather unpopular member who for some time had been suspected of pilfering from his own mess. Food was missing but there had been "no positive proof of his guilt. Last night, however, he was caught in the act of stealing rations from the general stock of his mess. A meeting of the Company was held to-day to consider his Case and it was decided, by a unanimous vote of the Company, to expel him. He was furnished with provisions sufficient, (allowing him the same ration the balance of us have) to last him from here to San Diego, and ordered him to go, and he has gone."[16]

Considering the late date—it was November—and the isolated location—in dangerous Indian country—expulsion in this case was a very severe punishment. It probably was not regarded as a death sentence but we cannot be sure. A great deal would have depended on the age, the physical condition, and the experience of the expellee. It is reasonable to suppose that most men would have survived. Some did under worse circumstances. One case, which

---

[14]For example, Lorch, "Gold Rush," p. 362n121.
[15]For example, entries for 12–13 June 1845, Howell, "Diary of Emigrant," p. 142.
[16]Entry for 6 November 1849, Simmons, *Notes*, p. 89.

provides an interesting twist on expulsion and how to survive, also occurred that same year on the southern trail but much further east. A company of New York forty-niners, when traveling between San Antonio and El Paso, sought the protection of a brigade of army engineers surveying a road in what was then unsettled wilderness. They thought it important for their safety to stay close to the military yet found it difficult after a member got into trouble with the commanding officer.

> One of our party (a Jew named Rose) was (by order of Maj[o]r [Jefferson] Van Horn) drummed out of Camp — he was condemned without a hearing, and thus disgracefully punished. — A little "brief authority" in the hands of a damned fool, is ever exercised injudiciously, and therefore (except by accident) allways injudiciously. . . . poor Rose cannot return to Camp except at night, or when the Troops are out of sight — We have determined that he shall not be driven entirely away.[17]

Usually expulsion was the only penalty inflicted. It was seldom coupled with another sanction. The case mentioned in the last chapter—the man on the southern trail who was ordered both whipped and expelled for committing a culpable homicide that the jury found not to be a capital offense[18] — was one of these exceptions to the general rule. Another was the punishment inflicted in 1849 on a man who was "most cruelly beaten for stealing & turned out of the company."[19]

---

[17]Entry for 25 July 1849, Eastland, "Diary and Letters," p. 111.
[18]See above, p. 169.
[19]Entry for 13 June 1849, *Geiger–Bryarly Journal,* p. 106.

Expulsion must have seemed a wonderfully simple punishment to those imposing it, because there was so little danger for a person put out of a train. Even the ownership of personal property created few problems for the expelling company. An expelled person was always allowed to take his personal property with him, his mules or horses, his wagon, his provisions, and his clothes. The only problems that ownership of personal property created was when the expellee owned too much or had no private means to transport what he had. There could also be a problem when a person owned too little. A member of an 1849 company was tried and convicted of "refusing to do duty." He was expelled. "At night they carried his trunk of clothing outside the guard and put him with it."[20] Apparently that was all he owned: no animals, and no share in a wagon.

Concurrent ownership, whether of mess, partnership, company, or joint-stock, was quite a different matter from personal property. After all, rights to concurrent property tied the expelled individual to the expelling group or to at least part of it. If the expellee owned rights in a mess or a wagon, he had claims on the other members of the mess or the other owners of the wagon and had to be compensated either in money, a proportional share of the provisions, or, if he insisted, with part of the team needed to haul the wagon. If he had purchased shares in the company, he owned property rights concurrently with every other member of the company, a connection which could get quite complicated if the draft animals and wagons had not been distributed to individuals or to partnerships, but were controlled by the officers or by majority vote.[21] A company's constitution could simplify matters by providing for forfeiture of rights and interests, including concurrent-property interests, upon conviction for a crime and expulsion.[22] In that case, what the

---

[20]Entry for 3 July 1849, Hall, "Diary," p. 7.
[21]*Law for the Elephant*, pp. 127–215.
[22]See sources cited, "Coercing the Elephant," p. 167*n*22.

expelled party took with him, aside from his personal clothing and valises, was up to majority decision. That also seems to have been the customary practice where there were no constitutions or when the constitution did not provide for forfeiture. In one instance occurring in 1849, a man "driven out of the Company" was "left [behind] after night with two mules,"[23] apparently voted him by the membership. Perhaps the animals were regarded as his equitable share of the concurrent property. Just as likely they were given him as a humane gesture to ensure his survival.

The problems of property were quite different when the expelled person was a principal owner. He might, for example, possess a wagon in which others were traveling or be the sole owner of the provisions. Then his messmates would either have to leave the company and go with him, or purchase their way into another mess.[24] Quite a different situation was faced by an expellee who had his wife and children along, at least before 1849 when he could expect to join another company within hours. During the sparse emigration of 1846, James Frazier Reed, whose expulsion was the most memorable banishment ever ordered by a California-bound company, faced this predicament. Without him his family and property would have been precariously exposed—at the mercy of the Nevada desert, the Sierras, and the Paiutes. All he could do was ask the company "to care for his family."[25] It is a story best left to the discussion of the reasons why people were expelled. It is the reasons for Reed's expulsion, not his family's immediate predicament, that makes his banishment the most interesting punishment in the history of the overland trail.

---

[23]Brown, *Memoirs*, p. 11; Brown, "Gold Seeker," p. 138.

[24]Which they most likely would do by contract, not with money, either agreeing to serve as a hired hand or promising future payment. See "Binding the Elephant."

[25]Morgan, *First Overland*, p. 441n72.

# 13 | Hanging the Elephant
## PUNISHMENT OF EXECUTION

Things were not always as one might expect on the overland trail. As the death penalty was a more complicated punisment for emigrants to impose than the punishment of expulsion, it might be thought that the problems of dividing or disposing of property would be more complicated for executions than for expulsions. Not so. Had James Frazier Reed been sentenced to die he would probably not have had to make arrangements for his family: the company that executed him would have been responsible for seeing them through. Of course, the emigrants did not think of the complexity of punishment in terms of property. For them death was the most complicated punishment. It was surely the most troublesome and awesome and, therefore, the one most frequently recounted and discussed. Emigrants who drove by graves of executed men thought the sight worth mentioning in their diaries. They might know nothing of the circumstances of the homicide and meet no one who could tell them about the execution, but the mere fact that summary and final justice had been meted out hundreds of miles from the nearest courts and prisons struck them with awe.

Those able to learn the details of executions often recorded the facts. Death by firing squad especially intrigued them. Two of the men discussed earlier,[1] who elected to be executed rather than leave their companies, were killed that way. In both cases the emigrants mustered squads of twelve men each. One of the condemned wrote a letter to his family and then "he pulled his Coat off, & step[p]ed off about four Rods, & told them he was ready. upon

---

[1]See above, pp. 164–65.

which the twelve fired & every ball entered his body, Killing him instantly."[2] In the second case the assembled emigrants "selected 12 men gave each a gun   6 loaded with Balls   6 with blank Cartridges   they fired and killed him."[3]

It might be thought that the six guns with blanks tell us something about sensitivities of the emigrants. More likely they tell only that many of these men had served in their state militia. Most likely none of them, not even veterans of the Mexican War, had seen a firing squad. But those who had been officers had read arms manuals describing how firing squads were conducted. Still, sensitivities must be given some due. An execution that reveals much about the sensibilities of nineteenth-century Americans was mentioned by several diarists. It was the death by firing squad of George Hickey for the killing of Elijah Davis along the Gila River in the southern route of the overland trail. Hickey had been tried by emigrants, found guilty, and sentenced to be shot. The jury, which had been drawn from three separate trains, "recommended that lots be cast for the selection of 12 men to fire the guns, which were to be stacked together and drawn by a blind-folded man and handed out one at a time to the executioners."[4] According to the account posted by the participants to inform other emigrants of what had happened, "A ticket was placed in a hat for each man, all blank but twelve, who were to shoot. 12 guns were loaded, 6 with powder & balls & 6 with blank charges, & all loaded secretly. They all fired at a signal given from one grave to another (about ten steps) & several balls entered the region of his heart. He died

---

[2]Entry for 5 July 1852, Bradley, *Daily Journal.*
[3]Entry for 16 May 1852, Short, "Diary." For other executions by shooting, see Mattes, *Narratives*, pp. 378, 345 (man is shot and woman "begged us to kill her"), p. 453 ("man shot for stealing horses 3 weaks [*sic*] ago.").
[4]C. C. Cox, "Notes and Memoranda of an Overland Trip from Texas to California," quoted in Foreman, *Marcy*, p. 299.

immediately."[5] By firing "from one grave to another," the notice
meant that the executioners had "dug his [Hickey's] grave on the
road side opposite Davis's & fired from Davis's grave,"[6] that is,
"Hickey stood near his grave & the executioners stood at the grave
of the murdered man, the distance accross the road or Wagon path
about 40 feet . . . & the next Flood in the Rio Gila will obliter-
ate every mark from the face of the earth of this murderer & his
victim."[7]

One reason some guns had been loaded with blanks may be
because the executioners had not been volunteers but had been
drafted by lottery. This was true of some of the other occasions
when half the firing squad had blank ammunition,[8] as, for instance,
the execution of Balsley who killed Beal on the main California
trail. "Some one got a number of tickets and put them in a hat
when each man drew a ticket   Those that drew one with a block
mark upon it had to shoot at him   10 men drew such tickets   One
man loaded [the] riffles   6 with ball and 4 with blank cartradge."
It is amazing, but one of the ten selected was David Dye, the messmate of Balsley and Beal who had been the lead witness to the
killing and whose testimony probably convicted Balsley. In an even
more remarkable turn of events, after Dye joined the firing squad,
Balsley named him as his and Beal's executor, trusting him to sell
their property and to send the proceeds to their families. We will
never know just how these relationships were worked out but one

---

[5]"Notice of Execution," signed by C. Mitchell, copied in entry for 29 November
1849, Eccleston, *Overland*, p. 217. It was reported that five out of the six guns which were
loaded struck Hickey. Entry for 15 August 1849, Bouldin, "Diary."

[6]Entry for 6 October 1849, Brisbane, *Journal*.

[7]Entry for 21 October 1849, Forsyth, "Journal," p. 87.

[8]For example, the "second case" discussed above. See above, p 182.

eyewitness believed that Dye accepted both duties, serving first as Balsley's executioner, and then as his executor.[9]

After the firing squad had been drawn, Balsley, the condemned man, led it

> a short distance from the tents and told them when he was ready he would hold up his right hand   he then knelt down with his face towards them   but they doing an unholy act could not look their victim in the face and told him that he must die with his back to them   He gave them one look and turned around and said a prayer   then turning again and looking at his <u>foes</u> in the face said "May the Lord forgive you for what you are about to do" held up his hand and fell pierced with 4 balls.[10]

A quite different account of the same execution was given by a second emigrant, one who had been a fellow member of the company to which Balsley and Beal had belonged. In fact, after Balsley and Beal had separated, Beal had joined this man's mess and was riding in his wagon when Balsley rode up and shot Beal, although for some reason the man is not reported to have testified at the trial. Perhaps he had been away from the wagon at the time. In any event, he barely discussed the trial of Balsley in his diary but wrote a remarkably long description of the execution. In contrast to the diarist just quoted, he was more interested in the executioners than in the condemned man. It appears from what he says that those conducting the execution sought to conform to what they likely thought was American practice.

---

[9]Entry for 14 June 1852, McKieran, *Diary.*
[10]Ibid.

[A] file of twelve men ware drawn from the company by ballott to execute the prisinar   Twelve guns were charged six with ball and six blank and placed in the hands of these men   no one knew who held the fatal guns   This being done the file of men under command of the fourman of the Jeury marched about four rods to the place whare the prisinar awaited them under a strong gard   The prisinar was then marched about eight rods to the road side with a blanket about his shouldars, by command the procession halted   The commander with the prisinar steped of[f] twelve payces in front of the file   The blanket which had hitherto bin about the prisionars shouldars was then spread on the ground upon which the prisinar knelt down with his back to the men   This was his chois   This being done the prisinar then caled for a man who had conversed with him upon his future destany and requested a prair of forgiveness   This man was one of the twelve who the prisinar knelt before for execution — He laid down his gun and with a bended knee did offer up [to] the Almighty God a prair in behalf of this retched man   The executioner then steped into his place and these words ware given (by the fourman)   make ready take aim — the prisinar gave the signal for fire by raising his right hand   this was his request   One sharp report of twelve rifels and all was over[11]

·

---

[11]Entry for 14 June 1852, Green, *1852 Diary*, p. 14.

The details may seem familiar. If so, that is the important point. We will never know whether the emigrants who directed this execution were copying what they had read of European procedures, what they heard from stories of the Mexican war, or what they had learned in their militia units. We can only be certain that they had in mind some pattern. The marching of the firing squad, the formality of the guard, the shouted commands, the stepping-off of set paces, the prayer, and the granting of a final request, however, may not have come from remembered, or half-remembered, "legal" executions east of the Missouri River. They were, more likely, a reaching for legitimacy, a groping by the emigrants to do what they thought American governments would do. Their attempt, whether well understood or only vaguely comprehended, was to obtain legality by maintaining solemnity and regularity through a re-creation of the recognizable.

If there was an odd feature to this particular execution, it was the role played by the foreman. For the foreman of the jury to lead the firing squad may be unprecedented. He also swore the witnesses and is said to have called them,[12] so his duties were more than merely those of presiding over the jury and reporting its verdict. His role may have been analogous to a sheriff's or a clerk of court's.

We are already familiar with a third case in which some guns held blank ammunition. It is the one where "Captain Kennedy" forced the issue by arresting a manslayer who was a "stranger" to his company and then had strangers try him. Kennedy also arranged for the man's execution, using what seems to have been the largest firing squad in the history of the overland trail.

> Twenty five armed men marched him one half mile
> to where his grave had been prepared. Fourteen of

---

[12]Entry for 13 June 1852, ibid., p. 13; Eaton, *Overland*, p. 222.

the guns were loaded with bullets and the rest with
blanks. When the signal was given they all fired the
prisoner falling backwards and dying within one
minute. It was a sad sight to look upon. We immediately laid him in his grave without even a rough
box.[13]

A memoir of the 1852 emigration, written years later, recalled
a firing squad of six men, three with loaded guns and three that
were empty. These men apparently did not know how to prepare
blank ammunition.[14] There was, in fact, no set method for executing those convicted of deliberate homicide. It is not surprising that
overland executions in this respect were in sharp contrast with overland trials. Many emigrants had seen trials and shared memories of
how they were conducted. As a result, though held years apart and
in different areas on the trail, overland-trail trials had many procedures in common. But the average emigrant knew little of
executions, especially executions by firing squad. Hence, aside from
efforts to avoid brutality and to create a semblance of legality, they
varied in detail.

There was one procedure adopted in a few executions that the
emigrants must have known departed from American practices.
That was when a person convicted of a capital offense was allowed
to pick the method of execution. Captain Kennedy, for example,
"[g]ave [the] prisoner his choice to be shot or hanged. He preferred
to be shot."[15] Another man allowed to select "preferred being shot,

---

[13]Entry for 8 July 1862, Scott, "Across the Plains." It is somewhat remarkable that
Kennedy could find so many executioners. It was reported in 1849 that a man convicted
of murder had to be released because "no one could be found to execute him." Mattes,
*Narratives*, p. 147 (quoting J. A. Daigh).

[14]Payette, *Northwest*, p. 525 ("Edson Marsh's Account").

[15]Entry for 7 July 1862, Scott, "Across the Plains."

and was forthwith."[16] Not everyone cared for the alternatives. "You can have your choice," a third defendant was told by a judge at the Humboldt Sink, "to be shot, or hanged to the uplifted tongue of a wagon. Which do you choose?" The condemned man ran. "'Shoot boys,' commanded the sheriff; . . . a chorus of shots sounded, and the court's sentence was executed."[17]

One overland court even permitted condemned men to select their own executioners. We might guess this would be a procedure only when the firing squad came entirely from the defendant's company and he knew them all. Not so. In the one documented case of this type, the condemned were not even emigrants but six white renegades, horse thieves, who had been pursued by men from several companies, arrested, tried, found guilty, and sentenced to death. Given a period of grace "to make any preparations they desired," they had time to become acquainted with their captors. They even "disposed of their possessions, consisting principally of their outfit, horses, saddles, and arms, each one giving what he had to bestow to those whom they [sic] might have taken a passing fancy." During the night between trial and execution, two escaped. "The next morning each of the four remaining was given the right to choose by whom he should be shot. There was but one refusal, and that was by the young fellow chosen by Badger, who positively refused. The judge then, as Badger would make no further choice, appointed one whom Badger accepted."[18]

There is only one account of this execution and, although it is unusually detailed, it gives no explanation for allowing such a

---

[16]Entry for 10 July 1862, Gould, "Journal," p. 23. Also, see Mattes, *Platte River Road*, pp. 79, 81.

[17]Maxwell, *Crossing the Plains*, p. 157.

[18]Burroughs, "Reminiscences," pp. 48–49. For the name "Badger" and its significance, see *Law for the Elephant*, pp. 25–26.

bizarre choice. But at least the executioners were spared the ordeal of looking into the faces of the men who had selected them. The prisoners "were placed in line, their eyes bandaged, their hands tied behind them and they were made to kneel down." An executioner apparently stood closely behind each, shooting directly into the skull of the man for whom he was responsible. This procedure was probably designed to keep the affair tidy, as indeed it did. "At a given sign, it was almost as if a single shot had been fired, and as if a single man had fallen, so near together was it that they gave up their lives."[19]

Although condemned felons preferred to be shot, their executioners preferred hanging. We lack the evidence for compiling statistics, but there is no doubt that in most executions firing squads were not used. Instead, the condemned were hanged.[20] It is a safe guess that most emigrants thought of hanging before shooting, as hanging was the capital punishment then employed by all the states which had the death penalty. It was less nasty; it took no more effort; and, since it involved many participants, its public sanction was usually as great as that of death by firing squad.

Again the emigrants attempted to follow remembered ceremony, although admittedly there are not many cases where the head of the condemned man is reported hooded.[21] Diaries also seldom mention a hangman, which implies that most hangings were col-

---

[19]Burroughs, "Reminiscences," p. 49.

[20]For reports (though not necessarily by eyewitnesses) of hangings, see entry for 23 June 1852, McAuley, "Record," p. 58; entry for 27 June 1852, Clark, "Overland," p. 263; entry for 30 June 1852, Coon, "Journal," p. 192; entry for 3 July 1852, Jones, *Passenger to California*; entry for 20 August 1859, Brown, *Journal of a Journey*, p. 46; Mattes, *Narratives*, pp. 342, 371, 385, 390, 392, 492, 501, 510.

[21]"I saw him after the rope was around his neck and cap over his face but I did not see him drop." Mattes, *Narratives*, p. 492 (Jane Bell, 1859).

lective affairs, conducted by a group rather than one or two individuals.[22] Numbers appear to have been, for example, involved in one execution where "a hangman's rope [was] brought into action by tying one end of it to the man's neck and the other was thrown over the limb of a tree and drawn taut." The writer unfortunately was not an eyewitness, but she seems to be saying that a number of men pulled the "other" end of the rope.[23]

The most common method of hanging was truly a cooperative effort. It occurred when no trees or structures were available from which to hang the condemned person. A gallows was then improvised by using the covered wagons. The implication of an 1852 account, reporting that the condemned man was "hung on our old waggon at sundown,"[24] is that one wagon was enough. Usually, however, they used two wagons, which meant that the owners of two wagons—as likely to have been messes of from four to eight men as to have been individuals—as well as other people, participated. The wagons were run together and the tongues were elevated "to form a tripod"[25] or, as one emigrant expressed it, "in the shape of a letter 'A',"[26] that is, they "put two waggon tongues up together and fastened them,"[27] "blocked the wheels,"[28] or had "the fore-wheels scotched with ox-yokes."[29]

There are two accounts of one hanging that employed wagon tongues for a gallows, neither of them eyewitness. We have already met the condemned man. He is the wagon owner who went hunt-

---

[22]Contrary: "The sheriff kicked the boxes from under him." See below, text to note 34.

[23]"Copy of Smith's Reminiscences," p. 4. The date was 4 July 1849.

[24]Entry for 23 June 1852, Clark, *Guide*; Eaton, *Overland*, p. 165. Similarly, see entry for 18 August 1859, McPherson, "Journal," part 3, col. 2.

[25]Thompson, "Reminiscences," p. 2.

[26]Entry for 5 July 1852, Conyers, "1852 Diary," p. 459.

[27]Mattes, *Narratives*, p. 345 (Samuel Chadwick, 1852).

[28]Dickinson, *Overland Journal* (recalling 1852 trip).

[29]Terrell, "Overland Trip," p. 79 (writing of 1852).

ing along the Sweetwater River with the boy or young man in his employ, returned without him, and reported the boy had gone to visit another train, was forced to go back, and, when the body was discovered, was tried, found guilty, and sentenced to be hanged.[30] "[A]s they had nothing to make a gallows out of," one emigrant explained, "they took two wagon tongues  put them point to point and set a chair in the mid[d]le and the man stood on same till the Rope was tied and then the chair was taken from under him."[31] In the second account the man stood on boxes rather than a chair.

> They made a gallows by running two or three wag-
> ons with their tongues together, so as to make a
> fork, then locked them so that they could not slip;
> the culprit was made to stand on some boxes and
> the rope put on his neck, and when all was ready the
> sheriff kicked the boxes from under him and he was
> launched into eternity. This is the way in which jus-
> tice is meted out on the Plains.[32]

It is evident that these executions were as much cooperative efforts as were firing squads, trials, and most arrests. If the condemned stood on a chair, someone had to lend the chair as well as the rope and the wagon tongues, someone had to steady him on the chair, someone had to fix the noose, and someone had to pull away the chair. If the condemned person sat on the back of a horse, someone had to furnish the animal, someone had to hold it, and someone had to drive it out from under him.[33]

---

[30]See above, pp. 94–95.

[31]Entry for 29 June 1852, Moreland, *Diary.*

[32]Entry for 29 June 1852, Thompson, *Crossing the Plains,* p. 56.

[33]Doubt about whether men were ever executed from wagon tongues has been expressed. Langum, "Pioneer Justice," p. 435*n*45. In addition to the incidents cited above, see Mattes, *Narratives,* pp. 348, 365, 372, 391, 499, 508.

A great deal could be made of this joint activity, although we should be careful not to push the argument too far. The evidence provides more surmise than proof, yet one conclusion is inescapable. A majority of emigrants expressed popular acceptance—if not actual approval—of overland punishments, including the penalty of death. This was expressed in several ways, and silent acquiescence may not have been the most common: an impressive number expressed support by active participation.

Another indication of collective activity was the orderliness of overland executions. As a rule, they were neither sadistic nor vengeful. The execution of those four white renegades shot for horse stealing is typical. They were treated respectfully, permitted to address the court, one was allowed to remain anonymous after saying he did not wish to disgrace his parents by revealing his family name,[34] and, after being condemned, they were given several hours to prepare themselves for death. "As soon as decency permitted," an eyewitness wrote, "they were buried and the crowd dispersed."[35]

An emigrant of 1850 stands out as an exception to the general rule of "decency" when he suggested that a convicted manslayer should have been boiled to death. He was upset because there had been a trial at which the deliberate nature of the killing had been proven. "But they let him go," the emigrant complained, "not because they thought him not guilty, but because they did not like the job of hanging him. They say he shall be tried in Cal[ifornia]. I expect that it made greatly in his favor there being no trees in the valley. Why didn't they put him in one of the hot springs?"[36] It was probably just as well he did not suggest such an idea to his fellow emigrants. They would not have thought him serious.

---

[34] *Law for the Elephant*, p. 26.
[35] Burroughs, "Reminiscences," p. 49.
[36] Entry for 13 August 1850, McKinstry, *Diary*, pp. 254–55.

# 14 | JUSTIFICATION OF CAPITAL PUNISHMENT

Diaries and letters of emigrants which mention capital punishment on the overland trail ignore, almost without exception, questions of justification or legality. An execution was an important event to be reported: little thought was given to authority.

"[T]oday," one diarist wrote in a typical entry, "we understand a man is to tried for murder & if found guilty is to be executed near the crest of the mountain."[1] It was, apparently, an event worth a notation, but one which the diarist did not think raised questions enough for him to record his own thoughts and reactions. Even pathetic circumstances were reported but not commented upon. One man convicted of murder, and sentenced to die, asked his triers "to whip him and let it go at that, they Paid no attention to this."[2] The diarist was apparently not interested in the merits of either the plea or the refusal. Other overland manslayers accepted the inevitability of trial and punishment. Elijah Brown was the man who stabbed to death a German near the Green River ferry. "In an instant," we are told, "Brown gave himself up & was put under Guard."[3] The emigrant reporting Brown's surrender gave no explanation, made no comment. He was not even surprised that a man would have voluntarily placed himself in the custody of fellow emigrants. And that was the general attitude: jurisdiction and authority were realities accepted, not technicalities questioned.[4]

---

[1] Entry for 4 July 1849, Steuben, *Journals.*
[2] Closing entry, 1852, Thorniley, *Diary.*
[3] Entry for 29 June 1849, Stitzel, *Diary.*
[4] For similar examples of not questioning the right to arrest and punish, see entry for 2 July 1849, Parke, *Diary,* p. 45; entry for 23 May 1852, Frizzell, *Journal,* p. 17; entry for 19 June 1852, Sawyer, "Journal," p. 97.

The main judgment our informants expressed or implied was approval. The eighteen-year-old bride of a Presbyterian minister passed the grave of Lafayette Tate. "He was tried by his company and then hung," she noted. "'Tis awful to think of his fate, yet it was just."[5] A seventeen-year-old drove by the grave of another man who had been hanged. "Vengeance however quickly followed him," she wrote, "and he was doomed to (*receive*) the penalty which his conduct so completely deserved."[6]

It is somewhat disappointing to find that lawyers and judges were just as taciturn. Addison Crane is representative. Admitted to practice in New York State, he had been a judge in Lafayette, Indiana, and later would become a judge in Oakland, California.[7] Like almost every other emigrant, he took overland justice for granted. On being told of a homicide, Crane recorded the details in his journal. "A Court and jury [were] formed," he concluded, the accused was "tried, found guilty, and hung on the Spot, the limb of a tree answering for a gallows, and two empty barrells for Scaffold."[8] Despite being both a lawyer and a judge, Crane raised no more questions than did other emigrants. The issue of justification—or even legality—did not concern him enough for comment.

It tells us something that one of the few emigrants to question the lawfulness of a punishment was motivated by a mistake of facts. Commenting on an execution that had taken place along the Gila River, he approved of the punishment but wondered about its legality. "From their own statement," he wrote, referring to an account of the affair posted by the men who had tried and executed the manslayer, "justice was administered though the Law was

---

[5]Entry for 16 June 1852, Hanna, *Journal*, p. 50.
[6]Entry for 30 June 1852, Scott, "Oregon Journal," p. 79.
[7]Crane, "Autobiography," p. 866; Eaton, *Overland*, p. 319.
[8]Entry for 24 June 1852, Crane, *Journal*.

violated. The case would have come under the jurisdiction of Old Mexico as the murder was committed in it."[9] Actually, the affair had occurred between Tucson and the Colorado River, in today's Arizona, which was then part of the United States.

There were exceptions to the general rule. Although hardly any emigrants questioned the legality of overland executions, a few wondered how to explain and justify punishments. One theory they came up with might have impressed, even if it did not persuade, a court of law. It was that individuals who committed crimes on the overland trail, just by venturing out onto the trail, had waived questions of jurisdiction. When they elected to cross the continent on the trail, emigrants voluntarily submitted themselves to what was termed "the execution of California laws." It did not matter that they might be hundreds of miles closer to the Missouri River than to California, "California laws" prevailed. It will be recalled that a thief was whipped on the west bank of the Missouri, just across from St. Joseph. He "implored his tormenters to desist and send him to state's prison." They replied that "he was a California emigrant & must submit to California laws."[10]

Another man accused of murder far out on the trail also "wanted to be taken back to a civilized country before being tried."[11] The emigrants refused. "[H]e had," it was said, "committed murder on the plains, he should be tried on the plains, and if found guilty, should be hung upon the plains."[12] Convicted, he was "hung on the spot."[13]

---

[9]Entry for 6 October 1849, Brisbane, *Journal.*

[10]Entry for 2 May 1850, McBride, *Diary.* See above, pp. 167–68. This theory may have been the justification for the hanging that occurred at Council Bluffs, within the jurisdiction of Iowa. Above, pp. 138–41.

[11]Eaton, *Overland,* p. 117. The place was near the crossing of La Bonte Creek, in the area of today's Orin, Wyoming. See generally, Duffin, "Miller-Tate Murder," p. 26.

[12]Entry for 17 June 1852, Clark, "Overland," p. 255.

[13]Eaton, *Overland,* p. 117.

Necessity was a second justification for summary justice on the overland trail. The emigrant quoted above, who said that murder on the plains deserved trial on the plains, defended the execution that took place on the grounds of necessity.

> The murder was proven fair and square, the jury prompt in its verdict, sentence pronounced immediately and the hangman's rope finished the job. We felt like giving three cheers that justice, quick and sure, was so promptly administered. Conservatives and law loving people may take exception to such proceedings; but let such come out into a wild country like this and expose themselves to any whim the ruffian may take to shoot or otherwise dispose of him and he will, I think, be as ready to take the law into his own hands as the most of men do on these plains.[14]

Necessity was so compelling a justification it practically forced upon emigrants the duty of punishing manslayers. Writing of the "orderly" trial and execution of a thief and killer at the Sink of Humboldt, an eyewitness labelled it "an action necessary."

> [I]t was justice conscientiously administered, without law — an action necessary under the circumstances. Its justification was fully equal to that of similar services performed by the Vigilante Committee, in San Francisco, within a year preceding. It was a matter the necessity of which was deplorable, but the execution of which was imposed upon those who were on the spot and uncovered the convincing facts.[15]

---

[14]Entry for 17 June 1852, Clark, "Overland," p. 255.
[15]Maxwell, *Crossing the Plains*, p. 159.

Reflecting on the execution of Hickey on the Gila River, a forty-niner concluded that it was less the isolation, or the distance from constituted law enforcement, that made the necessity than it was the conditions of life on the overland trail that thrust upon emigrants the duty to act as executioners. "[I]t may appear strange in fact much Stranger than Fiction that such deeds & such sudden retribution should follow in those Wilds & solitudes," he wrote, "but men carry their evil passions with them wherever they go & here on this prolonged trip there is sufficient [word missing] to derange the most Equible temper."[16]

The imperative of necessity had an important side effect. Perhaps because they felt necessity left them no choice, emigrants not only justified trial and punishment but more easily reached the conclusion that what they did was just and "fair." When an emigrant used the expression "lynch law" it seldom meant condemnation. Commenting on one of the hangings from elevated wagon tongues, a diarist was typical of almost every other emigrant who reported hearing of an execution. He approved of it because "men on the plains" had no alternative, and—perhaps—the fact that there was no alternative convinced him that "justice" had been done. "Some of the men of the plains," he later recalled, "seemed to think that there was no law on the frontier and that they could do as they pleased, but that is not a country for that way of doing things, for Judge Lynch invariably gave justice."[17]

Arguments for the necessity to punish led emigrants to a third justification: security, or what could be called self-preservation or social protection. Explaining why some members of his train had volunteered to pursue and arrest a manslayer, a forty-niner argued: "Several murders had been committed on the road, and all felt the

---

[16]Entry for 21 October 1849, Forsyth, "Journal," p. 87.
[17]Ingrim, "Gold Mines," p. 4.

necessity of doing something to protect themselves, where there was no other law but brute force."[18] "Without law or officers of the law," another emigrant wrote of a capital punishment, "there was no other course to pursue consistent with safety to the living."[19] Arriving overland in a gold-mining community during 1850 a Methodist minister explained the unusual name of the place, "Hangtown." It came, he wrote, "from the fact Judge Lynch found it necessary to administer summary Justice or absolute Anarchy would probably have resulted."[20]

Like the justification of necessity, the motivation of security was thrust upon the emigrants by the circumstances of the overland trail. There was a shared, felt need to preserve the group, to protect the tiny, itinerant society from disintegration. Somewhere in the Utah desert during the lonely emigration of 1846

> [a] disagreeable altercation took place between two members of our party about a very trivial matter in dispute, but threatening fatal consequences. Under the excitement of angry emotions, rifles were levelled and the click of the locks, preparatory to discharging the death-dealing contents of the barrels, was heard. I rushed between the parties and ordered them to hold up their pieces, and cease their causeless hostility towards each other. I told them that the life of every individual of the party was, under the circumstances in which we were placed, the property of the whole party, and that he who raised a gun to take away a life, was, perhaps inconsiderately, worse than a common enemy or a

---

[18]Entry for 3 July 1849, Delano, *Life*, p. 124; Delano, *Across the Plains*, p. 52.
[19]Thompson, "Reminiscences," p. 2.
[20]Sharp, *Brief Notes*, p. 53.

traitor to all of us, and must be so considered in all future controversies of this nature, and be denied all further intercourse with us.[21]

The motivation of security was not limited to the survival, well-being, and harmony of the immediate wagon train in which the emigrants were traveling. It was extended to the entire emigration. Joseph Newton Burroughs was a member of the jury, in a case previously discussed, that found several white renegades guilty of horse-stealing in the wilderness of today's southern Idaho. The jurors knew their verdict meant death and they fully appreciated the severity of the penalty. "Now," Burroughs wrote, "I must relate the fact that perhaps there were none present who were not extremely sorry that there was no other way open to deal with them, except to let them go free, but none that I ever heard of expressed themselves in favor of that."

> It was a serious, solemn occasion for the judge. There was no question of their guilt, but they could not be turned over to a regular court of law for there was none in possibly hundreds of miles, and there was no way in which they could be secured against further carrying out their avowed purpose of robbing and stealing and possible murder; though up to this time, so far as could be learned, no one had been killed by them, they claimed on their examination that they intended to do their work without killing if they could — but after all to condemn men to death for stealing and robbing only was an extreme penalty. But to turn them loose to prey upon the emigration that was yet to pass along the

---

[21]Entry for 7 August 1846, Bryant, *Journal,* p. 190.

road was not to be thought of, and the court's decision was that the guilty were to be shot.[22]

Perhaps no other emigrant developed the theory of justification
of overland punishment as extensively as did Burroughs. The
length of his discussion is surprising, even more so because it was
in a case of confessed white renegades. Except for Mormons, we
might have expected that their plight as condemned men would
have troubled emigrants less than any other category of criminals,
even Indians and mountain men. Burroughs justified the punishment on grounds of both necessity and security. It was necessity
created by having no alternative to the death penalty, and it was
security for the entire "emigration that was yet to pass along the
road," not just for his company or the companies in the immediate vicinity. One other justification at least was implied by
Burroughs. It was that of popular approval, a justification also
occasionally expressed by other emigrants. "The judge's decision,"
Burroughs wrote, "was approved, so far as I ever knew, universally
by those present, of whom there were more than one hundred at
the time of its rendering."[23]

There were two aspects to popular approval, one minor, the
other important. The first was implied by Burroughs. Emigrants
who actively participated in the process of punishing overland
offenders found justification for their actions in the support they
received from other emigrants, especially support openly manifest-
ed by those companies who stopped and actively participated, with
words and actions, in both the trial and the execution. Second, and
more significantly, was the validity obtained from numbers. With
popular support explicitly voiced by those numbers came a sense of
both legitimacy and legality, a sense reinforced by the almost uni-

---

22Burroughs, "Reminiscences," p. 48.
23Ibid.

versal assumption that overland trials were "fair" and overland executions were "regular."

In addition to popular participation, emigrants deliberately sought to establish justification, validity, legitimacy, and legality for punishments—especially executions—by notoriety. Not only the trials but all the executions were conducted in the open. Much more to the point was the concerted practice of publicity. Consideration should be given to the purpose the emigrants had in mind when they put headboards over graves, to inform those who were coming along behind that the dead man had been shot, or hanged, and for what crime. Some of these headboards have been quoted above. One frequently noticed during the 1852 emigration was that of Leanadas or Leon Balsley, whose trial and execution have both been discussed. After his death at the hands of a firing squad, he was buried and, one witness reported, "this inscription riten on a board and placed at his head Leanadas Balsley was tryed condemned and shott for the murder of Mather Beel June 14th, 1852 Both of Barn (Barren) County Kentucky."[24] Nine days later another passerby recorded that the headboard read: "Leon Balsley, shot June 14th, 1852, for the murder of Matthias Beal, June 12th, 1852, both of Boone Co., Kentucky."[25]

The Balsley headboard was one of many. It deserves special attention from us only because of certain information it may have contained. It was later reported that in addition to Balsley's identity and "the cause of his death," the board listed "the names of the jurors who tried him, and also the names of his executioners."[26] Unfortunately these facts are part of a story printed in a California newspaper, and no known diarist, writing an account on the day of passing the grave, mentioned seeing these names. If we knew for

---

[24]Entry for 14 June 1852, Green, *1852 Diary*, p. 14.
[25]Entry for 23 June 1852, Fox, "Memorandum," p. 22.
[26]*The El Dorado News*, quoted in Eaton, *Overland*, p. 224.

certain that names of the jurors and the executioners were included in the public notice, we could draw more confident conclusions about the significance that those overland travelers at least, who wrote them down, attached to notoriety as a way of strengthening the legitimacy and legality of executions.[27] Why would the men who convicted, condemned, and shot Balsley post their identification unless it was to give their actions additional legitimacy by separating those actions from lynching? They established legitimacy in two ways: by the regularity of their proceedings and by publicity.

One lawyer, writing of the overland trail, summed up the theory of notoriety when he said of a party of executioners, "To make everything regular, as they conceived it, they made a formal report of what was done, published it by posting [it] on the highway, and proclaiming it to those with whom they came in contact."[28] He was referring to another incident that has been discussed in some detail above, the homicide, trial, and execution on the Gila River on the southern route in 1849. Historians have been able to discuss this affair in greater detail than any other overland crime and punishment because it was the one to which the participants gave the most publicity. They posted what other emigrants referred to as "a history"[29] or "a paper,"[30] a detailed account of the stabbing, the death, the arrest, the trial, and the execution.

If, on one hand, the purpose of the notice was to publicize the event, it certainly succeeded. Just about every forty-niner diarist who saw the notice, and whose journal has survived, copied the

---

[27]There is, however, one posting reported that was "signed by the judge and jury" but apparently not by the executioners. Also in 1852, it was the case where an emigrant stabbed his partner who was eating breakfast. Terrell, "Overland Trip," p. 79. For the case, see above, pp. 120–21.

[28]Foreman, *Marcy*, pp. 298–99n23.

[29]Entry for 15 August 1849, Bouldin, "Diary"; Hayes, *Diary*, p. 156.

[30]Entry for 5 November 1849, Brainard, "Journal."

facts, some verbatim. If, on the other hand, the purpose of the notoriety was to establish legitimacy by an overt report associating the execution with the familiar, the accepted, the anticipated, the legitimate, and the legal, it also succeeded. No extant diarist criticized the execution or lamented the fate of the condemned man.[31]

Legitimacy was not the only object those jurors had in mind when they posted the "notice" of the execution. By publicizing punishment emigrants were seeking to obtain approval through openness. In addition they had another purpose in mind. At least some of the emigrants were motivated in part by the hope that punishment would deter future crime.

The expectation of deterrent effect was summed up by one overland traveler, on hearing that four men accused of horse stealing had been hanged near Fort Kearny. "This, we hope, will prove a salutary warning to all who may have been disposed to act the part of prairie marauders."[32] An army officer was present at an emigrant meeting called in July 1849 to see what should be done about a killing that had occurred near the Green River. When the majority voted to send after and arrest the manslayer, the officer was said to have "seconded the views of the emigrants, in order to protect them against similar assassinations."[33] In both of these cases the speakers had to have been thinking of deterrence. Failure to pursue, capture, and punish would have led to "similar assassinations" if other potential manslayers were led to think that they too could escape being penalized for their transgressions.

The hanging of Lafayette Tate for deliberate homicide is a good example of how emigrants used punishment as a deterrent. We are

---

[31]For a list of diarists copying the "notice" or reporting seeing it, see "Coercing the Elephant," pp. 194–95n151, n153.

[32]Entry for 27 April 1859, Patterson, "Diary," p. 105.

[33]Entry for 3 July 1849, Delano, *Life*, p. 124; Delano, *Across the Plains*, p. 52. For the facts of this case, see above, pp. 101–02.

fortunate that two diarists, present at the trial and execution, wrote extensive accounts.[34] But even if we did not have these eyewitness accounts we would know about his offense and execution because they were given the usual notoriety. As one emigrant noted, a "large headboard described the horrible crime and hanging,"[35] an "example," another emigrant wrote, "to thousands who may chance to stop and read the inscription,"[36] implying that she thought the headboard was meant to deter. She may have been correct. After Tate had been hanged, the people directing his punishment had sought to stigmatize his memory as infamous, surely as a warning, and perhaps as a deterrent, to others. Judge Crane, who passed the headboard a month later, understood that Tate's body "was allowed to hang all night and [was] buried in the morning."[37]

Crane must have received the information third- or fourth-hand. The account on the headboard, it would seem, did not mention an infamous burial, and other diarists passing the scene do not mention that Tate's corpse was exposed for a time as a mark of shame. It could have happened, however, for the practice was not unknown on the overland trail. Going up the North Platte River beyond Fort Laramie, an 1852 emigrant "past the place to day on big timber creek whare thare was three men hung a few day[s] ago & they was left to the lim so much for that."[38] Also in this year, another overland traveler had heard of a hired man who killed his employer and employer's son by cutting their throats and tossing the bodies behind some logs. After selling their property to a

---

[34]Entry for 14 June 1852, McKieran, *Diary*; entry for 14 June 1852, Green, *1852 Diary*, p. 14; above, pp. 80–81, 96, 99–100, 123.

[35]Ingrim, "Gold Mines," p. 8; Eaton, *Overland*, pp. 118–19.

[36]Entry for 16 June 1852, Richardson, *Journal*, p. 65; Duffin, "Miller-Tate Murder," p. 28.

[37]Entry for 24 June 1852, Crane, *Journal*. For Crane on the Tate homicide, see above, p. 194.

[38]Entry for 7 July 1852, Lewis, *Book*, p. 63.

Frenchman and some Indians, the manslayer fled back toward the Missouri River.[39] The emigrants "caught him and [as] there been trees handy here he was hung and left there and there was a board put up of the murder and he was left hanging in the tree and there was a board put up saying fresh meat for sale."[40] "Saw a notice of a man being hung for murder and robbery," another passerby wrote, probably also referring to the Tate notice although he gave a different date for the killing. "The notice was headed, 'Dried beef for sale, wholesale or retail.'"[41]

Judge Crane may have been mistaken about Lafayette Tate's body being suspended from his gallows tree all night, or it may be that he had confused one humiliation with another. We do not know whether or not Tate was left hanging until morning but we do know that Tate, like another executed man put in the ground near Humboldt Sink "*sans ceremonie,*"[42] was not given the decent burial accorded just about every other executed manslayer. Part of his sentence had been that "his remains [be] buried but 1 foot below the sod so that his Body should become the prey of wolves & other animals." An emigrant who passed the spot twenty-one days after Tate had been hanged, "noticed his grave from which one of his bones protruded forth and his hair was strewed around the grave. It was a shocking sight."[43] It was supposed to be shocking, a sight deliberately contrived to impress passing emigrants with the awesomeness of punishment on the overland trail.

---

[39]This case is described above, p. 99.

[40]Entry for 2 July 1852, Chadwick, *Travels.* Chadwick's other diary says "they followed the man . . . and fetched him back and hung him [from] a tree and left him there putting up a board of the [*sic*] marked fresh meat to sell, so you see we have linch laws on this trip." Entry for 2 July 1852, Chadwick, *Diary*; Eaton, *Overland,* pp. 150–51.

[41]Entry for 26 June 1852, Kerns, "Journal," p. 167.

[42]Maxwell, *Crossing the Plains,* p. 158.

[43]Entry for 6 July 1852, Verdenal, "Journal," p. 22.

There is at least one other recorded instance of an executed manslayer being sentenced to a shallow grave,[44] but even if Tate's burial had been unique and not representative of overland penology, it underlines the importance of deterrence as one of the purposes of overland punishment. It may, however, not be the entire story, for deterrence was not the only possible purpose for marking a felon's body with infamy. Retribution—the vengeful wrath of an outraged emigration—is another purpose the emigrants may have had in mind. At least to say so is to offer a suggestion that is plausible and jibes with popular notions of frontier vigilante justice. It is, admittedly, less provable than other motivations, and what evidence we have makes its validity doubtful.

A search through extant accounts reveals hardly a trace of *lex talionis* (retaliation in kind) legal philosophy. Reading between the lines, we might suggest that the many references to "justice" being done on the overland trail referred to the certainty of punishment rather than to the fairness, regularity, or legitimacy of the proceedings. This interpretation, however, would be stretching words to fit our preconceptions of nineteenth-century frontier attitudes. Whenever we encounter overland punishment, its purpose seems to be the maintenance of order, the deterrence of antisocial acts, and the enforcement of the rules of social behavior that the emigrants had long respected as "law."

Recall the manslayer on the southern route who presented evidence at his trial that "modified the affair some": as a result he avoided the death penalty and was, instead, sentenced "to have 50 lashes and to be expelled from the train."[45] One eyewitness—the

---

[44]The sentence was given to Balsley who was executed for killing Beal. His grave was ordered to be one and a half feet deep. Entry for 14 June 1852, McKieran, *Diary.*

[45]See above, pp. 124–25, 168–69.

one already quoted as saying that had the defendant been tried east of the Missouri he would been sentenced to the penitentiary "in any state in the Union"—became annoyed on discovering that the flogging of the convicted man did not meet his expectations. At least he thought the punishment too private and too lenient. It was not so much the lack of pain that upset him, but more that the executioners had eschewed the public humiliation he expected would be part of the punishment. Notoriety had been avoided, and so had some harshness.

> I saw a little knot of men a short distance down the Nimbres — on enquiring I learnt it was putting the sentence in execution against Gadson, was somewhat surprised at the privacy of the concern — publicity being a part of the punishment, as I understood, but I suppose they wished to save the poor lamb's feelings as much as possible. The punishment was inflicted by a sick man (or rather, one very weak & just recovering from sickness) — the instrument a willow switch.[46]

One conclusion that should not be drawn from this account is that the convicted man was being spared by his friends. The company to which he and his victim both belonged had handed him over to strangers for trial and, it may be assumed, for punishment. In fact, the chief responsibility for the trial seems to have been taken by the company to which the victim's aunt and uncle, as well as the diarist finding fault with the process, belonged. This company was, quite likely, also responsible for inflicting the penalty. The diarist just quoted seems to have been unhappy because the convict was whipped in private which meant that the punishment did not

---

[46]Entry for 8 September 1849, Powell, *1849 Diary*, p. 106.

receive the "publicity" he thought was "part" of it, although whether he wanted it for deterrence or for notoriety he did not say. It is possible that the men administering the punishment believed the whipping too harsh a substitute for the prison term that might have been imposed back home. From either perspective, talionic revenge was not the purpose of that overland punishment.

## 15 | IMPERATIVE OF HARMONY

*Preserving the Elephant*

We must not conclude that the emigrants just quoted, who wanted severe punishment for crimes committed on the overland trail, were eccentrics. The diarist who said a manslayer could have been shoved into a boiling spring and the person who complained that a whipping was done in privacy were not unusual. Overland punishments were more likely to be criticized because they were too lenient than too harsh. It was not just emigrants who said so. Historians, too, have charged that overland sanctions were too mild. They have been particularly critical of expulsion, faulting it both as a penalty too freely used[1] and a punishment that did not really punish.[2] A lawyer historian has recently argued that the punishment of expulsion was not a legal sanction. It was, instead, employed by emigrants to evade the task of imposing real sanctions.[3] "Banishment," he writes, "should be looked at, then, as an avoidance of judicial action and not as that action itself."[4] Many of those out on the trail also thought expulsion did not penalize. When the manslayer at the Green River ferry who resisted trial was put out of the "waggons,"[5] an emigrant wrote that "nothing" had been done to punish him. "[T]he Co[mpany] to which he belonged discharged him & Left him sit[t]ing on his Trunk Near By the river."[6]

---

[1]Langum, "Pioneer Justice," pp. 428–29.

[2]Or allowed "murderers . . . to continue unmolested." Read, "Diseases," p. 273.

[3]Langum, "Pioneer Justice," p. 439.

[4]Ibid., p. 427.

[5]See above, pp. 165–66, 193.

[6]Entry for 30 June 1849, Stitzel, *Diary*, p. 149. Other emigrants expressed annoyance that expelled offenders were allowed to depart taking animals and a pack. For example, James Lyne quoted in Potter, "Introduction," p. 106*n*27.

There are at least two perspectives from which the punishment of expulsion, as it was administered on the overland trail, can be evaluated. One is the physical perspective—the lack of danger, hardship, or even relative inconvenience incurred—from which it can be plausibly argued that expulsion "was not a punishment."[7] To sustain this contention, however, requires a peculiarly narrow definition of punishment and a very restricted idea of the function of law. The argument assumes that retribution is the purpose of punishment rather than that punishment is but a tool serving law and that the purpose of law is the good of the whole group, the preservation of the body politic.

It must again be emphasized that for most emigrants, at least between 1849 and 1860, expulsion did not mean physical suffering or even exposure to danger. But the ease with which an individual could join another company, or travel within sight of other emigrants, must not mislead us into thinking expulsion was not an effective sanction. We will gain greater insight into the purpose of expulsion on the overland trail if we consider ease of social movement not just from the perspective of a culprit expelled by his companions but from the perspective of discipline within overland companies. After all, from one point of view, ease of social movement between trains could have been a cause of disunity. It could have permitted emigrants to defy company authority without the fear of suffering any consequence more serious than that of being expelled and having to find another train with which to travel. Only one case need be considered to illustrate how social mobility could undermine discipline.

---

[7]"It should be remembered that such banishment was not a punishment; from 1846 onward, wagon trains were relatively numerous, and particularly as the parties were frequently breaking up and reforming of their own accord, without regard to banishment, it was not difficult for the expelled party to join another train. Almost everyone ejected was allowed to take his animals, wagons, supplies, and gun." Langum, "Pioneer Justice," p. 427.

It was ordered, among other regulations, that the teams retain permanently the order in which they had fallen into line on the first day [and] . . . that the procession should be operated as a sort of endless chain, each team in its turn occupying the lead one day and dropping to the rear the next day. . . . The driver — James McCartney, a resolute South Bender — who enjoyed the post of honor the first day, insisted on retaining the same position on the next day, and he did, in spite of all expostulations and peremptory commands to the contrary. A court martial was ordered; but the recalcitrant was inexorable. He simply scouted the authority of that grave tribunal, and thereafter drove and encamped at a convenient distance from the main body, thus largely profiting by the supposed advantages of the organization, while wholly relieved of its duties and inconveniences.[8]

From a quite different perspective—one emphasizing the penological purposes of expulsion rather than its physical ease—it is readily apparent that overland companies also took advantage of social mobility to alleviate their own problems of internal friction. It made the sanction of expulsion easier to administer and, therefore, one that might be applied in many circumstances. Even within messes members were expelled to end continual bickering. Or, following a fight, one member might shift to a different mess within the same company. An emigrant of 1852 reported mess changes occurring at least twice in one month in the train with which he

---

[8]Leeper, *Argonauts*, pp. 14–16 (1849).

traveled.[9] Somewhat analogously, a company became quite upset at the brutal manner in which an Englishman treated his teenage daughter during the 1842 emigration. One man asked a family to take the daughter under its protection. While the father was out hunting, the daughter was transferred to that family's wagon which, along with several others, separated from the company and drove off.[10]

The fact that the person being punished did not care whether he was expelled from his company is not important. It was also irrelevant to the company expelling him whether he cared or not. Making the culprit suffer was, at best, a secondary purpose of punishment. Far more important was to heal the body politic and keep it whole. If the objective of overland banishment was to maintain harmony within the group, it must be judged on those terms and not by more popular notions about the purposes of penology.[11]

Although many emigrants understood that the relatively numerous emigrations from 1849 onward made expulsion less retributive than some people might have liked, they also realized that the very ease with which a discontented person could leave one company for another contributed to social harmony by avoiding potential violence. By "throwing out" individuals for fighting, slacking off, or just being involved in a "difficulty,"[12] harmony could be restored.

---

[9]Two men travelling in the train "came to Blows," one "took his part of the Team and all his goods and Chattels" and "Spliced in With Wheeler the Captain of our Train." A month later, "two Partners of our train, had a falling out about their affairs and Clifford took his goods and Chattels from Maclures Wagon and Joined Highram Leinvilles Wagon of our train." Entries for 14 May, 12 June 1852, Thorniley, *Diary*.

[10]Giffen, *Pioneer*, p. 39.

[11]See Langum, *Law and Community*, pp. 75, 79; Moore, *Law as Process*, pp. 56, 117, 124–25.

[12]For example, Eaton, *Overland*, p. 165.

It will be recalled that Edwin Bryant, who went overland in 1846, contended that justice on the trail was somewhat of a mockery because a delinquent could always appeal a conviction to the entire company and might have his punishment set aside. As was then suggested,[13] Bryant missed the point of overland punishment. He thought the convicted culprit, by winning reversal of his sentence, defeated the retributive and deterrent purposes of criminal adjudication. He should have considered the appeal from the perspective of other members of the company. By the very act of making an appeal, the wrongdoer was saying that he wished to remain in the company. If the group decided the appeal was sincere, forgiveness served the same end as did expulsion—restoration of harmony.

Harmony was also the social value or penal objective we should use when evaluating companies that overlooked a transgression when the transgressor said he was sorry.

> I was sent out to guard cattle against attacks of Indians, and being very tired, I laid down with my head on a large stone and unintentionally fell asleep. For this I was censured by a meeting of the company, but my honest regrets expressed for the occurrence saved me from being placed on extra duty as a punishment for my dereliction of duty.[14]

It simply would be wrong to think the young man used a slick tongue to escape punishment. It is worth repeating that when a wrongdoer asked for forgiveness, or a person convicted of a violation appealed his conviction to the entire company, they were stating explicitly that they wished to remain members. Of course,

---

[13]See above, pp. 110–11.
[14]Pfouts, "Autobiography," p. 21.

their fellows understood that wrongdoers also wished to avoid penalties, and appreciated that if the company was to impose the penal sanctions mandated for the offenses it might experience social disruption. Punishment, even extra guard duty, could leave hard feelings and, therefore, disharmony in the body politic. Forgiveness, following a plea to remain part of the group, restored harmony and it is not farfetched to contend that the first principle of overland criminology was the restoration of social harmony.

Some overland companies codified forgiveness—or, emphasizing the penology purpose, they codified the imperative of harmony. The constitution of a Missouri company, for example, provided:

> Any delinquency or failure of duty may be excused, or forgiven, except cowardice or refusal to do duty, for which the company shall expel the offender — going to sleep on guard, or abandoning post before relief is sent, shall be punished by causing the offender to perform camp duty the day following the offence.[15]

Of interest is not so much the fact that a constitution drafted in part by a lawyer[16] institutionalized the concept of excuse or forgiveness for any delinquency except the four mentioned. More pertinent for this discussion is the legislative history of the clause penalizing "sleep on guard" or "abandoning post." At first these crimes had been punished by "camp duty the day following." After there had been two trials—one in which the defendants were accused of "abandoning post" and sleeping on guard duty, and the other for "abandoning post"—the company's membership was persuaded that the sanction of extra camp duty was too harsh for every

---

[15]Constitution of the Holt County Mining Company (1849), in McLeod, *Diary*, p. 22.
[16]James Craig, one of three men to write the constitution and the company's captain, was a lawyer. Ibid., pp. 20–22.

214

violation, at least when the company believed the "repentance" that the convicted parties had expressed at their trials was sincere.

In the first of the two trials a brace of men were accused, one of leaving his post when on duty, the other of sleeping while on guard.

> Both pleaded guilty to the charge, expressed their regret, stated that fatigue and a want of knowledge of the rules led them to act so. The company deeming such to have been the cause by a unanimous vote suspended the article in the constitution bearing on their case.
>
> The captain then addressed the delinquents, showing the misfortunes that might have arisen for such wilful negligence [and] hoped by their future good conduct they would prove the sincerity of their present declarations of repentance.[17]

Expressions of regret and contrition carried the day for these two men. Lack of "intentional desire" to violate the rules saved the defendant in the second of the two cases. "[C]harged with leaving his post as herdsman," he pointed out that the animals he had been guarding had been between the river and his wagon. Under the circumstances he had not imagined that going to the wagon could be desertion. A committee of two appointed by the captain to investigate the facts in the case found sufficient evidence to support the charge of desertion, "yet the com[mittee] were of opinion that the violation of the rule arose from a misconception of the duty required, and not from any intentional desire."[18] Someone moved that the rule be suspended, the motion carried, and the man was excused. It was also voted that the captain reprimand the defendant but he refused, saying it was

---

[17]Entry for 14 May 1849, ibid., p. 37.
[18]Entry for 19 May 1849, ibid., p. 39.

unnecessary. There was a second motion that the constitution be amended, "deeming it better to have no rule of the sort, since it became a dead letter, from the almost impossibility of car[ry]ing it into effect."[19] The motion was adopted and the constitution amended in the form "as it now reads."[20]

Lawyers might correctly claim that, in this case, there was no need to amend the constitution. They might argue that the constitution could always be suspended and that, as the two trials indicated, it probably always would be, at least when the accused pleaded no intent, expressed regret, and prayed forgiveness. But accusation and trial can be disruptive and disharmonious in small, confined groups such as overland companies. They could cause anxiety and perhaps resentfulness, so it is not surprising the membership decided to eliminate a potential source of tension and bitterness. By repealing mandatory expulsion they were not condoning the actions of those who had no excuse or lacked contrition, for the constitution still provided that "refusal to do duty" was an expellable offense. The person who would not perform his duty threatened the harmony of the train. The person who violated the rule yet was sorry and asked forgiveness did not.

Emigrants knew the distinction. Harmony was so vital to their social well-being, their physical security, and their survival that it shaped penal policy. It also shaped social behavior. There were cases of expulsion imposed entirely for the purpose of securing harmony.[21] One of the most drastic occurred during the emigration of 1846. Oregon and California emigrants were traveling in a single train when two Oregon-bound emigrants sharing the same wagon

---

[19]Entry for 19 May 1849, McLeod, *Note Books.*
[20]Entry for 19 May 1849, McLeod, *Diary,* p. 40.
[21]Or, in a comparable situation, a hired hand might be dismissed and "[a]ll feel much relieved as he was a person of ungovernable temper." Entry for 6 July 1853, Williams, *Journal.*

had a falling out.[22] Bryant, who was with the California-bound part of the expedition, told what happened.

> The two individuals at variance about their oxen and wagon, were emigrating to Oregon, and some eighteen or twenty wagons, now travelling with us, were bound to the same place. It was proposed, in order to relieve ourselves from the consequences of disputes in which we had no interest, that all the Oregon emigrants should, in a respectful manner and a friendly spirit, be requested to separate themselves from the California emigrants, and start on in advance of us. This proposition was unanimously carried, and the spirit in which it was made prevented any bad feeling, which otherwise might have resulted from it. The Oregon emigrants immediately withdrew their wagons from the *corral* and proceeded on their way.[23]

There can be no misreading of Bryant. The two groups did not separate for any of the reasons which caused the breakup of hundreds of other overland traveling companies: too many members, too little grass, or disagreements about the speed of travel or whether to journey on Sundays. They separated because the California emigrants wished to be free of quarrels between persons with whom they did not have to travel and with whom, in any case, they would not be traveling for about half of the trip. The importance that they attached not only to separating but to doing so in a harmonious manner is highly revealing.

---

[22]Entry for 2 June 1846, McKinstry, "Diary 1846," p. 210. Also, see A. B. Rabbeson's account, in Morgan, *First Overland*, p. 405n40.

[23]Bryant, *Journal*, reprinted in Morgan, *First Overland*, p. 405n40.

Through expulsion emigrants hoped to end not merely existing or past trouble. They also expelled potential trouble. An illustration is provided by a shooting, the facts of which have already been quoted in detail. It concerned the "Kentuckian" who shot "Mr. Bush." The two men quarreled and the Kentuckian retired to a tent. Bush entered the tent and kicked the Kentuckian in the mouth while he was down. The Kentuckian reached for a gun and shot Bush, wounding him badly but not killing him. The company expelled the Kentuckian.[24]

The facts, admittedly, are ambiguous, but one way they can be read indicates that the Kentuckian shot Bush in self-defense. He was on the ground, under attack, and reached for a weapon; he had been the defender, Bush the aggressor. Yet it was the Kentuckian, not Bush, who was expelled. We should not express surprise or wonder if the account we have of the facts might be mistaken. That the Kentuckian was put out of the company is no puzzle. It is immaterial whether the Kentuckian had been wholly innocent of provoking the incident, and had had no choice but to defend himself by using deadly force. Once Bush had recovered, trouble between the two could have flared up again. Because of his wounds, the company could not expel Bush: it had to take him along. It was the Kentuckian who could be expelled. We would be wrong to protest and say that it was the innocent man who was being punished. The Kentuckian had shot Bush. It does not matter whether he had a choice or whether he was forced to do so to save his life. The fact remains that he had shot Bush but not killed him and, potentially, his very presence risked trouble. By remaining, the Kentuckian threatened the social harmony of the train, and in that respect was not a guiltless man.

The argument could be pushed further. It was not merely potential trouble the company sought to avoid by expelling the

---

[24]See above, pp. 171–72.

Kentuckian; it sought also to eradicate a sense of trouble and violence. A troublemaker was to be avoided as much as trouble itself, and so was a reminder of past conflict. A manslayer expelled from his company petitioned to be admitted to a second train. He was rejected. "The murderer," an emigrant explained, "doubtless thought he had got ahead of the report, but I happened to get wind of it — charged him with murder — he owned it, mounted his horse and put forward."[25] A party passing through Mexico was approached by another expelled manslayer, who claimed he had acted in self-defense and offered to pay anyone who would transport his effects. Because of the homicide, "we declined to carry his Provisions or to permit him to follow us."[26]

It has been suggested by a well-known student of the overland trail that the expelled manslayers were being ostracized; that others along the trail, when they refused to allow them to join their companies, were reinforcing the sanction of expulsion.[27] Although that explanation is plausible, a better interpretation is that they were concerned with social harmony. A convicted criminal introduced a sense of uneasiness; a reminder not only of violence past, but a presence of violence in their midst. We can see this happening in another case with which we are already familiar. Holmstead, it will be recalled, killed Dunmore, a fellow member of a Wisconsin company. The facts indicated justifiable homicide, for he had been acting in self-defense, and that was what a jury of strangers would rule when Holmstead was tried for murder and was acquitted.[28] Even so, and even before the trial was held, several wagons withdrew from the train. They belonged to emigrants who "would not travel with them [Holmstead's company] longer on account that they did

---

[25]Mattes, *Platte River Road*, p. 79.
[26]*Quaker Forty-Niner*, p. 226.
[27]Mattes, *Platte River Road*, p. 79.
[28]See above, pp. 143–44; entry for 15 July 1852, Chadwick, *Travels.*

219

not like to travel with Holmstead because he had killed Dunmore."[29]

James Frazier Reed was less fortunate than Holmstead, as we have seen in a case also previously mentioned. A part of the body politic did not withdraw from him; he was forced to withdraw from the entire body politic. He is the best-known expellee in the history of the overland trail and his story the most fateful because, after he was banished, his train became trapped by the Sierra snows and the Donner tragedy occurred. Some members of the party froze to death, some starved, and others became cannibals. "Had I remained with the company," Reed later argued, "I would have had the whole of them over the mountains before the snow would have caught them; and those who got through have admitted this to be true."[30] A convincing argument could be made that Reed was probably right.

Reed was traveling with an isolated and quite small party when he killed a man named John Snyder. They were going down the Humboldt River, the most precarious and distressing stretch of the California part of the overland trail, when Reed acted under circumstances that appear to have been "justified."[31] Accounts differ as to how the fight started but, according to a lawyer who undertook a thorough investigation while there were still several eyewitnesses, Reed attempted to stop a fight between Snyder and another man. An angry Snyder then struck Reed

---

[29]Entry for 15 July 1852, Chadwick, *Travels*.

[30]Letter from James Frazier Reed to Gersham Keyes, 2 July 1847, in Morgan, *First Overland*, p. 304.

[31]"No other portion of the History of the Donner Party, as contributed by the survivors, has been so variously stated as this Reed-Snyder affair. Five members of the party, now living, claim to be eye-witnesses. The version of two of these . . . is the one here published. In the theory of self-defense they are corroborated by all the early published accounts. This theory was first advanced in Judge J. Quinn Thornton's work in 1849, and has never been disputed publicly until within the last two or three years." McGlashen, *Donner Party*, pp. 45–46.

with the butt end of his heavy whip-stock. This blow was followed in rapid succession by a second, and a third. As the third blow descended, Mrs. Reed ran between her husband and the furious man, hoping to prevent the blow. Each time the whip-stock descended on Reed's head, it cut deep gashes. He was blinded with the blood which streamed from his wounds, and dazed and stunned by the terrific force of the blows. He saw the cruel whip-stock uplifted, and knew that his wife was in danger, but had only time to cry "John! John!" when down came the stroke full upon Mrs. Reed's head and shoulders. The next instant John Snyder was staggering, speechless and death-stricken. Reed's hunting-knife had pierced his left breast.[32]

A Virginia lawyer, who went to Oregon in 1846, the same year the Donner party went to California, and who was appointed a supreme court judge in 1847, was the first person to investigate the Snyder killing for purposes of publication. He concluded that Reed had drawn his knife before he was hit by the whipstock, "without, however, attempting to use it, and told Snyder that he did not wish to have any difficulty with him." Snyder, whose threats had motivated Reed to draw the knife, replied "that he would whip him, 'any how.'" The lawyer-investigator also thought Reed stabbed Snyder before Snyder struck Mrs. Reed but not before Snyder struck him.[33] By either account, juries in the nineteenth century could have readily ruled that Reed had acted in self-defense.

If overland emigrants ever had reasons for overlooking a homicide it would have been the Reed–Snyder killing. The members of

---

[32]Ibid., p. 45.
[33]Thornton, *California Tragedy*, p. 20.

the Donner party would have been justified even if Reed had not been able to claim self-defense. He had not set out to harm Snyder, nor had he indicated any intention that he wished to slay him, "immediately showing great remorse for it was known that he and Snyder had been friends."[34] More to the point, all those present knew full well that they were in a most perilous situation, and badly needed every available man if they were ever to reach California. Yet the killing of Snyder was not overlooked. We may not be surprised that Reed was not executed; but should we be surprised that he was banished from the train?

There can be little doubt, from the evidence gathered both in the last century and in this,[35] that the first reaction of a majority of the company with which Reed and Snyder had been traveling was to hang Reed. The membership was far too small to have held an overland trial or even to have conducted an impartial investigation, and there were no other trains coming along to whom they could have turned for a "stranger" verdict. The argument in favor of executing the manslayer, therefore, was more popular than deliberative, more "political" than "judicial." That is how it has generally been treated by students of the 1846 migration. Snyder had been well liked.[36] Reed was not.[37] "Snyder," one account contends, "had been vastly popular, while the haughty Reed was correspondingly disliked."[38]

We must be careful not to jump to obvious conclusions that may cause us to miss essential elements of the story. One fact that is easy to overlook is that Reed's friends had good reasons to defend him, even with force, and these reasons could have been persuasively argued in a court of law. Another is that the majority—if, in fact,

---

[34]McGlashan, *Donner Party*, p. 47.

[35]By Dale Morgan in his two-volume collection of documents from the 1846 emigration.

[36]McGlashan, *Donner Party*, pp. 43–44, 48.

[37]Thornton, *California Tragedy*, p. 20.

[38]Stewart, *Ordeal by Hunger*, p. 52.

it really would have hanged Reed had there been no opposition—
may not have felt that it was accepting a compromise when it agreed
to expulsion as an alternative to execution. At least one historian
who has studied the Donner tragedy has claimed that the majority
expected banishment to be a death sentence. Reed was given only a
horse, saddle, and clothes to get him across the mountains.

> It was contemplated, by those who insisted that
> Reed be hanged, that the sentence of banishment
> would result in his death, and so they agreed to the
> banishment sentence. That Reed could cross the
> wild trackless range of mountains in the mid winter,
> alone and without food, seemed almost impossible,
> as it was intended he should go without food or gun.

That part of the sentence was frustrated when Reed's wife and a
male friend "followed Reed and brought him his gun with ammunition and some food."[39]

That, at least, is one explanation, although it does not enjoy
much support from overland-trail historians. It is just as plausible
to argue that Reed's banishment was not dissimilar to, but shared
points in common with, all the other overland expulsions of which
we know. That the company was divided need not prove that social
values were not a factor in the decision, or even that the decision
was more political than legal. It may only prove the closeness of
the facts. Even if there had been a stranger jury available to try the
case, Reed's stabbing of Snyder would have presented the jury with
a question not easily resolved even with the hindsight of historical
evidence. Of course, much would have depended upon who testified, what members of the party happened to have been on the
spot when the killing occurred. There was, first of all, the issue of
whether Reed had created the situation of danger by intervening

---

[39]Stookey, *Fatal Decision*, pp. 127–28.

in a fight between two other men. Had he drawn his knife before he was struck? Had he been obliged to retreat at a moment when it might reasonably be supposed his wife was in mortal peril?

Perhaps the better explanation is that both politics and facts had forced the stalemate, and if Reed's expulsion was a compromise, it was as much a legal as a political compromise driven, in part, by the imperative of harmony. Consider the issue from the perspective of Reed's supporters. It appears that at least two men said that his actions did not merit execution. To the extent that they remained steadfast, he could not have been hanged without further conflict. The majority, therefore, agreed to expulsion. His departure may not have restored the degree of social harmony produced by other overland banishments, but it did restore the appearance of harmony by removing the presence of a manslayer. The appearance of harmony was as necessary for legal as for political ends. It avoided potential bloodshed. The absence of the manslayer made those who felt he should have been executed not only less apprehensive, but more socially at ease as they continued the trip westward.

To say that expulsion was not punishment in the Reed case would be to contend either that only a talionic retribution—death or a severe whipping—could have atoned for Snyder's killing or that expulsion was not a punishment. To make either argument is to miss the purpose of punishment on the overland trail.

Aside from the political need to abate passions, it made little pragmatic sense to expel James Frazier Reed. If ever an overland party needed every man it was the Donner party. It especially needed the leader who had been most responsible for what progress the group had so far made. Yet Reed was expelled. Personal relationships alone simply cannot explain the actions. The homicide victim, a hired teamster driving the wagon of another man, had been traveling alone, while Reed was traveling with his family. Reed's departure created complications for other members of the train and brought problems that must have touched them all. Yet

Reed was put out, sent ahead without arms at a place where the trail was very lonely, very perilous, and at a time, as everyone knew, when the snows were coming.

It would have been in the interest of all the other members of the train to have allowed Reed to remain with the party, at least until they had crossed the Sierras and were out of danger. They did not do so, and the question historians have failed to ask is, why not?

One plausible explanation is the same one that has been previously suggested for some lesser offenses. It is that Reed was expelled because his presence was disruptive, an uncomfortable suggestion of trouble, violence, and disharmony. Even if he had remained on his best behavior, Reed was a daily reminder of anger and death, of a body politic out of control. In reply, it might be argued that harmony could not possibly have been a consideration in Reed's expulsion. By putting out a family man, knowing that the family would remain, the group was inviting, not eliminating, hostility. Reed's wife and daughters were certain to be less cooperative with the party, and their resentment could prove disruptive, perhaps even more disruptive than Reed's own presence would have been had he not been expelled.[40]

If preservation of harmony was the overriding purpose of overland punishment, one might expect men traveling with families not to be expelled. Reed, however, was not only expelled; he was expelled alone, without his family. To have sent his wife and daughters with him during the sparse 1846 emigration, even had he been given guns, ammunition, and provisions, would have meant their likely

---

[40]In the only other situation of mortal danger that has come to attention, a seventeen-year-old, on 27 July shot and killed a man who had been shooting at him. "The boy being too fond of the old man[']s nice little Girl aged 13 years." On 28 and 29 July the company to which they both belonged became involved in Indian warfare. Trains around them were attacked and several people were killed. Despite the danger, and despite the fact that the seventeen-year-old was needed as a guard and a gun man, he was hanged on the 29th. It seems that he had no family along. Entries for 27, 28, 29, 30 July 1859, Snow, "Diary," pp. 205–206.

deaths. Later, when crowds along the overland trail made conditions of travel far safer, we might expect that families of expellees would have been banished with them. That happened for many antisocial actions but apparently not for homicide. Several groups executed manslayers despite the presence of their wives and children.

If the wife could be "sent back," as reported in one case,[41] the threat of disharmony was avoided. Opportunities of doing so, however, were rare. In an 1852 case an emigrant who had a wife and four children along was found guilty of a homicide. The family depended "upon this man for their lives," yet he was hanged. The company had to provide the woman with "a driver to finish the journey."[42]

That same year a man, said to be "the principal owner of the train,"[43] was hanged in the presence of his wife and two children. The company was at Devil's Gate in central Wyoming and the family could not be "sent back." They had to continue with the company, some of whose members—if the words "principal owner" mean what they should—would, after the execution, be in the employ of, or in a fiduciary relationship to, the woman. Moreover, she attempted to assert her authority and stop the execution. When the man was about to be hanged, "She Came along and Jerked the Rope that was intended to hang her Husband from one of the Committee Men, but they soon got another Rope."[44] Finally there was one other factor making it likely she could cause

---

[41]See above, pp. 82–83.

[42]Meeker, *Ventures and Adventures*, p. 30. Meeker's account is not reliable. Langum, "Pioneer Justice," p. 435*n*45. One historian has cited this case as an example of overland injustice, apparently for no other reason than that a woman and her children were involved. Mattes, *Platte River Road*, p. 80.

[43]Entry for 29 June 1852, Dalton, "Diary," p. 18; Eaton, *Overland*, p. 165; Mattes, *Platte River Road*, p. 79.

[44]Last entry for 1852, Thorniley, *Diary*.

trouble during the remainder of the trip. She seems to have been accompanied by her brothers.[45] Yet despite all of this, the executioners, some of whom most likely were her hired men, went through with the execution.

There are other facts that put the execution at Devil's Gate of this husband–father–brother-in-law within the theory of harmony. For one thing, although arrested by members of his own train, he had been tried, convicted, sentenced, and hanged by emigrants from a number of companies.[46] Most jurors and executioners, therefore, were not traveling with the woman and her brothers and did not have to be concerned with their presence for the remainder of the trip. Secondly, the crime had been especially vicious. It was the killing of the boy "Charlie" who angered his employer when he scratched the stock of the man's gun. The man then lured the boy off hunting, killed him in cold blood, and attempted to conceal the act.[47] The atrocity was so extreme it was impossible the emigration would have felt at ease traveling with the man. Security and a sense of doing right for the boy required that the people who judged the killing and determined punishment should ignore the wife's pleas. They could not have been satisfied expelling the manslayer. Despite the family considerations, despite the dependency that some of the hired hands had on the property of the man they were executing, and despite the fiduciary relationship they might now have with the woman, the legal norms of the day required that the manslayer be put to death, and he was.

The pattern is somewhat fuzzy and may have to remain that way. It does not do to force consistency where none exists. There were always exceptions to the rule. When a crime was brutal or

---

[45]Entry for 2 July 1852, Chadwick, *Travels*.
[46]Last entry for 1852, Thorniley, *Diary*.
[47]See above, pp. 94–95, 122.

offended the sensibilities of the emigrants, retribution may have been on the minds of the executioners. But in most cases retribution was not thought of and may never—or only rarely—have been one of the purposes of overland punishment.

The man who acted in self-defense, wounded his assailant but spared the aggressor's life, might himself have to leave the train should the wounded man remain. Harmony within the group, not retribution, was the motivating consideration.

Several factors had to be weighed when the emigration of 1846 expelled James Frazier Reed. The members of the expelling train were seriously diminishing their own chances of survival as they needed both his strength and his leadership. In addition, his wife would be socially alienated from the majority during the remainder of the trip. Yet a man had died. There must have been something unbearable or at least civilly unstabilizing about traveling with a manslayer. A cancer on the body politic had to be excised, and at the risk of another source of disharmony—a bitter wife—the majority sought social harmony by removing a man whose presence would have been a reminder of violent homicide.

The sanctions decreed by overland emigrants may not have been what lawyers, historians, or students of vigilantism would term punishment. But emigrants were seldom lawyers and even more seldom philosophers. "We met several men returning today," an emigrant of 1850 wrote on the early date of 14 May. "They have seen the *Elephant*, and not two hundred miles out."[48] Most emigrants did not turn back. They continued on until they reached the Pacific slopes. They had all gone to see the elephant, but they were nineteenth-century Americans and they did not go far before discovering that their elephant was the law.

---

[48]Entry for 14 May 1850, Read, "Overland Diary," p. 31.

# 16 | Knowing the Elephant
CONCLUSION

On his first Sunday on the overland trail, a twenty-five-year-old Irish American physician from Grafton, Illinois, paused to wonder why he had become part of the great 1849 rush to California. "Was it the love of gold that induced me to leave every thing that makes life desirable — home, kindred and friends," he asked himself, "or was it that I might for a time be free from the restraints of society and the varieties of life?" Two months, two weeks, and two days later, he was going by the American Falls about thirty miles west of the Hudson's Bay Company's trading post, Fort Hall. It was his twenty-sixth birthday and at last, he decided, he knew why he was on the overland trail. "I left the States and started on this trip," the man concluded, "because I had become tired of Society and its restraints having learned by experience that it is artificial. I determined therefore to leave it and try for a while the life of liberty and unrestrained indulgence, the future will show the results."[1]

We need not puzzle over this man's erroneous notions. They were part of American ideas at that time. People knew that to enjoy a "life of liberty and unrestrained social indulgence" one went to the wild west. Alexis De Tocqueville apparently believed this. And he is important for he was the first observer to study, report on, describe, and analyze what he considered to be the unique law-mindedness of nineteenth-century Americans. He developed his theory before any emigrants had ventured onto the overland trail but at a time when people were beginning to realize that wagons might be taken all the way to Oregon. "Those Americans who go

---

[1]Entries for 7 May, 23 July 1849, Kirkpatrick, *Journal*, pp. 4, 22.

out far away from the Atlantic Ocean, plunging into the West, are adventurers impatient of any sort of yoke, greedy for wealth, and often outcasts from the states in which they were born," he wrote. "They arrive in the depths of the wilderness without knowing one another. There is nothing of tradition, family feeling, or example to restrain them. Laws have little sway over them, and mores still less."[2] Even in the 1990s students of Americana repeat this vision of the westward movement: that the settlers were without customary restraints or a sense of lawmindedness, that they lived not by rule of law but rule of force.

It is a view of the American past that has too long focused on only one aspect of the evidence. Looked at from the perspective of the lawmindedness of the average person seeking out new lands to the west, it is evident that throughout all of American history—whether going from the Atlantic coast to the untamed wilderness along the Connecticut River, or from the Missouri River to the Pacific coast—westward settlers have always carried with them their traditions, their customs, and their law.[3] Of course, scholars of violence and of the "wild west" have seen matters differently. For them the overland emigrants who arrested, tried, and executed manslayers had not been enforcing law. They had, rather, been committing murder by lynching their victims; or perhaps, more accurately, that those who conducted trials and executions on the overland trail are analogous to vigilantes conducting "drumhead trials."[4]

---

[2]Tocqueville, *Democracy in America*, p. 376.

[3]A trend that started with the first English settlers crossing the Atlantic Ocean to New England. See for example, Allen, *In English Ways*; Powell, *Puritan Village*.

[4]The term "drum-head" trial is, strictly speaking, not inaccurate when applied to overland prosecutions, for drumhead trials were courts-martial held during a military march for an infraction requiring immediate example. It has, however, been applied to overland trials with a more pejorative connotation in mind. See for example, Mattes, *Platte River Road*, p. 79; Mattes, *Narratives*, pp. 375, 400, 550, 553.

When discussing violence in the westward movement writers have been too apt to oversimplify the past. Just as every homicide is called "murder" no matter what the circumstances or whether the killing would be culpable at common law, so every act of citizen self-help is cited to prove the rule of force over the rule of law. When, however, we cut away the myths of how the west must have been or should have been, and instead ask what overland emigrants thought they were doing, we learn they were average citizens, bringing with them out onto the plains the society they did not want to leave behind. They went west to live by the rules, the controls, and the restraints by which they had lived before—law, order, and the morality of Christian civilization.[5]

It would be unsafe to draw too broad a lesson. It is important that we do not make more of the argument than our evidence can sustain. The diaries, accounts, letters, and reminiscences written by the emigrants who crossed the plains and mountains from the Missouri River to the Pacific Ocean do not tell us how trials were conducted on the overland trail. What they tell us is, however, perhaps more important—how the emigrants thought trials should be conducted. It is their sense of justice, their understanding of judicial fairness, and their respect for the rights of individuals that are delineated by their words and attitudes. Whether they lived up to their own standards is not the same question. Legal realities should not be confused with legal values.

Whether the diarists' attitudes toward fairness and their capacity to understand law is indicative of attitudes and capacities of average nineteenth-century Americans is a question that cannot be answered with the definitiveness historians would wish. We learn enough from the writings of emigrants to know what the average overland diarist thought of homicide, punishment, procedural fair-

---

[5] *Law for the Elephant.*

ness, and judicial decorum. But how close the ideas, values, principles, and lawmindedness of the average emigrant diarist were to
those of the average American citizen need not be precisely mea-
sured. The reflected image is sharp enough, even though fuzzy at
the edges. We have a good idea who these overland travelers were,
who left us their views about crime and their thoughts about punishment; but we cannot be certain how closely they matched the
general American population. For one thing, of course, they were
all literate. They were also disproportionately male, as were most
emigrants, at least those going to California. Although quite a few
hired hands kept diaries,[6] most diarists, even if down on their luck,
were probably from the middle class. Some of them were city-
dwellers or had grown up in the towns around Boston or New
York, yet the bulk came from mostly rural, but not necessarily agri-
cultural, communities.[7]

Perhaps the most cautious conclusion is that the attitudes of
the emigrants toward the judicial process, and the consistency with
which they appealed to legal principles, were more indicative of
those of the average American than those of "frontiersmen." One
small lesson they teach is how nonfrontiersmen acted on the frontier. The broader historical lesson they teach is of Americans who
consciously strove to carry beyond the line of forward settlement a
mode of social behavior and legal conduct which they had learned
during a remembered youth in the towns and cities they left behind
in body but not in spirit.

One word must be emphasized, and that word is "behavior."
Behavior is the operative concept—the key idea for understanding
what we have learned of crime and punishment on the overland

---

[6]Most notably for this study, McKieran, *Diary*. For others, see sources cited,
"Prosecuting the Elephant," p. 349*n*129.

[7]Goodrich and Davidson, "Wage-Earner," p. 154*n*111.

trail. It is the taught, remembered, respected, and shared legal behavior that we have been examining—not the implementation of particular legal concepts, rules, doctrines, maxims, or principles. An emigrant of 1857 made the point differently, when he described the overland trail as crossing an area "where there was no law to govern, other than the character and natural bent of individuals."[8] One manifestation of that "natural bent" by overland emigrants was legal behavior. It was a legal behavior that avoided acts of violence,[9] allocated precious resources according to shared notions of property rights rather than by force,[10] and, when crime occurred, dealt with offenses not by vengeance but by applying the remembered trappings of a partly understood judicial process.

Leaving Independence, Missouri, as part of the 1846 emigration, Charles T. Stanton wrote home, telling his family and friends not to worry for his safety. There was little danger, he assured them, "as we go in such large crowds that we shall be law unto ourselves and a protection unto each other."[11] Stanton was correct. He and his fellow overland emigrants, sharing remembrances of a respected judicial process, would indeed become a law unto themselves.

---

[8]Maxwell, *Crossing the Plains*, p. 95.

[9]*Law for the Elephant*, pp. 335–64; "Paying for the Elephant."

[10]*Law for the Elephant*, pp. 127–215; "Sharing the Elephant;" "Dividing the Elephant."

[11]Letter from Charles T. Stanton to Philip R. Stanton, 12 May 1846, printed in Morgan, *Second Overland*, p. 533.

# Acknowledgements

Leave from teaching responsibilities at New York University School of Law was provided by the Filomen D'Agostino Greenberg and Max E. Greenberg Faculty Research Fund at New York University School of Law, and by John Sexton, dean of New York University School of Law. The index is the work of the dedicated Patricia Allen Smith, formerly of Billings and now at the Huntington Library. Cite and substance investigation was assumed by Barbara Wilcie Kern of East Ninth Street near the corner of Broadway and Eighth Street, and by R. B. Bernstein (known in other acknowledgments as Richard B. Bernstein) of Remsen Street, across the river in Brooklyn. For any errors contact them and not the author.

The proofreading was entirely completed in New Hampshire. Theodore J. Finnegan of Madbury Road did a valiant job of staying awake while every section, including the "Copyright Acknowledgement" was read aloud. Ann Reid of the General Sullivan house caught the mistakes the Colonel missed.

Research at the Huntington Library is always a joy, and writing this book was made much easier by the gracious and wonderfully competent staff, ever ready to assist at any stage of progress: Peter Blodgett, Kelli Ann Bronson, Jill Cogen, Carolyn Powell, Frances Rouse, Carrie Sailiers, and Elsa Sink. A very special debt is owed to two librarians from beyond the gardens of the Huntington. At the Denver Public Library, Bruce Hanson showed that incomparable collections can be located in palatial hideaways. Michael Meier, at the National Archives, made a valiant try far beyond the call of duty to uncover the still elusive orders common sense ensures us that Washington had to have sent the commanders of Fort Kearny and Fort Laramie, directing them about the army's duties and responsibilities toward civilians on the overland trail.

Careful, painstaking research has prevented what might well have been serious error. It was at first thought that Sir William Holdsworth should be credited with the observation that "Bad law is too high a price to pay for good history." That might have been printed as part of this book had not Mark F. Altmeyer discovered that what Holdsworth actually said was, "For certainty in law a little bad history is not too high a price to pay." It was rather, Franklin Pierce who, in an address to the New Hampshire Chapter of the Exiles at Hopewell, coined the aphorism, "Bad law is too high a price to pay for good history." Interestingly, as Altmeyer also discovered, it was Franklin Pierce who made the memorable claim, "Bad history may make good law, but bad law never makes good history."

John Phillip Reid

# Copyright Acknowledgement

*The author is grateful to the following libraries for permission to quote from the works listed below.*

University of Arkansas Libraries, Special Collections Division, Fayetteville: Alfred D. King, "Journal of Southern Route" (ms.).

The Bancroft Library, University of California, Berkeley: Henry Sheldon Anable, "Journal Kept by H. S. Anable while on the plains' in 1852" (ms. C-F 137: 1); Henry Austin, "1849 Diary" (ms. C-F 157); Amos Batchelder, "Journal of a Tour Across the Continent of N. America . . . in 1849" (ms. C-B 614); James H. Compton, "Diary" (ms. C-F 224); D. C. Dickinson, "Journal" (ms. 75/98C); Katherine Dunlap, "Journal [1864]" (ts. photostat P-I 109); John Robert Forsyth, "Journal of a Trip from Peoria, Ill. to California on the Pacific in 1849" (ts. microfilm C-F 50); Isaac Julian Harvey, "To California in 1850" (ms. C-D 5091A); Benjamin Hayes, "Diary of Benja. Hayes' Journey overland from Socorro to Warner's Ranch from Oct. 31, 1849 to January 14, 1850" (ms. C-E 79); Charles A. Kirkpatrick, "Journal . . ." (ms. C-D 207); John N. Lewis, "My Book" (ms. P-A 335); Byron N. McKinstry, "Gold Rush Diary . . . , 1850–1852" (ts. microfilm); Richard Martin May, "A Sketch of a Migrating Family to California" (ms. C-F 182); H. M. Powell, "Diary of 1849–1852" (ms. C-F 115); H. M. Powell, "1849 Diary" (ms.); Caroline L. Richardson, "Journal" (ms. C-F 102); Frances H. Sawyer, "Overland to California: Notes from a Journal kept by Ms. Frances H. Sawyer, in a Journey across the Plains, May 9 to August 17, 1852" (ts. C-F 103 transc.); E. C. Springer, "Daybook" (ms. microfilm 69/142); William North Steuben, "Journals" (ms. C-F 183); Jacob Stitzel, "Overland Diary, Mar. 20–Aug. 26, 1849" (microfilm 66-6800); N. H. Stockton, "Journals" (ts. C-F 135); Dr. T., "Journal of his Experience Crossing the Plains in 1849" (ms. C-B 383:1); John F. Verdenal, "Journal Across the Plains 1852" (ts.).

The Beinecke Rare Book and Manuscript Library, Yale University, New Haven, Connecticut: Nancy Jane Bradley and Henry Bradley, "A Daily Journal Kept by N. J. and H. Bradley on an Overland Trip to California, in the Spring & Summer of 1852" (ms. Western Americana Collection #45); Philip F. Castleman, "Diary of P[hilip] F. Castleman While Crossing the Plains to California from the time he left St. Joseph, Mo., With a Seeth [Sketch?] of his Trip from Home Which Was in Larue Co. Ky to St. Joseph Mo. 1849" (ms. Western Americana Collection #S-745); John Clark, "The California Guide" (ms. Western Americana Collection #83); B. F. Dowell, "Journal (in a letter to 'Greensville' dated 27 September 1850)" (ms. Western Americana Collection #142); Simon Doyle, "Journals and Letters of Simon Doyle" (ms. Western Americana Collection #144); Perry Gee, "Journals of Travels Across the Plains to California" (ms. Western Americana Collection #213); D. S. I. Grow, "Diary (letter to A. Richardson)" (ms.); S. L. Grow, "Journal" (ms. Western Americana Collection #235); John Lawrence Johnson, "Overland to Oregon in 1851" (ms. Western Americana Collection #274); "Journal of the Granville Overland Company" (ms. Western Americana Collection #228); Moses F. Laird, "Moses F. Laird's Book: A Journal to a few Turns of my Life: Different Situations: Travels, &c." (ms. Western Americana Collection #290); Thomas Cotton Lewis, "Notes" (ms. Western Americana Collection #302); James Lyne, "Letters" (ms. Western Americana Collection #312); Joseph Middleton, "Across the Plains from Independence to the Humboldt" (ts. Western Americana Collection #S-39); "Letter from Charles G. Moxley to [his sister] Emily Moxley" (ms. Western Americana Collection #S-712); Silas Newcomb, "Journal of Silas Newcomb of Madison Wisconsin, 1 April 1850 to 31 March 1851" (ms. Western

Americana Collection #359); R. H. P. Snodgrass, "Journal of the Trip from Piqua, Ohio to Sacramento California across the Plains in 1852 with an appendix containing Prices ancient & new of Various Subjects" (ms. Western Americana Collection #432); William T. Stackpole, "Journal of a trip towards California commenced Apl 4th 1849" (ms. Western Americana Collection #S-1006); P. C. Tiffany, "Journal" (ms. & ts. Western Americana Collection #474).

The California Historical Society, San Francisco, California: Anonymous, "Diary of an Unknown Scout Accompanying a Company of Covered Wagon Emigrants from St. Joseph, Missouri, to California, May 2, 1852" (ts.); Fidelia March Bowers, "An Account of the Wagon Train Mastered by Solomon Tetherow" (ts. OV 10549); Joseph Newton Burroughs, "Reminiscences of 1856 Overland Journal" (ts. & ms. 269); James S. Cowden, "Diary Kept by J. S. Cowden on His Trip 'Overland' from Iowa to Cal. in 1853 with Ox Teams and Wagons" (ms. photostat 465); "Letters of Thomas B. Eastland to Josephine Eastland" (ms. VMS 19); Eliza Ann McAuley [Egbert], "Mother's Diary: The Record of a Journey Across the Plains in '52" (ts. & ms. 645); Jasper Morris Hixson, "Diary of Jasper Morris Hixson May 1–August 6, 1849" (ts. & ms. 1002); "Copy of Elizabeth Drusilla Robinson Smith's Reminiscences" (ms. & ts. 1994); "William North Steuben and His Journal, 1849–1850" (Harry E. Rutledge, ed., ts. PAM 4610); John William Watts, "Diary written while Crossing the Plains in 1850" (ms. 2273).

The California State Library, Sacramento, California: J. C. Buffum, "Diary of J. C. Buffum, 1847–1854" (ms.); Robert Chalmers, "Diary" (ms.); William E. Chamberlain, "Diary" (ms.); Jared Fox, "Memorandum of a Trip from Dalton, Sauk County, Wisconsin, to Oregon and California, April 12, 1852–Aug. 12, 1854 (copied from the original by Ruth Grimshaw Martin)" (ts.); Alpheus N. Graham, "Journal kept by Alpheus N. Graham from Coles County Illinois to California in the Year 1852" (ts.); Mary

Jane Guill (Mrs. John Hudson Guill), "The Overland Diary of a Journey from Livingston County, Missouri, to Butte County, California May 5 to September 5, 1860" (ts.); O. J. Hall, "Diary of a Forty Niner" (ts.); "Copy of Diary of William Johnston, Huntington, Pa." (ts.); Micajah Littleton, "Journal of a Trip Across the Plains From Independence, Missouri, to California May 11, 1850–October 11, 1850" (ts.); H. R. Mann, "Portion of a Diary of H. R. Mann, 1849" (ts.); Alexander B. Nixon, "Journal of the Pacific Ocean" (ms., 2 vols.); John Sharp, "Brief Notes Recorded by John Sharp, Methodist Minister, Concerning his Life and including His Arrival in Placeville, August 31, 1850" (ms.); John C. Thorniley, "Diary of Overland Journey in 1852" (ms.); Robert Milton Wilson, "A Chronicle of the Migration of Robert M. Wilson, S. E. Wilson, S. M. Wilson, and L. G. Liler, from Osage County, Missouri, to California in 1850" (ts.).

Dartmouth College Library, Hanover, New Hampshire: Joshua D. Breyfogle, "Diary" (ms. 165).

Denver Public Library, Western History Department, Denver, Colorado: Mendall Jewett, "Journal to and from California of Dr. Mendall Jewett" (ts.).

The Holt-Atherton Pacific Center for Western Studies, University of the Pacific, Stockton, California: "Diary of Alpheus Richardson Crossing the Plains in 1852" (ms. & ts. R521).

The Henry E. Huntington Library and Art Gallery, San Marino, California: George Belshaw, "Journey from Indiana to Oregon—Journal of George Belshaw, March 23 to September 27, 1853" (ts. HM 16765); Lorenzo Dow Chillson, "Diary" (ms. HM 4293); Addison M. Crane, "Journal of a Trip Across the Plains in 1852" (ms. HM 19333); J[oshua?] H. Drake, "Diary, 1849–1851" (ms. film 580); Isaac Foster, "A Journal of the Route to Alta California" (ts. HM 16995); Charles G. Gray, "An Overland Passage from Independence Mo. to San Francisco, Cal. in 1849" (ms. HM 16520); [Letter from] John T. Kinkade to

James and Hannah Kinkade, 11 July 1849 (ms. HM KI 85); Israel Shipman Pelton Lord, "Journal of 1849 . . ." (ms. HM 19408); William S. McBride, "Diary" (ms. HM 16956); John S. McKieran, "Diary" (ms. microfilm #422); Charles R. Parke, "Notes Crossing the Plains" (ms. HM 16996); William Tell Parker, "Notes by the Way" (ms. HM 30873); Joseph Pownall, "Overland Diary and Letterbook" (ms. PW 553); William Rowe, "Ho for California: Personal Reminiscences of William Rowe, Sr. of an Overland Trip from Rochester, Wisconsin, to California in 1853 in Company with 'Lucky' Baldwin" (ts. HM 19027); W. W. Sullivan, "Crossing the Plains in 1862" (ts. HM 16772); Dr. Edward Alexander Tompkins, "Expedition to California" (photocopy FAC 222); Joseph Warren Wood, "Diaries of Crossing the Plains in 1849 and Life in the Diggings from 1849 to 1853" (ms. HM 318).

The State Historical Society of Iowa, Iowa City: Jane A. Gould, "Her Journal: Oregon–California Trail 1862" (mimeograph); Letter from Alphonso B. Newcomb to Solurous Wakeley, 13 July 1850 (ms.); Albert G. Paschal, "Diary of Albert G. Paschal, Overland Trip to California with Ox Team in the Year 1850" (ts.).

The Kansas State Historical Society, Library and Archives Division, Topeka, Kansas: Godfrey C. Ingrim, "Starting Out for the Gold Mines" (ts.); Henry Shombre, "Diary" (ms.).

Lane County Historical Society, Eugene, Oregon: Enos Ellmaker, "Autobiography of Enos Ellmaker" (ts.); "An Organizational Account of the Wagon Train Captained by Solomon Tetherow, 1845. [The Oregon Society Journal reporting Bylaws of the Oregon Emigrating Society Constitution 5 May 1845]" (ts.); "Savannah Company Journal" (ts.); Catherine Amanda Stansbury Washburn, "Journal of Catherine Amanda Stansbury Washburn: Iowa to Oregon, 1853" (ts.).

Library of Congress, Manuscripts Division, Washington, D.C.: Clark W. Thompson, "Letters" (ts.).

Missouri Historical Society Archives, St. Louis, Missouri: "Letter of Hunt to Messrs. Keemle and Field, May 2, 1849, published in St. Louis *Weekly Reveille*" (ts. copy Oregon-California Collection); Lydia A. Rudd, "Notes by the Wayside Enroute to Oregon" (ts. copy Oregon-California Collection); James Tate, "Copy of Diary of Colonel James Tate 1849" (ts. Oregon-California Collection).

National Archives, Washington, D.C.: "Fort Laramie Orders," RG 393, Part V, entry 11; "General Orders—United States Army General Orders," RG 393, Part I, entry 54; "Laramie Letters Received," RG 393, Box 1, U.S. Army Continental Commands 1821–1920; "Sixth Military Department Letter Book," RG 393, Part I, entry 46.

Nebraska State Historical Society, Division of Library/Archives, Lincoln, Nebraska: John H. Benson, "Forty Niner: From St. Joseph to Sacramento" (ts. & ms. MS0713).

The Newberry Library, Chicago, Illinois: George P. Burrall, "A Trip Across the Plains in 1849" (ts.); William Thompson, "Reminiscences of a Pioneer" (ts. Fort Laramie Journals, vol. 4); J. A. Wilkinson, "Journal: Across the Plains in 1859" (ms.).

The Ohio Historical Society, Archives/Library Division, Columbus, Ohio: Robert L. Sharp, "Travel Diary" (ms. VFM 3188).

The Oregon Historical Society Library, Portland, Oregon: Cecilia Emily McMillan Adams, "Journal" (ts. 1508); Benjamin Franklin Dowell, "Copy of his Journal" (ms. 209); "Letter from George Marshall to wife and children, 11 May 1850" (ms. photocopy 1500); Jesse Moreland, "Rev. Jesse Moreland's Diary Tennessee to Oregon 1852" (ms. 1508); Paris Swazey Pfouts, "Autobiography" (ts. 297); Hamilton Scott, "A Trip Across the Plains" (ts. 596); T. J. Stites, "Journey of Travels" (ts. 1508); John S. L. Taylor, "California Journal" (ts. 17); Sarah Sutton, "Diary" (ts., Fort Laramie Journals, Vol. 4).

The University of Oregon, Department of Special Collections, Eugene, Oregon: Isom Cranfill, "Overland Journal" (ms. & ts.); Medorem Crawford, "Pocket Diary 1863" (ms.); V. A. Williams, "Journal" (ms.).

Princeton University Libraries, Princeton, New Jersey: William Brisbane, "Journal of a Trip Or Notes of One From Fort Levenworth to San Francisco, Via Santa Fe in 1849" (ms.); Patrick H. McLeod, "1849 Going to California" (ms.); Patrick H. McLeod, "Notebooks" (unbound ms. NB 1–5); James O. Rayner, "Journal of a Tour from Iowa to Oregon" (ts.); Erasmus N. Taylor and John W. Taylor, "Letters written to their families from Placeville, California" (ms.).

The Stanford University Libraries, Stanford, California: James E. Bouldin, "Diary of Captain James E. Bouldin" (ts.).

Eastern Washington State Historical Society Research Library and Archives, Spokane, Washington: Benjamin Burgunder, "Reminiscences of Benjamin (Ben) Burgunder About 1916" (ts.); Andrew Jackson Griffith, "Hancock County, Illinois to California in 1850. The Diary of Dr. Andrew Jackson Griffith" (ts.).

Washington State Historical Society, Special Collections Division, Tacoma, Washington: Jay Stillman, "Recollections of a Trip Across the Plains in 1852" (ts.).

University of Washington Libraries, Seattle, Washington: Amelia Knight, "Journal Kept on the Road from Iowa to Oregon" (ms.); Michael F. Luark, "Diary" (ms.); David McDonald, "A Story of Crossing the Plains in 1865" (ms.).

Western Historical Manuscript Collection, University of Missouri, Columbia, Missouri: Samuel Matthias Ayres, "Letters from Dr. Samuel Matthias Ayres to Priscilla Frances Ayres" (ts. #995, vol. XXIX-760); Elijah Preston Howell, "Diary" (ms. C1675); Joseph R. Simmons, "Notes of Travel: Adventures of a Party of Missourians who Travel Overland from Missouri to California, A.D. 1849" (ms. C1259); T. J. Stites, "Journal of Travels from Putham County, Missouri, to Portland, Oregon, May 8, 1862 to October 1, 1862" (ts. C995, vol. XIII:395).

State Historical Society of Wisconsin, Library and Archives, Madison, Wisconsin: David Brainard, "Journal of the Walworth County Mutual Mining Company, commencing March the 20th, 1849" (ts.); Samuel Chadwick, "Samuel Chadwicks Travels to California in 1852" (ms.); John Dalton, "Diary of John Dalton, 1852" (ts.); Charles G. Schneider, "Memorandum 1852" (ts. trans. from German ms.); George Washington Short, "Diary of George Washington Short of Waukesha, Wisconsin, Covering his Trip to and from California in 1852–53" (ts.); H. D. Williams, "Original Diary kept by H. D. Williams when he crossed the plains to California in 1859" (ts.).

# Short-Title List

Adams, "Diary"
  Cecilia Emily McMillen Adams, "Crossing the Plains in 1852," *Transactions of the Thirty-Second Annual Reunion of the Oregon Pioneer Association for 1904* (1905): 288–329.

Adams, "Journal to Oregon"
  Cecilia Emily McMillen Adams, "Journal," (ts. 1508, Oregon Historical Society).

Adams and Blank, "Diary"
  Cecilia Adams and Panthenia Blank, "Diary," in 5 *Covered Wagon Women*, pp. 256–312.

Allen, *Canvas Caravans*
  Eleanor Allen, *Canvas Caravans*. Portland, Ore.: Binfords and Mort, 1946.

Allen, *In English Ways*
  David Grayson Allen, *In English Ways: The Movement of Societies and the Transferral of English Local Law and Custom to Massachusetts Bay in the Seventeenth Century*. Chapel Hill: University of North Carolina Press, 1981.

Allyn, "Journal"
  "Journal of Henry Allyn, 1853," *Transactions of the Forty-Ninth Annual Reunion of the Oregon Pioneer Association* (1924): 372–435.

Anable, *Journal*
  Henry Sheldon Anable, *Journal Kept by H. S. Anable while on the "plains" in 1852* (ms. C-F 137:1, Bancroft Library).

Anderson, *Letters*
  *Letters of Charles Lewis Anderson to his wife* (ms. P-G 266, Bancroft Library).

Anon., "Diary"
> Anonymous, "The Diary of an Unknown Scout Accompanying a Company of Covered Wagon Emigrants from St. Joseph, Missouri, to California, May 2 1852" (ts. 59A, California Historical Society).

Applegate, "Cow Column"
> Jesse Applegate, "A Day with the Cow Column" (address before Oregon Pioneer Association, 1876), in *Frontier Experience*, pp. 98–103.

Austin, *Diary*
> Henry Austin, *1849 Diary of Henry Austin* (ms. photocopy, C-F 157, Bancroft Library).

Ayres, "Letters"
> Letters from Dr. Samuel Matthias Ayres to Priscilla Frances Ayres (ts. #995, vol. XXIX-760, 1850, Western Historical Manuscript Collection, Columbia, Mo.).

Banks, *Diary*
> John Edwin Banks, *Diary*, in *The Buckeye Rovers in the Gold Rush: An Edition of Two Diaries*. Howard L. Scamehorn, ed. Athens: Ohio University Press, 1965.

Barry, "Notes to Clark"
> Louise Barry, "Notes" to Clark, "Overland."

Batchelder, *Journal*
> Amos Batchelder, *Journal of a Tour Across the Continent of N. America ... in 1849* (ms. C-B 614, Bancroft Library).

Becker, "Introduction"
> Robert H. Becker, "Introduction and Notes," to Christy, *Road*, pp. 1–13.

Belshaw, "Diary Kept"
> "Diary Kept by Mrs. Maria A. Belshaw," edited by Joseph Ellison, printed in *New Spain and the Anglo-American West:*

*Historical Contributions Presented to Herbert Eugene Bolton —
Volume II: The Anglo-American West.* Lancaster, Pennsylvania:
Privately Printed, 1932, pp. 219–43.

Belshaw, "Journey"
"Journey from Indiana to Oregon — Journal of George
Belshaw, March 23 to September 27, 1853" (ts. HM 16765,
Huntington Library).

Benson, "Forty Niner"
John H. Benson, "Forty Niner: From St. Joseph to
Sacramento" (ts., ms. 0713, Nebraska State Historical Society,
Lincoln).

Bidlack, *Letters*
Russell E. Bidlack, *Letters Home: The Story of Ann Arbor's Forty-
Niners.* Ann Arbor, Mich.: Ann Arbor Publishers, 1960.

Bidwell, *Journey*
*A Journey to California, 1841 — The First Emigrant Party to
California by Wagon Train: The Journal of John Bidwell.* Francis
P. Farquhar, ed. Berkeley, Calif.: Friends of the Bancroft
Library, 1964.

Bieber, *Southern Trails*
*Southern Trails to California in 1849.* Ralph P. Bieber, ed.
Glendale, Calif.: The Arthur H. Clark Company, 1937.

"Binding the Elephant"
John Phillip Reid, "Binding the Elephant: Contracts and Legal
Obligations on the Overland Trail," 21 *American Journal of
Legal History* (1977): 285–315.

*Boston-Newton*
*The Boston-Newton Company Venture: From Massachusetts to
California.* Jessie Gould Hannon, comp. Lincoln: University of
Nebraska Press, 1969.

Bouldin, "Diary"

James E. Bouldin, "Diary of Captain James E. Bouldin" (ts., Special Collections Department, Stanford University Libraries).

Bowers, "Account"
Fidelia March Bowers, "An Account of the Wagon Train Mastered by Solomon Tetherow" (ts., OV 10549, California Historical Society).

Bradley, *Daily Journal*
Nancy Jane Bradley and Henry Bradley, *A Daily Journal Kept by N. J. & H. Bradley on an overland Trip to California, in the Spring & Summer of 1852* (ms., Western Americana Collection 45, Yale University).

Brainard, "Journal"
David Brainard, "Journal of the Walworth County Mutual Mining Company, commencing March the 20th, 1849" (ts., Wisconsin Historical Society).

Breyfogle, *Diary*
Joshua D. Breyfogle, *Diary* (ms. 165, Dartmouth College Library).

Brisbane, *Journal*
William Brisbane, *Journal of A Trip Or Notes of One From Fort Levenworth to San Francisco, Via Sante Fe in 1849* (ms., Princeton University).

Brooks, "Plains Across"
Noah Brooks, "The Plains Across," 63 (New Series 41) *The Century Magazine* (1902): 803–20.

Brown, "Gold Seeker"
John Evans Brown, "Memoirs of An American Gold Seeker," 2 *Journal of American History* (1908): 129–54.

Brown, *Journal of a Journey*
James Berry Brown, *Journal of a Journey Across the Plains in 1859*. George R. Stewart, ed. San Francisco: Book Club of California, 1970.

Brown, "Journal to California"
Adam Mercer Brown, "Over Barren Plains and Rock-Bound Mountains." David M. Kiefer, ed. 22 *Montana* (Autumn 1977): 16–29.

Brown, *Memoirs*
John E. Brown, *Memoirs of a Forty-niner.* Katie E. Blood, ed. New Haven, Conn: Associated Publishers of American Records, 1907.

Brown, *Wagon Train Journal*
William Richard Brown, *An Authentic Wagon Train Journal of 1853 from Indiana to California.* Barbara Wills, ed. Mokelumne Hill, Calif.: Horseshoe Printing, 1985.

Bruff, *Journals*
*Gold Rush: The Journals, Drawings, and Other Papers of J. Goldsborough Bruff, Captain, Washington City and California Mining Association, April 2, 1849–July 20, 1851.* Georgia Willis Read and Ruth Gaines, eds., with a forward by F. W. Hodge. 2 vols. New York: Columbia University Press, 1944.

Brundage, "Diary"
"Diary of T. J. Brundage," in *Trailing the Campfires.* Elisa Spear Edwards, ed. Sheridan, Wyoming: Sheridan Chapter Daughters of the American Revolution, 1935, pp. 8–11.

Bryant, *Journal*
Edwin Bryant, *What I Saw in California: Being the Journal of a Tour by the Emigrant Route and South Pass of the Rocky Mountains, across the Continent of North America, The Great Desert Basin, and Through California in the Years 1846, 1847.* New York: D. Appleton & Company, 1848. rep. ed., Lincoln: University of Nebraska Press, 1985.

Bryarly, *Diary*
Wakeman Bryarly, *Diary,* in *Geiger-Bryarly Journal.*

Buffum, *Diary*
Diary of Jos. C. Buffum 1847–1854 (ms., California State Library).

Burbank, "Diary and Journal"
Augustus Ripley Burbank, "Diary and Journal of a Trip to California by Overland" (ts. copy 2, Oregon Collection, University of Oregon).

Burgunder, "Reminiscences"
Benjamin Burgunder, "Reminiscences of Benjamin (Ben) Burgunder About 1916" (ts., Eastern Washington State Historical Society, Spokane).

Burrall, "Trip"
George P. Burrall, "A Trip Across the Plains in 1849" (ts., Newberry Library).

Burrell, *Diary*
Mary Burrell, "Council Bluffs to California, 1854," in 6 *Covered Wagon Women*, pp. 228–55.

Burroughs, "Reminiscences"
Joseph Newton Burroughs, "Reminiscences of 1856 Overland Journey" (ts. #269, California Historical Society).

Caldwell, "Notes"
Dr. [T.G.?] Caldwell, "Notes of a Journey to California by Fort Hall Route, June To Oct[obe]r 1849, Found in Mountains," in Bruff, *Journals*, 2:1250–69.

Castle, "Belshaw Journey"
Gwen Castle, "Belshaw Journey, Oregon Trail, 1853," 32 *Oregon Historical Quarterly* (1939): 217–39.

Castleman, *Diary*
Diary of P[hilip] F. Castleman While Crossing the Plains to California Commencing from the time he left St. Joseph, Mo.,

*With A Seeth of his trip from home which was in Larue Co. Ky to St. Joseph Mo.* (1849) (ms., Western Americana Collection, S-745, Yale University).

Chadwick, *Diary*
Samuel Chadwicks Travels to California in 1852 (ms., Wisconsin Historical Society).

Chadwick, *Travels*
Samuel Chadwicks Travels to California in 1852 (ms., Wisconsin Historical Society).

Chalmers, *Diary*
Robert Chalmers, *Diary* (ms., California State Library).

Chamberlain, *Diary*
William Edwin Chamberlain, *Diary* (ms., California State Library).

Chillson, *Diary*
Lorenzo Dow Chillson, *Diary* (ms. HM 4293, Huntington Library).

Christy, *Road*
Thomas Christy's Road Across the Plains: A Guide to the Route from Norman Crossing, Now Omaha, Nebraska, to the City of Sacramento, California. Robert H. Becker, ed. Denver: Fred A. Rosenstock, 1969.

Clapp, *Journal*
John T. Clapp, *A Journal of Travels to and from California with Full Details of the Hardships and Privations; Also a Description of the Mines, Cities, Towns, &c.* Kalamazoo, Mich.: Geo. A. Fitch & Co., 1851.

Clark, *Guide*
John Clark, *The California Guide* (ms. #83, Western Americana Collection, Yale University).

Clark, "Overland"
> John Hawkins Clark, "Overland to the Gold Fields of California in 1852: The Journal of John Hawkins Clark, Expanded and Revised From Notes Made During the Journey." Louise Barry, ed. 11 *Kansas Historical Quarterly* (1942):227–96.

Cleland, "From Louisiana"
> Robert Glass Cleland, ed. "From Louisiana to Mariposa," 18 *Pacific History Review* (1949):24–32.

Cleland, *Rushing*
> Robert Glass Cleland, "From Louisiana to Mariposa," in *Rushing for Gold.* John Walton Caughey, ed. Berkeley: University of California Press, 1949, pp. 24–32.

Clough, *Diary*
> Aaron Clough, *Diary of Overland Journey to Oregon, May 15–December 15, 1862* (ms., microfilm, Oregon Historical Society).

"Coercing the Elephant"
> John Phillip Reid, "Coercing the Elephant: Punishment and Correctional Behavior on the Overland Trail," in *Criminal Science in a Global Society: Essays in Honor of Gerhard O.W. Mueller.* Littleton, Colo.: Fred B. Rothman & Co., 1994, pp. 163-212.

Coke, *Ride*
> Henry J. Coke, *A Ride Over the Rocky Mountains to Oregon and California with a Glance at Some of the Tropical Islands, including the West Indies and the Sandwich Isles.* London: Richard Bentley, 1852.

Cole, *Early Days*
> Gilbert L. Cole, *In the Early Days Along the Overland Trail in Nebraska Territory, in 1852.* Kansas City, Mo.: Franklin Hudson Publishing Company, [1905].

Compton, *Diary*
James H. Compton, *Diary* (ms. C-F 224, Bancroft Library).

Conyers, "1852 Diary"
"Diary of E. W. Conyers, a Pioneer of 1852," *Transactions of the Thirty-Third Annual Reunion of the Oregon Pioneer Association June 15, 1905* (1906): 423–512.

"Copy of Smith's Reminiscences"
"Copy of Elizabeth Drusilla Robinson Smith's Reminiscences" (ts. #1994, California Historical Society, San Francisco).

Cook, "Diary Letters"
Louisa Cook, "Letters from the Oregon Trail, 1862–1863," in 8 *Covered Wagon Women*, pp. 30–57.

Cooke, "Letters"
Lucy Rutledge Cooke, "The Letters of Lucy R. Cooke," in 4 *Covered Wagon Women*, pp. 214–95.

Coon, "Journal"
Polly Crandall Coon, "The Journal of Polly Lavinia Coon," in 5 *Covered Wagon Women*, pp. 177–206.

Cosad, *Diary*
David Cosad, *Journal of a Trip to California by the Overland Route and Life in the Gold Diggings During 1849–1850* (ms., California Historical Society).

Coupler, "Crossing the Plains"
J. C. Coupler, "Crossing the Plains from St. Joseph, Mo. to San Francisco" (ts. #1508, Oregon Historical Society).

*Covered Wagon Women*
*Covered Wagon Women: Diaries & Letters from the Western Trails 1840–1890*. Kenneth L. Holmes, ed. and comp.: with David C. Duniway on volume five. 11 vols. Glendale, Calif. and Spokane, Wash.: The Arthur H. Clark Company, 1983–1993.

Cowden, *Diary*
*Diary Kept by J[ames] S. Cowden on his Trip "Overland" from Iowa to Cal. in 1853 with Ox Teams and Wagons* (Photostat ms. #465, California Historical Society).

Crane, "Autobiography"
Addison Moses Crane, "Memoir Written By Himself," in M. W. Wood, *History of Alameda County, California* (1883): 865–69.

Crane, *Journal*
Addison M. Crane, *Journal of a Trip Across the Plains in 1852* (ms. HM 19333, Huntington Library).

Cranfill, *Journal*
Isom Cranfill, *Overland Journal* (ms. & ts., Oregon Collection, University of Oregon).

Crawford, *1863 Diary*
Medorem Crawford, *Pocket Diary 1863* (ms., Oregon Collection, University of Oregon).

Cross, "Journal"
Osborne Cross, "The Journal of Major Osborne Cross," printed in Settle, *March,* pp. 31–272.

Dalton, "Diary"
"Diary of John Dalton, 1852" (ts., Wisconsin Historical Society).

Davis, "California Diary"
Sarah Davis, "Diary from Missouri to California, 1850," in 2 *Covered Wagon Women*, pp. 174–206.

Davis, "Diary of 1852"
"Diary of Mr. Davis, 1852," in *Transactions of 37th Annual Reunion of the Oregon Pioneer Association* (1910): 355–81.

Davis, "Introduction and Notes"
James E. Davis, "Introduction" and Notes to Parke, *Diary.*

Decker, *Diaries*
   *The Diaries of Peter Decker: Overland to California in 1849 and
   Life in the Mines 1850–51.* Helen S. Giffen, ed. Georgetown,
   Calif.: Talisman Press, 1966.

Delano, *Across the Plains*
   Alonzo Delano, *Across the Plains and Among the Diggings: A
   Reprint of the Original Edition.* New York: Wilson-Erickson
   Inc., 1936.

Delano, *Life*
   A. Delano, *Life on the Plains and Among the Diggings; Being Scenes
   and Adventures of an Overland Journey to California: with
   Particular Incidents of the Route, Mistakes and Sufferings of the
   Emigrants, the Indian Tribes, the Present and the Future of the Great
   West.* Auburn and Buffalo: Miller, Orton & Mulligan, 1854,
   reprinted Ann Arbor, Mich.: University Microfilms, Inc., 1965.

"Diary of Robert Lee Sharp"
   "Diary of Robert Lee Sharp, Sugar Grove, Fairfield County,
   Ohio, Made while Crossing the Plains to the Gold Fields in
   California," printed in William Hale Sharp, *Life and Diary of
   Robert Lee Sharp: Naturalist and Geologist Pioneer and
   Statesman.* n.i., [1938], pp. 17–46.

Dickinson, *Overland Journal*
   D. C. Dickinson, *Journal* (ms. 75/98c, Bancroft Library).

Dinwiddie, *Journal*
   *Overland from Indiana to Oregon: The Dinwiddie Journal.*
   Margaret Booth, ed. *Sources of Northwest History*, no. 2.
   Missoula: State University of Montana, 1928.

"Dividing the Elephant"
   John Phillip Reid, "Dividing the Elephant: The Separation of
   Mess and Joint Stock Property on the Overland Trail," 28
   *Hastings Law Journal* (1976): 73–92.

Dowell, *Journal*
  Benjamin Franklin Dowell, *Copy of his Journal* (ms. #209,
  Oregon Historical Society).

Dowell, *Letter Journal*
  B. F. Dowell, *Journal* (in a Letter to "Greensville" dated 27
  September 1850) (ms., Western Americana Collection 142,
  Yale University).

Doyle, *Journals and Letters*
  Simon Doyle, *Journals and Letters of Simon Doyle* (ms.,
  Western Americana Collection #144, Yale University).

Dr. T., *Journal*
  Dr. T., *Journal of his Experience Crossing the Plains in 1849* (ms.
  C-B 383:1, Bancroft Library).

Drake, *Diary*
  J[oshua?] H. Drake, *Diary 1849–1851* (ms. film 580,
  Huntington Library).

Duffin, "Miller-Tate Murder"
  Reg. P. Duffin, "The Miller-Tate Murder and the John F.
  Miller Grave," 5 (#4) *Overland Journal* (Fall 1987): 24–31.

Dunlap, "Journal"
  Katherine Dunlap, "Journal [1864]" (ts., photostat P-I 109,
  Bancroft Library).

Dutton, "Journal and Letters"
  "Across the Plains in 1850: Journal and Letters of Jerome
  Dutton," 9 *Annals of Iowa* (July–October 1910): 447–83.

Eastland , "Diary and Letters"
  "To California Through Texas and Mexico: The Diary and
  Letters of Thomas B. Eastland and Joseph G. Eastland, his
  Son," 18 *California Historical Society Quarterly* (1939):
  99–135: 229–50.

Eastland, *Letters*
Letters of Thomas B. Eastland to Josephine Eastland (ms. VMS19, California Historical Society).

Eaton, *Overland*
Herbert Eaton, *The Overland Trail to California in 1852*. New York: G. P. Putnam's Sons, 1974.

Eccleston, *Overland*
*Overland to California on the Southwestern Trail 1849: Diary of Robert Eccleston*, George P. Hammond and Edward H. Howes, eds. Berkeley: University of California Press, 1950.

*Edmund Booth*
*Edmund Booth Forty-Niner: The Life Story of a Deaf Pioneer. Including Portions of his Autobiographical Notes and Gold Rush Diary, and Selections from Family Letters and Reminiscences.* Stockton, Calif.: San Joaquin Pioneer and Historical Society, 1953.

Egbert, "Record"
Eliza Ann McAuley [Egbert], "Mother's Diary: The Record of a Journey Across the Plains in '52" (ts. 645, California Historical Society).

Ellmaker, "Autobiography"
"Autobiography of Enos Ellmaker" (ts., reproduced by Lane County Historical Society, 1962).

Epperson, "Journal"
Lucretia Lawson Epperson, "A Journal of our Trip, 1864," in 8 *Covered Wagon Women*, pp. 164–98.

Fish, *Daily Journal*
Mary C. Fish, *Daily Journal Written During An Overland Journey to California* (ms. C-F 140, Bancroft Library).

Foreman, *Marcy*
Grant Foreman, *Marcy & the Gold Seekers: The Journal of Captain R. B. Marcy, with an Account of the Gold Rush over the Southern Route*. Norman: University of Oklahoma Press, 1939.

Forsyth, "Journal"
    John Robert Forsyth, "Journal of a Trip from Peoria, Ill. to
    California on the Pacific in 1849" (ts., microfilm, C-F 50,
    Bancroft Library).

*Fort Laramie Orders*
    National Archives, RG 393, Part V, Entry 11, vols. 1–4, Fort
    Laramie, Wyoming.

*Foster Family*
    *The Foster Family: California Pioneers*. Lucy A. Foster Sexton,
    ed. Santa Barbara, Calif.: Schauer Printing Studio, 1925.

Foster, "First Diary"
    Reverend Isaac Foster, "A Journal of the Route to Alta
    California," in *Foster Family*, pp. 14–97.

Foster, "Journal"
    Isaac Foster, "A Journal of the Route to Alta California" (ts.
    HM 16995, Huntington Library).

Fox, "Memorandum"
    Jared Fox, "Memorandum of a Trip from Dalton, Sauk
    County, Wisconsin, to Oregon and California, April 12,
    1852–Aug. 12, 1854 (copied from the original by Ruth
    Grimshaw Martin)" (ts., California State Library).

Franklin, "Journal to California"
    "Journal of William Riley Franklin to California from Missouri
    in 1850." Homer Franklin, Sr., and Homer Franklin, Jr., eds.
    46 *Annals of Wyoming* (Spring 1974): 47–74

Frizzell, *Journal*
    *Across the Plains to California in 1852: From the Little Wabash
    River in Illinois to the Pacific Springs of Wyoming. Journal of
    Mrs. Lodisa Frizzell*. Victor Hugo Paltsits, ed. New York: New
    York Public Library, 1915.

Froncek, "Winterkill"
Thomas Froncek, "Winterkill, 1846: The Tragic Journey of the Donner Party," 28 *American Heritage* (1976): 28–41.

*Frontier Experience*
*The Frontier Experience: Readings in the Trans-Mississippi West.* Robert V. Hine and Edwin R. Bingham, eds. Belmont, Calif.: Wadsworth Publishing Co., 1963.

*Frontier Guardian*
*The Frontier Guardian and Iowa Sentinel,* Kanesville, Iowa.

Gardner, *Journal to California*
Daniel B. Gardner, *Journal to California April 1850* (ms., Library of Congress).

Gee, *Journal*
Perry Gee, *Journal of Travels Across the Plains to California* (ms., Western Americana Collection #213, Yale University).

Gee, "Journal of Travels"
Perry Gee, "Journal of Travels Across the Plains to California in 1852 With Notes by the Way and an Account of Four Months Experiences at the Gold Diggings" (ts., Western Americana Collection #213, Yale University).

Geer, "Diary"
"Diary of Mrs. Elizabeth Dixon Smith Geer," *Transactions of the 35th Annual Reunion of the Oregon Pioneer Association* (1908): 153–78.

*Geiger-Bryarly Journal*
*Trail to California: The Overland Journal of Vincent Geiger and Wakeman Bryarly.* David Morris Potter, ed. New Haven: Yale University Press, 1945.

*General Orders*
National Archives. United States Army General Orders. RG 393, Pt. I, Entry 54, vols. 71 and 74.

Gibbs, "Diary"
George Gibbs, "The Diary of George Gibbs," printed in Settle, *March,* pp. 273–327.

Giffen, *Pioneer*
Helen S. Giffen, *Trail-Blazing Pioneer: Colonel Joseph Ballinger Chiles.* San Francisco: John Howell Books, 1969.

Goldsmith, *Overland*
Oliver Goldsmith, *Overland in Forty-Nine: The Recollections of a Wolverine Ranger after a Lapse of Forty-Seven Years.* Detroit: The Author, 1896.

Goodrich and Davison, "Wage-Earner"
Carter Goodrich and Sol Davison, "The Wage-Earner in the Westward Movement," in *Pivotal Interpretations of American History.* Carl N. Degler, ed. vol. 1. New York: Harper and Row, 1966, pp. 111–58.

Goodridge, "Morman Diary"
"The Diary of Sophia Lois Goodridge," in *2 Covered Wagon Women,* pp. 213–34.

Gould, *Diary*
Charles Gould, *Diary,* in *Boston-Newton.*

Gould, "Journal"
Jane A. Gould, "Her Journal: Oregon-California Trail 1862" (Mimeograph, State Historical Society of Iowa, Des Moines, Iowa.).

"Governance of the Elephant"
John Phillip Reid, "Governance of the Elephant: Constitutional Theory on the Overland Trail," 5 *Hastings Constitutional Law Quarterly* (1978): 421–43.

Graham, "Journal"
Alpheus N. Graham, "Journal kept by Alpheus N. Graham From Coles County Illinois to California in the Year 1852" (Positive photostat of a ts., California State Library).

*Granville Company Journal*
  *Journal of the Granville Overland Company* (ms., Western
  Americana Collection #228, Yale University).

Gray, "Oregon Journal"
  "Notes and Documents: Gray's Journal of 1838." Clifford M.
  Drury, ed. 29 *Pacific Northwest Quarterly* (July 1938): 277–82.

Gray, *Passage*
  Charles G. Gray, *An Overland Passage from Independence Mo. to
  San Francisco, Cal. in 1849* (ms. HM 16520, Huntington Library).

Green, *1852 Diary*
  *Diary of Jay Green: Covering the Period May 1, 1852 to July 27,
  1852, During the Crossing of the Plains and Mountains in a
  Journey from Duncan's Ferry, Missouri, to Hangtown (Placerville)
  California.* Stockton, San Joaquin, Calif.: San Joaquin Pioneer
  and Historical Society, 1955—The Fifth Publication of the
  Society.

Griffith, "Diary of 1850"
  Andrew Jackson Griffith, "Hancock County, Illinois to
  California in 1850. The Diary of Dr. Andrew Jackson Griffith"
  (ts., Eastern Washington State Historical Society, Spokane).

Grow, *Journal*
  S. L. Grow, *Journal* (ms., Western Americana Collection #235,
  Yale University).

Grow, *Letter Diary*
  D. S. I. Grow, *Diary* [Letter to A. Richardson] (ms., Yale
  University).

Guill, "Diary"
  Mary Jane Guill (Mrs. John Hudson Guill), "The Overland
  Diary of a Journey from Livingston County, Missouri, to Butte
  County, California May 5 to September 5, 1860" (ts.,
  California State Library).

Gundlach, *Minutes*
    John H. Gundlach, *Minutes of my trip to California* [1850]
    (ms., "Journal of a Trip to California", Missouri Historical
    Society, St. Louis).

Hafen and Young, *Fort Laramie*
    LeRoy R. Hafen and Francis Marion Young, *Fort Laramie and
    the Pageant of the West, 1834–1890.* Lincoln: University of
    Nebraska Press, 1938.

Hale, "1849 Diary"
    Israel F. Hale, "Diary of Trip to California in 1849," 2
    *Quarterly Society of California Pioneers* (June 1925): 61–130.

Hall, "Diary"
    O. J. Hall, "Diary of a Forty Niner" (ts., California State Library).

Handsaker, "Journal"
    Samuel Handsaker, "Journal of an Overland Trip to Oregon"
    (ts., Huntington Library, Fac. 590).

Hanna, *Journal*
    Esther Belle McMillan Hanna, *Journal,* in Allen, *Canvas
    Caravans.*

Harker, "Letters"
    [Letters of George Miffen Harker to St. Louis *Weekly Reveille,*]
    "Morgan Street to Old Dry Diggings 1849," 6 *Glimpses of the
    Past* (1939): 35–76.

Harvey, *To California*
    Isaac Julian Harvey, *To California in 1850* (ms. C-D 5091A,
    Bancroft Library).

Hastings, *Emigrant Guide*
    Lansford W. Hastings, *The Emigrants' Guide to Oregon and
    California* (facsimile of 1845 ed.; Charles Henry Carey, ed.)
    Princeton: Princeton University Press, 1932.

Hayes, *Diary*
> *Diary of Benj. Hayes' Journey overland from Socorro to Warner's Ranch from Oct. 31 1849 to January 14, 1850* (ms. C-E 79, Bancroft Library).

Herndon, *Crossing the Plains*
> Sarah Raymond Herndon, *Days on the Road: Crossing the Plains in 1865.* New York: Burr Printing House, 1902.

Hewitt, *Across*
> Randall H. Hewitt, *Across the Plains and Over the Divide: A Mule Train Journey from East to West in 1862, And Incidents Connected Therewith.* New York: Argosy-Antiquarian Ltd., 1964.

Hickman, *Overland Journey*
> *An Overland Journey to California in 1852: The Journal of Richard Owen Hickman.* M. Catherine White, ed. *Sources of Northwest History* No. 6, Missoula: State University of Montana, 1929.

Hillyer, "Journal"
> "From Waupun to Sacramento in 1849: The Gold Rush Journal of Edwin Hillyer." John O. Holzhueter, ed. 49 *Wisconsin Magazine of History* (1966): 210–44.

Hines, "Oregon Diary"
> Celinda Hines, "Life and Death on the Oregon Trail," in 6 *Covered Wagon Women*, pp. 81–130.

Hinman, *Pretty Fair View*
> *"A Pretty Fair View of the Eliphent"* or, *Ten Letters by Charles Hinman Written During His Trip Overland From Groveland, Illinois, to California in 1849 and his Adventures in the Gold Fields in 1849 and 1850.* Collon Storm, ed. Chicago: Gordon Martin, 1960.

Hixson, "Diary"
>   "Diary of Jasper Morris Hixson May 1–August 6, 1849" (ts. 1002, California Historical Society)

Hough, "Overland Diary"
>   "The 1850 Overland Diary of Dr. Warren Hough," 46 *Annals of Wyoming* (Fall 1974): 207–16.

Howell, *Diary*
>   Elijah Preston Howell, *Diary* (ms. #C1675, Western Historical Manuscript Collection, Columbia, Mo.).

Howell, "Diary of Emigrant"
>   John Ewing Howell, "Diary of An Emigrant of 1845," 1 (#3) *Washington Historical Quarterly* (April 1907): 135–58.

[Huntley,] *California*
>   [Henry Vere Huntley], *California: Its Gold and Its Inhabitants*, vols. 1 and 2. London: T. C. Newby, 1856.

Hutchings, *Journal*
>   *Seeking the Elephant, 1849: James Mason Hutching's Journal of his Overland Trek to California Including his Voyage to America, 1848 and Letters from the Mother Lode*. Shirley Sargent, ed. Glendale, California: Arthur H. Clark Company, 1980.

Ingalls, *Journal*
>   E. S. Ingalls, *Journal of a Trip to California by the Overland Route Across the Plains in 1850–51*. Waukegan, Ill.: Tobey & Co., 1852.

Ingrim, "Gold Mines"
>   Godfrey C. Ingrim, "Starting Out for the Gold Mines" (ts., Kansas State Historical Society).

Jewett, "Journal to California"
>   Mendall Jewett, "Journal to and from California of Dr. Mendall Jewett" (ts., Denver Public Library).

Johnson, *Overland*
John Lawrence Johnson, *Overland to Oregon in 1851* (ms., Western Americana Collection #274, Yale University).

Johnston, "Diary"
"Copy of Diary of William H. A. Johnston, Huntington, Pa." (ts., California State Library).

Jones, "Diary"
Carlton Jones, "Diary" (photostat, 348, Western Historical Manuscript Collection, Columbia, Mo.).

Jones, *Passenger to California*
Evans O. Jones, *Passenger to California* (ms., C-F 212, Bancroft Library).

Kerns, "Journal"
John T. Kerns, "Journal of Crossing the Plains to Oregon in 1852," *Transactions of the Forty-Second Annual Reunion of the Oregon Pioneer Association* (1917): 148–93.

King, *Journal*
Alfred D. King, *Journal of Southern Route* (ms., Special Collections Division, University of Arkansas Libraries, Fayetteville).

Kirkpatrick, *Journal*
*Journal of Charles Alexander Kirkpatrick 1849* (ms. C-D 207, Bancroft Library).

Kleinsorge, "Diary"
"Charles Kleinsorge: Missouri to California, 1854." Edward Bode, ed. 76 *Missouri Historical Review* (1982): 421–46.

Knight, "Woman's Diary"
Amelia Stewart Knight, "Diary of Mrs. Amelia Stewart Knight," in Schlissel, *Women's Diaries*, pp. 199–216.

Koch, "Big Circle"
> William E. Koch, "The Big Circle Back to Kansas," *The Kansas Magazine* (1966): 52–57.

Laird, *Book*
> Moses F. Laird, *Moses F. Laird's Book: A Journal to a few Turns of My Life: Different Situations: Travels. &c.* (ms., Western Americana Collection #290, Yale University).

Langum, *Law and Community*
> David J. Langum, *Law and Community on the Mexican California Frontier: Anglo-American Expatriates and the Clash of Legal Traditions, 1821–1846.* Norman: University of Oklahoma Press, 1987.

Langum, "Pioneer Justice"
> David J. Langum, "Pioneer Justice on the Overland Trails," 5 *Western Historical Quarterly* (1974): 421–39.

Langworthy, *Scenery*
> Franklin Langworthy, *Scenery of the Plains, Mountains and Mines.* Paul C. Phillips, ed. Princeton: Princeton University Press, 1932; rep. ed. New York: De Capo Press, 1972.

*Laramie Letters Received*
> National Archives, RG 393 Records of the U.S. Army Continental Commands, 1821–1920, Fort Laramie, Wyoming, Letters Received 1850–1889, Box 1.

Lavender, *Westward*
> David Lavender, *Westward Vision: The Story of the Oregon Trail.* Lincoln: University of Nebraska Press, 1963.

*Law For Elephant*
> John Phillip Reid, *Law for the Elephant; Property and Social Behavior on the Overland Trail.* San Marino, Calif.: Huntington Library, 1980.

Leeper, *Argonauts*
> David Rohrer Leeper, *The Argonauts of 'Forty-Nine: Some Recollections of the Plains and the Diggings.* South Bend, Ind.: J. B. Stoll & Co., 1894.

Lewis, *Book*
> John N. Lewis, *My Book* (ms. P-A 335, Bancroft Library).

Lewis, *Notes*
> Thomas Cotton Lewis, *"Memorandum or Notes" of Thos. C. Lewis & Son* (ms., Western Americana Collection #302, Yale University).

Littleton, "Journal"
> Micajah Littleton, "Journal of a Trip Across the Plains From Independence, Missouri, to California May 11, 1850 — October 11, 1850" (ts., California State Library).

Lockley, *Captain Tetherow*
> Fred Lockley, *Captain Sol. Tetherow Wagon Train Master: Personal Narrative of his Son, Sam. Tetherow, who Crossed the Plains to Oregon, in 1845, and Personal Narrative of Jack McNemee, who was born in Portland, Oregon, 1848, and whose Father built the fourth House in Portland.* Portland, Oregon: Privately Printed, [1925].

Lockley, "Migration of 1845"
> Fred Lockley, "The McNemees and Tetherows with the Migration of 1845: Organization Documents to That Migration," 25 *Quarterly Oregon Historical Society* (1924): 353–77.

Loomis, *Journal*
> Leander V. Loomis, *A Journal of the Birmingham Emigrating Company: The Record of a Trip from Birmingham, Iowa, To Sacramento, California, in 1850.* Edgar M. Ledyard, ed. Salt Lake City: Legal Printing Co., 1928.

Loomis, *Memorandum*
> Charles O. Loomis, *Memorandum or Travils to California* (ms., Southwestern Museum).

Lorch, "Gold Rush"
> Fred Lorch, "Iowa and the California Gold Rush of 1849," 30 *Iowa Journal of History and Politics* (1932): 307–76.

Lord, *Journal*
> Israel Shipman Pelton Lord, *Journal of 1849* [composed partly of clippings entitled, "California Correspondence" Written By Dr. Lord for *The Western Christian*, Elgin, Kane County, Illinois] (ms. HM 19408, Huntington Library).

Loring, "Report"
> "Official Report of Colonel William Wing Loring," 15 October 1849, printed in Settle, *March*, pp. 331–43.

Loughary, "Diary"
> Harriet A. Loughary, "'Travels and Incidents,' 1864," in 8 *Covered Wagon Women*, pp. 118–62.

Luark, *Diary*
> Michael F. Luark, *Diary* (ms., University of Washington).

Luark, *Late Diary*
> Michael F. Luark, *Diary of Overland Journey, Indiana to Olympia, Washington, 1853 Written by Him in Late Life & Based on His Original Diary* (ms., University of Washington).

Lyne, *Letters*
> James Lyne, *Letters* (ms., Western Americana Collection #312, Yale University).

McAuley, "Record"
> Eliza Ann McAuley, "The Record of Eliza Ann McAuley," 4 *Covered Wagon Woman*, pp. 36–81.

McBride, *Diary*
> William S. McBride, *Diary* (ms. HM 16956, Huntington Library).

McClure, "Journey"
: "Diary of A[ndrew] S. McClure of the Journey Across the Plains, May 7–October 15, 1853" (ts., California State Library).

McDonald, "A Story"
: David McDonald, "A Story of Crossing the Plains in 1865" (ts., University of Washington).

McGlashen, *Donner Party*
: C.F. McGlashen, *History of the Donner Party: A Tragedy of the Sierra.* 2nd ed. San Francisco: A. L. Bancroft, 1880; rep. ed., Stanford, Calif.: Stanford University Press, 1940.

McKieran, *Diary*
: John S. McKieran, *Diary* (ms., microfilm #422, Huntington Library). [The origin of this diary is unknown. The microfilm was deposited in the Huntington Library by Allan Nevins as if it were an unrestricted gift. Attempts to discover other owners have been made but have failed to uncover any further information.]

McKinstry, *Diary*
: *The California Gold Rush: Overland Diary of Byron N. McKinstry, 1850–1852, With a Biographical Sketch and Comment on a Modern Tracing of His Overland Travel by His Grandson Bruce L. McKinstry.* Glendale, Calif.: The Arthur H. Clark Company, 1975.

McKinstry, "Diary"
: "Gold Rush Diary of Byron N. McKinstry, 1850–1852" (ts., microfilm, Bancroft Library).

McKinstry, "Diary 1846"
: George McKinstry, "Diary," printed in Morgan, *First Overland,* pp. 203–15.

McLane, "Leaves"
    Dr. Allen McLane, "Leaves From a Pencil'd Journal, Found on
    Road (1849), From Mud Lake to the Pass - S. Nevada," print-
    ed in Bruff, *Journals*, 2:1269–71.

McLeod, *Diary*
    Patrick H. McLeod, *1849 Going to California* (ms., Princeton
    University).

McLeod, *Note Books*
    Patrick H. McLeod, *Note Books* (notebooks numbered 1, 2, 3,
    4, and 5, unbound, ms., Princeton University).

McMillan, "Reminiscences"
    Marcus McMillan, "Reminiscences" (ms., University of
    Washington).

McPherson, "Journal"
    William Gregg McPherson, "Journal," *Orange Daily News*,
    Orange, California, (part 1) 9 August 1937, p. 2; (part 2) 10
    August 1937, p. 5; (part 3) 11 August 1937, p. 5; (part 4) 12
    August 1937, p. 5; (part 5) 16 December 1937, p. 5; (part 6)
    17 December 1937, p. 6.

McWilliams, *Recollections*
    *Recollections of John McWilliams His Youth Experiences in
    California and the Civil War.* Princeton: Princeton University
    Press, n.d.

Madsen, *Shoshoni Frontier*
    Brigham D. Madsen, *The Shoshoni Frontier and the Bear River
    Massacre.* Salt Lake City: University of Utah Press, 1985.

Mann, "Portion"
    "Portion of a Diary of H. R. Mann, 1849" (ts., California
    State Library).

Marshall, *Letter to Wife and Children*
Letter from George Marshall to wife and children, 11 May 1850 (ms. photocopy, 1500, Oregon Historical Society).

Mattes, *Narratives*
Merrill J. Mattes, *Platte River Road Narratives: A Descriptive Bibliography of Travel Over the Great Central Overland Route to Oregon, California, Utah, Colorado, Montana, and Other Western States and Territories, 1812–1866.* Urbana: University of Illinois Press, 1988.

Mattes, *Platte River Road*
Merrill J. Mattes, *The Great Platte River Road: The Covered Wagon Mainline Via Fort Kearny to Fort Laramie.* Lincoln: Nebraska State Historical Society, 1969.

Maxwell, *Crossing the Plains*
Wm. Audley Maxwell, *Crossing the Plains Days of '57: A Narrative of Early Emigrant Travel to California by the Ox-Team Method.* San Francisco: Sunset Publishing House, 1915.

May, *Migrating Family*
Richard Martin May, *A Sketch of a Migrating Family to California* (ms. Bancroft Library, C-F 182).

Meeker, *Ventures and Adventures*
Ezra Meeker, *The Busy Life of Eighty-Five Years of Ezra Meeker: Ventures and Adventures, Sixty-Three Years of Pioneer Life in the old Oregon Country: An Account of the Author's Trip Across the Plains with an Ox Team, 1852; Return Trip, 1906–07; His Cruise on Puget Sound, 1853; Trip Through the Natchess Pass, 1854; Over the Chilcoot Pass; Flat-boating on the Yukon, 1898. The Oregon Trail.* Seattle: The Author, 1916.

Menefee, "Travels"
Arthur M. Menefee, "Travels and Adventures Across the Plains 1857" (ts., California State Library).

"Menefee's Travels"
"Arthur M. Menefee's Travels Across the Plains, 1857," 9
*Nevada Historical Society Quarterly* (Spring 1966): 5–28.

Middleton, "Across the Plains"
Joseph Middleton, "Across the Plains from Independence to
the Humboldt" (ts., Western Americana Collection S-39, Yale
University).

Miles, *Journal*
William Miles, *Journal of the Sufferings and Hardships of Capt.
Parker H. French's Overland Expedition to California.*
Chambersburg, Penn.: Printed at the Valley Spirit Office,
1851.

Minto, "*Oregon Trail*"
"Reminiscences of Honorable John Minto, Pioneer of 1844," 2
*Quarterly of the Oregon Historical Society* (1901): 119–67.
[Continued in John Minto, "Reminscences of Experiences on
the Oregon Trail in 1844. — II," in *id.*, 209–54].

Moore, *Law as Process*
Sally Falk Moore, *Law as Process: An Anthropological Approach.*
London: Routledge & Kegan Paul, 1978.

Moorman, *Journal*
*The Journal of Madison Berryman Moorman, 1850–1851.* Irene
D. Paden, ed. San Francisco: California Historical Society,
1948.

Moreland, *Diary*
Jesse Moreland, *Rev. Jesse Moreland's Diary Tennessee to Oregon
1852* (ms. 1508, Oregon Historical Society).

Morgan, *First Overland*
*Overland in 1846: Diaries and Letters of the California-Oregon
Trail.* Dale L. Morgan, ed. Vol. I. Georgetown, Calif.:
Talisman Press, 1963.

Morgan, "Green River Ferries"
Dale L. Morgan, "The Ferries of the Forty-Niners: Part III—
Section 1. The Green River Ferries," 32 *Annals of Wyoming*
(1960): 51–69; "The Ferries of the Forty-Niners: Part III—
Section 2. The Ferries of Sublette Cutoff," 32 *Annals of
Wyoming* (1961): 167–203.

Morgan, "Notes to Overland"
Dale L. Morgan, "Notes," in Morgan, *First Overland*, pp.
369–457; "Notes," in Morgan, *Second Overland*, pp. 743–99.

Morgan, *Second Overland*
*Overland in 1846: Diaries and Letters of the California-Oregon
Trail.* Dale L. Morgan, ed. Vol. II. Georgetown, Calif.:
Talisman Press, 1963.

Morgan, *Trip*
Martha M. Morgan, *A Trip Across the Plains in the Year 1849,
with Notes of a Voyage to California by Way of Panama.* San
Francisco: Pioneer Press, 1864.

*Mountain Men*
*The Mountain Men and the Fur Trade of the Far West:
Biographical Sketches of the Participants by Scholars of the Subject
and with Introductions by the Editor.* Le Roy R. Hafen, ed. 10
vols. Glendale, Calif.: The Arthur H. Clark Company,
1965–1972.

Moxley, *Correspondence*
Letter from Charles G. Moxley to [his sister] Emily Moxley
(ms., Western Americana Collection #S-712, Yale University).

Munkres, "Plains Indian Threat"
Robert L. Munkres, "The Plains Indian Threat on the Oregon
Trail before 1860," 40 *Annals of Wyoming* (1968): 193–221.

Muscott, "Letters"
: "Letters of John M. Muscott to Ebenezer Robbins Published in the *Rome [New York] Sentinel*" (ts., California Historical Society, San Francisco).

Ness, *Journal*
: Richard Ness, *Overland Diary to California* (ms., Western Americana Collection #S-709, Yale University).

Newcomb, *Journal*
: *Journal of Silas Newcomb of Madison Wisconsin, 1 April 1850 to 31 March 1851* (ms., Western Americana Collection #359, Yale University).

Newell, "Report on Indians"
: Robert Newell, " A Report on the Indians of Sub-Agency First District South of the Columbia, August 10th, 1849," printed in *Robert Newell's Memoranda: Travles in the Teritory of Missourie, Travle to the Kayuse War, together with a Report on the Indians South of the Columbia River.* Dorothy O. Johansen, ed. and intro. Portland, Ore.: Champoeg Press, 1959, pp. 144–59.

Nixon, *Journal*
: Alexander B. Nixon, *Journal of the Pacific Ocean* (ms., 2 vols., California State Library).

Page, *Wagons*
: Elizabeth Page, *Wagons West: A Story of the Oregon Trail.* New York: Farrar & Rinehart, 1930.

Parke, *Diary*
: Charles Ross Parke, M.D., *Dreams to Dust: A Diary of the California Gold Rush, 1849–1850.* James E. Davis, ed. Lincoln: University of Nebraska Press, 1989.

Parke, *Notes*
: Charles R. Parke, *Notes Crossing the Plains* (ms. HM 16996, Huntington Library).

Parker, *Notes*
    William Tell Parker, *Notes by the Way* (ms. HM 30873, Huntington Library).

Parkman, *Oregon Trail*
    Francis Parkman, Jr., *The Oregon Trail.* David Levin, ed. New York: Penguin Books, 1982.

Parrish, "Crossing in 1844"
    Edward Evans Parrish, "Crossing the Plains in 1844," in *Transactions of the Sixteenth Annual Reunion of the Oregon Pioneer Association for 1888.* Portland, Ore., 1889, pp. 82–122.

Parsons, "Journal"
    "The Journal of Lucena Parsons," in 2 *Covered Wagon Women,* pp. 239–94.

Paschal, "Diary"
    "Diary of Albert G. Paschal, Overland Trip to California with Ox Team, in the Year 1850" (ts., State Historical Society of Iowa, Iowa City).

Patterson, "Diary"
    "Diary of E. H. N. Patterson," in *Overland Routes to the Gold Fields, 1859 From Contemporary Diaries.* LeRoy R. Hafen, ed. Glendale, Calif.; The Arthur H. Clark Company, 1942, pp. 59–197.

Payette, *Northwest*
    B. C. Payette, *The Northwest.* Montreal: Privately Printed for Payette Radio Limited, 1964.

"Paying for the Elephant"
    John Phillip Reid, "Paying for the Elephant: Property Rights and Civil Order on the Overland Trail," 41 *Huntington Library Quarterly* (1977): 37–64.

Peacock, *Letters*
> *The Peacock Letters, April 7, 1850, to January 4, 1852: Fourteen Letters Written by William Peacock to His Wife, Susan, Who Remained Behind at Chemung, Illinois, While He Journeyed to California in a Covered Wagon Train, Endured Months of Disheartening Labor in the Gold Fields, and Prepared to Return to Her, a Sadly Disillusioned Man.* Stockton, Calif.: San Joaquin Pioneer & Historical Society, 1950.

Perkins, *Gold Rush Diary*
> *Gold Rush Diary, Being the Journal of Elisha Douglass Perkins on the Overland Trail in the Spring and Summer of 1849.* Thomas D. Clark, ed. Lexington: University of Kentucky Press, 1967.

Pfouts, "Autobiography"
> Paris Swazey Pfouts, "Autobiography" (ts. 297, Oregon Historical Society).

Pigman, *Journal*
> *The Journal of Walter Griffith Pigman.* Ulla Staley Fawkes, ed. Mexico, Missouri: Walter G. Staley, 1942.

Potter, "Introduction"
> David Morris Potter, "Introduction and Footnotes" to *Geiger-Bryarly Journal,* pp. 1–73.

Powell, *1849 Diary*
> H. M. Powell, *Diary of 1849–1852* (ms. C-F115, Bancroft Library).

Powell, *Puritan Village*
> Sumner Chilton Powell, *Puritan Village: The Formation of a New England Town.* Middletown, Conn.: Wesleyan University Press, 1963.

Pownall, *Letter Book*
> Joseph Pownall, *Overland Diary and Letter Book* (ms. PW 553, Huntington Library).

Pritchard, *Diary*
 *The Overland Diary of James A. Pritchard from Kentucky to
 California in 1849.* Dale L. Morgan, ed. Denver: F. A.
 Rosenstock—The Old West Publishing Company, 1959.

"Prosecuting the Elephant"
 John Phillip Reid, "Prosecuting the Elephant: Trials and
 Judicial Behavior on the Overland Trail," 1977 *Brigham Young
 University Law Review* (1977): 327–50.

Putnam, *Journal*
 *The Journal of Royal Porter Putnam.* Porterville, Calif.: Farm
 Tribune, 1961.

*Quaker Forty-Niner*
 *A Quaker Forty-Niner: The Adventures of Charles Edward
 Pancoast on the American Frontier.* Anna Paschall Hannum, ed.
 Philadelphia: University of Pennsylvania Press, 1930.

Rahm, "Copy of Diary"
 Louisa Moeller Rahm, "Copy of Diary of Louisa Moeller
 Rahm" (ts., Washington State Historical Society, Tacoma).

Ramsay, "Diary"
 "Alexander Ramsay's Gold Rush Diary of 1849," 18 *Pacific
 Historical Review* (1949): 442–68.

Rayner, *Journal*
 James O. Rayner, *Journal of a Tour from Iowa to Oregon* (ts.,
 Princeton University).

Read and Gaines, "Introduction"
 Georgia Willis Read and Ruth Gaines, "Introduction and
 Critical Notes," in Bruff, *Journals.*

Read, "Diseases"
 Georgia Willis Read, "Diseases, Drugs, and Doctors on the
 Oregon-California Trail in the Gold Rush Years," 38 *Missouri
 Historical Review* (1943–1944): 260–76.

Read, "Overland Diary"
George Willis Read, "Diary," in *A Pioneer of 1850: George Willis Read 1819–1880*. Georgia Willis Read, ed. Boston: Little Brown, 1927, pp. 17–100.

Reber, *Journal*
*The Journal of Thomas Reber*. Albert M. Tewksbury, ed. (ts., Master's Thesis, Claremont College, 1935).

Reid, "Diary"
"The Diary of Bernard J. Reid, Esq., Written by Him during His Journey Overland to California in '49" (ts., Western Pennsylvania Historical Society, Pittsburgh).

Reid, *Diary*
*Overland to California with the Pioneer Line: The Gold Rush Diary of Bernard J. Reid*. Mary McDougall Gordon, ed. Stanford, California: Stanford University Press, 1983.

"Replenishing the Elephant"
John Phillip Reid, "Replenishing The Elephant: Property and Survival on the Overland Trail," 79 *Oregon Historical Quarterly* (Spring 1978): 64–90.

"Reveille Letters"
"Letter of Hunt to Messrs. Keemle and Field, May 2, 1849," published in *St. Louis Weekly Reveille*, p. 3. (ts., Oregon-California Collection, Missouri Historical Society, St. Louis).

Rhodes, "Journal"
"Joseph Rhodes and the California Gold Rush," Merrill J. Mattes, ed., 23 *Annals of Wyoming* (January 1951): 52–71.

Richardson, "Diary of 1852"
"Diary of Alpheus Richardson Crossing the Plains in 1852" (ts. R521, Holt-Atherton Pacific Center for Western Studies, University of the Pacific).

Richardson, *Journal*
Caroline L. Richardson, *Journal* (ms. C-F 102, Bancroft Library).

Ringo, "Journal"
Mary Ringo, "The 1864 Journal," in 8 *Covered Wagon Women*, pp. 204–28.

Robinson, *Journey*
*The Robinson-Rosenberger Journey to the Gold Fields of California, 1849–1850: The Diary of Zirkle D. Robinson.* Francis Coleman Rosenberger, ed. and intro. Iowa City: The Prairie Press, 1966.

Rowe, "Ho For California"
"Ho For California: Personal Reminiscences of William Rowe, Sr. of an Overland Trip from Rochester, Wisconsin to California in 1853 in Company with 'Lucky' Baldwin" (ts., copied from narrative as published in the Waterville, Wisconsin *Post*, May and June, 1905, ms. HM 19027, Huntington Library).

Rudd, "Notes"
Lydia A. Rudd, "Notes by the Wayside Enroute to Oregon" (ts., Oregon-California Collection, Missouri Historical Society Archives, St. Louis).

Rudd, *Notes by the Wayside*
Lydia Allen Rudd, *Notes by the Wayside Enroute to Oregon* (ms., HM 27517, Huntington Library).

Rudd, "Woman's Diary"
Lydia Allen Rudd, "Woman's Diary," in Schlissel, *Women's Diaries*, pp. 187–98.

Rumer, *Wagon Trains*
Thomas A. Rumer, *The Wagon Trains of '44: A Comparative View of the Individual Caravans in the Emigration of 1844 to Oregon.* Spokane: The Arthur H. Clark Company, 1991.

"Savannah Company Journal"
"An Organizational Account of the Wagon Train Captained by Solomon Tetherow, 1845" (ts., reproduced by the Lane County Historical Society, 1960).

Sawyer, "Journal"
Frances Sawyer, "The Journal of Frances Sawyer," in 4 *Covered Wagon Women*, pp. 85–115.

Sawyer, "Notes from a Journal"
"Overland to California: Notes from a Journal kept by Mrs. Frances H. Sawyer, in a Journey across the Plains. May 9 to August 17, 1852" (ts. C-F 103 Transc., Bancroft Library).

Schlissel, *Women's Diaries*
Lillian Schlissel, *Women's Diaries of the Westward Journey*. New York: Schocken Books, 1982.

Schneider, *Memorandum*
Charles G. Schneider, *Memorandum 1852* (ms., Wisconsin Historical Society. Text is from English typescript translated from the German).

Scott, "Across the Plains"
Hamilton Scott, "A Trip Across the Plains" (ts. 596, Oregon Historical Society).

Scott, "Letters"
Scott Sisters, "Scott Letters to Illinois," in 5 *Covered Wagon Women*, pp. 141–72.

Scott, "Oregon Journal"
Abigail Jane Scott, "Journal of a Trip to Oregon," in 5 *Covered Wagon Women*, pp. 39–138.

Searls, *Diary*
Niles Searls, *The Diary of a Pioneer, and other Papers, Being the Diary Kept by Niles Searls on his Journey from Independence, Missouri, to California*. San Francisco: Pernan-Walsh Printing Co., 1940.

Settle, "Introduction"
Raymond W. Settle, "Introduction" to Settle, *March*, pp. 13–30.

Settle, *March*
*The March of the Mounted Riflemen: First United States Military Expedition to Travel the Full Length of the Oregon Trail from Fort Leavenworth to Fort Vancouver, May to October, 1849.* Raymond W. Settle, ed. Glendale, Calif.: The Arthur H. Clark Company, 1940.

"Sharing the Elephant"
John Phillip Reid, "Sharing the Elephant: Partnership and Concurrent Property on the Overland Trail," 45 *University of Missouri-Kansas City Law Review* (1976): 207–22.

Sharp, *Brief Notes*
John Sharp, *Brief Notes Recorded by John Sharp, Methodist Minister, Concerning his Life and including His Arrival in Placeville, August 31, 1850* (ms., California State Library).

Sharp, *Travel Diary*
Robert L. Sharp, *Travel Diary* (ms. VFM 3188 microfilm, Robert L. Sharp Papers, Ohio Historical Society).

Sheperd, *Journal*
James S. Sheperd, *Journal of Travel Across the Plains to California, and Guide to the Future Emigrant.* Racine, Wisc.: Mrs. Rebecca Sheperd, 1851 (Reprinted 1945).

Shombre, *Diary*
Henry Shombre, *Diary* (ms., Kansas State Historical Society).

Short, "Diary"
"Diary of George Washington Short of Waukesha, Wisconsin, Covering his Trip to and from California in 1852–53" (ts., Wisconsin Historical Society).

Simmons, *Notes*
>J. R. Simmons, *Notes of Travel: Adventures of a Party of Missourians who Travel Overland from Missouri to California, A.D. 1849* (ms. C1259, Western Historical Manuscript Collection, Columbia, Mo.).

Sixth Military Department
>National Archives. United States Army General Orders. RG 393, Pt. I, Entry 52, Volumes 72 and 73 ["Order Book," Head Quarters 6th Military Department].

Sixth Military Department Letter Book
>National Archives. RG 393, Pt.1, Entry 46, Volumes 12 and 13 DM.

Smith, *Journal of Trip*
>C. W. Smith, *Journal of a Trip to California Across the Continent From Weston, Mo., To Weber Creek, Cal. in the Summer of 1850*. R. W. G. Vail, ed. New York: Cadmus Book Shop, 1920.

Snodgrass, *Journal*
>R. H. P. Snodgrass, *Journal of the Trip from Piqua, Ohio to Sacramento California across the Plains in 1852 with an appendix Containing Prices ancient & news of Various Subjects* (ms., Western Americana Collection #432, Yale University).

Snow, "Diary"
>"Diary of Taylor N. Snow, Hoosier Fifty-Niner." Arthur Homer Hayes, ed. 28 *Indiana Magazine of History* (1932): 193–208.

Snyder, "Diary"
>"Diary of Jacob R. Snyder," 8 *Society of California Pioneers Quarterly* (December 1931): 224–60.

Springer, *Day Book*
  E. C. Springer, *Day Book* (ms., microfilm, 69/142, Bancroft Library).

Stackpole, *Journal*
  William T. Stackpole, *Journal of a trip towards California commenced Apl 4th 1849* (ms., Western Americana Collection S-1006, Yale University).

Staples, "Diary"
  David Staples, "Diary," in *Boston-Newton*, p. 144.

Steele, *Across the Plains*
  John Steele, *Across the Plains in 1850*. Joseph Schafer, ed. Chicago: The Caxton Club, 1930.

Stephens, *Jayhawker*
  L. Dow Stephens, *Life Sketches of a Jayhawker of '49*. San Jose, California: Notta Brothers, 1916.

Steuben, "Journal"
  "William North Steuben and His Journal, 1849–1850." Harry E. Rutledge, ed. (ts. PAM 4610, California Historical Society).

Steuben, *Journals*
  William North Steuben, *Journals* (ms. C-F 183, Bancroft Library).

Stewart, *California Trail*
  George R. Stewart, *The California Trail: An Epic with Many Heroes*. New York: McGraw-Hill Book Company, 1962.

Stewart, *Ordeal by Hunger*
  George R. Stewart, *Ordeal by Hunger: The Story of the Donner Party*. New York: Henry Holt and Company, 1936 (reprinted, Lincoln: University of Nebraska Press, 1986).

Stillman, "Recollections"
  Jay Stillman, "Recollections of a Trip Across the Plains in 1852" (ts., Washington State Historical Society, Tacoma).

Stites, "Journal"
    T. J. Stites, "Journal of Travels From Putham County,
    Missouri, to Portland, Oregon, May 8, 1862 to October 1,
    1862" (ts., C995, vol. XIII, 395, Western Historical
    Manuscript Collection, Columbia, Mo.).

Stites, "Journal of Travels"
    T. J. Stites, "Journal of Travels" (ts. 1508, Oregon Historical
    Society, Portland).

Stitzel, *Diary*
    Jacob Stitzel, *Overland Diary, Mar. 20 — Aug. 26, 1849*
    (microfilm 66-6800, Bancroft Library).

Stockton, "Journals"
    N. H. Stockton, "Journals" (ts., C-F 135, Bancroft Library).

Stookey, *Fatal Decision*
    Walter M. Stookey, *Fatal Decision: The Tragic Story of the
    Donner Party.* Salt Lake City: Deseret Book Company, 1950.

Sullivan, "Crossing"
    W. W. Sullivan, "Crossing the Plains in 1862" (ts. HM 16772,
    Huntington Library).

Sutton, "Diary"
    Sarah Sutton, "Diary" (ts., "Fort Laramie Journals, Vol. 4," Fort
    Laramie National Historical Site, Fort Laramie, Wyoming).

Swain, "Letters"
    William Swain, Letters to his Wife and his Brother, in J. S.
    Holliday, *The World Rushed In: The California Gold Rush
    Experience.* New York: Simon and Schuster, 1981.

Swan, "Letters"
    "Documents: Letters of a Forty-Niner [Chauncey Swan]."
    Mildred Thorne, ed. 47 *Iowa Journal of History* (1949): 63–77.

Tate, "Diary"
"Copy of Diary of Colonel James Tate 1849" (ts., Oregon-California Collection, Missouri Historical Society, St. Louis).

Taylor, "California Journal"
John S. L. Taylor, "California Journal" (ts. 17, Oregon Historical Society).

Taylor, *Eldorado*
Bayard Taylor, *Eldorado or Adventures in the Path of Empire.* New York: Alfred A. Knopf, 1949.

Taylor, *Letters*
Letters of Erasmus N. Taylor and John W. Taylor, written to their families, from Placerville, California (ms., Princeton University).

Taylor, "Letters"
"Documentary: Letters of S. H. Taylor to the Watertown [Wisconsin] Chronicle," 22 *Quarterly of the Oregon Historical Society* (1921): 117–60.

Terrell, "Overland Trip"
Joseph Christopher Terrell, "Overland Trip to California in '52 with Extracts from my Old Diary," in Capt. J. C. Terrell, *Reminiscences of the Early Days of Fort Worth.* Fort Worth: Texas Printing Co., 1906.

Thompson, *Crossing the Plains*
Origen Thompson, *Crossing the Plains: Narrative of the Scenes, Incidents and Adventures Attending the Overland Journey of the Decatur and Rush County Emigrants to the 'Far-off' Oregon, in 1852.* Greensburg, Ind.: Orville Thompson Printer, 1896.

Thompson, "Letters"
Clark W. Thompson, *Letters* (ts., Library of Congress).

Thompson, "Reminiscences"
William Thompson, "Reminiscences of a Pioneer" (ts., "Fort Laramie Journals, vol 4," Fort Laramie National Historic Site, Fort Laramie, Wyoming).

Thorniley, *Diary*
John C. Thorniley, *Diary of Overland Journey in 1852* (ms., California State Library).

Thornton, *California Tragedy*
J. Quinn Thornton, *The California Tragedy*. With a foreword by Joseph A. Sullivan. Oakland, California: Biobooks, 1945.

Tiffany, *Diaries*
P. C. Tiffany, *Diaries* (ms., Western Americana Collection #474, Yale University).

Tiffany, *Journal*
P. C. Tiffany, *Journal* (ms. and ts. 474, Beinecke Library, Yale University).

Tobie, "Meek"
Harvey E. Tobie, "Stephen Hall Meek," in 2 *Mountain Men*, pp. 225–40.

Tocqueville, *Democracy in America*
Alexis De Tocqueville, *Democracy in America*. J. P. Mayer, ed., George Lawrence, trans. Garden City, New York: Doubleday, 1969

Todd, "Foreword"
Edgeley Woodman Todd, "Foreword, Introductions, and Footnotes," to Wayman, *Diary*.

Tompkins, *Expedition*
Dr. Edward Alexander Tompkins, *Expedition to California* (photocopy FAC 222, Huntington Library).

Udell, *Incidents*
  John Udell, *Incidents of Travel to California, across the Great Plains: Together with the Return Trips through Central America and Jamaica; to which are Added Sketches of the Author's Life.* Jefferson, Ohio: Printed for the Author, at the Sentinel Office, 1856.

Unruh, *Plains*
  John D. Unruh, Jr., *The Plains Across: The Overland Emigrants and the Trans-Mississippi West, 1840–60.* Urbana: University of Illinois Press, 1979.

Unruh, *Plains Across*
  John D. Unruh, *The Plains Across: The Overland Emigrants and the Trans-Mississippi West, 1840–1860* (Unpublished Ph.D. dissertation, University of Kansas, 1975).

Verdenal, "Journal"
  John M. Verdenal, "Journal Across the Plains 1852" (ts., Bancroft Library).

Washburn, *Journal*
  *The Journal of Catherine Amanda Stansbury Washburn: Iowa to Oregon,* 1853 (ts., reproduced by Lane County Historical Society, 1967).

Watts, *Diary*
  John William Watts, *Diary written While Crossing the Plains in 1850* (ms. 2273, California Historical Society).

Wayman, *Diary*
  *A Doctor on the California Trail: The Diary of Dr. John Hudson Wayman from Cambridge City, Indiana, to the Gold Fields in 1852.* Edgeley Woodman Todd, ed. Denver: Old West Publishing Co., 1971.

Webb, *Trail*
  Todd Webb, *The Gold Rush Trail and the Road to Oregon.* Garden City, N.Y.: Doubleday, 1963.

Webster, *Gold Seekers*
Kimball Webster, *The Gold Seekers of '49: A Personal Narrative of the Overland Trail and Adventures in California and Oregon from 1849 to 1854.* Manchester, N.H.: Standard Book Company, 1917.

White, *Forty-Niners*
Stewart Edward White, *The Forty-Niners: A Chronicle of the California Trail and Eldorado.* New Haven: Yale University Press, 1918.

White, "Oregon Letter"
"To Oregon in 1852: Letter of Dr. Thomas White, La Grange County, Indiana, Emigrant," Oscar O. Winther and Gayle Thornbrough, eds. 23 (no.1) *Indiana Historical Society Publications* (1964).

Wilkins, *An Artist*
John F. Wilkins, *An Artist on the Overland Trail: The 1849 Diary and Sketches of John F. Wilkins.* John Francis McDermott, ed. San Marino, Calif.: Huntington Library, 1968.

Wilkinson, *Across the Plains*
J. A. Wilkinson, *Journal: Across the Plains in 1859* (ms., Newberry Library).

Williams, *Journal*
V. A. Williams, *Journal* (ms., Oregon Collection, University of Oregon).

Williams, "Original Diary"
"Original Diary kept by H. D. Williams when he crossed the plains to California in 1859" (ts., State Historical Society of Wisconsin).

Wilson, "Chronicle"
Robert Milton Wilson, "A Chronicle of the Migration of Robert M. Wilson, S. E. Wilson, S. M. Wilson, and L. G. Liler, from Osage County, Missouri, to California, in 1850" (ts., California State Library).

Wood, *Diaries*
Joseph Warren Wood, *Diaries of Crossing the Plains in 1849 and Life in the Diggings from 1849 to 1853* (ms. HM 318, Huntington Library).

Wood, "Journal of a Trip"
Elizabeth Wood, "Journal of a Trip to Oregon 1851 [copied from the *Peoria Weekly Republican*, January 30, 1852, and February 13, 1852]," 27 *Oregon Historical Quarterly* (1926): 192–203.

Woodhams, "Diary"
"The Diary of William H. Woodhams, 1852–1854: The Great Deserts or Around and Across." Charles W. Martin, ed. 61 *Nebraska History* (1980): 1–101.

Yager, "Diary"
James Pressley Yager, "Diary of a Journey across the Plains," 13 *Nevada Historical Society Quarterly* (no. 1): 5–19, (no. 2): 19–39, (no. 3): 27–48, (no. 4): 27–52, and 14 *Nevada Historical Society Quarterly* (no. 1): 27–54, (no. 2): 33–54 (1970–1971).

Young, *Log*
"Sheldon Young's Log 1849 Joliet Illinois to Rancho San Francisquito California," printed in Margaret Long, *The Shadow of the Arrow*. Caldwell, Idaho: Caxton Printers, 1941, pp. 241–68.

Zieber, *Diary*
Albert Zieber, *Diary* (ms., Oregon Collection, University of Oregon).

# Index

Coleman, M., 14($n$32)

Collective unconscious, 125

Colorado River, 195

Columbia River, 37

Common law, overland, 119–20

Companies, joint-stock, 114; definition of, 103; vs. traveling companies, 103–4; and ownership, 178

Companies, traveling, 3, 9–10, 20, 31, 39, 50, 58, 97–98, 102, 104, 112, 149, 174$n$10, 213, 216; disputes within, 6, 11–12, 15–16, 103–9, 171, 172, 198–99, 210–12 and $nn$ 7, 9, 217; and competition for trail position, 19–21; leaders of, 22, 32, 41$n$13, 96, 104, 111, 150, 161; judicial process within, 25, 95, 103–5, 108–9, 111, 113, 118–20, 164, 178; punishment within, 33, 163, 170, 207; and women, 14, 102; and property, 103, 178; families among, 74, 170; partners of, 86, 103, 144–46, 178; definition of, 103; executive councils of, 108–9; and executions, 125, 188; and expulsion, 171–75, 173$n$9, 177, 179; and social harmony, 173; and ease of joining, 210 and $n$7

—bylaws and constitutions of, 104$n$6, 105–6, 109, 114, 158–64 and $nn$ 4, 8–11, 174–75, 214–16 and $n$15; prohibitions in, 92–93, 128 and $n$ 38; drafting of, 92$n$5, 103, 112–13, 158$n$3, 216; provisions of, 108, 112–13, 178, 179; authority of, 125–26

—and crime, 32–34, 42–43, 86, 106, 168–69; of homicide, 85, 86, 100, 123, 154, 162, 186–88; and pursuit of criminals, 41, 96, 188. *See also* Fiduciary relationships; Juries and jurors; Legal behavior; Passengers; Punishment; Quarreling; Violence

Compton, James H., 127($n$37)

Concurrent property. *See* Property

Condemned men, 188, 189 and $n$21

Conflicts, overland. *See* Antisocial behavior; Quarreling

Conversion. *See* Stealing

Conyers, E. W., 2 and $n$9, 62($n$22), 126–27($nn$ 35, 36), 190($n$26)

Cook, Louisa, 76($n$13)

Cooke, Mr. (father of Lucy Rutledge Cooke), 4–5

Cooke, Lucy Rutledge, 4–5 and $n$18

Cooke, William, 4–5

Coon, Polly Crandall, 77($n$16), 80($n$26), 189($n$20)

Cooperation. *See* Social behavior

Corpse, described as meat, 205 and $n$40

Cosad, David, 14($n$29)

Council Bluffs, Iowa. *See* Kanesville

Coupler, J. C., 25($n$1)

Courts: availability of, 25, 73; and
    acquittals, 63, 108, 110–11, 149
    and *n* 44, 219; and preliminary
    hearing vs. formal trials, 64–65,
    149, 177; and courts-martial,
    64, 71*n*56; 175, 230*n*4; authori-
    ty of, 65, 103, 108–10; federal,
    66, 69; and convictions, 68–69,
    71, 178, 213–14; models for,
    108, 117–20, 125 and *n*32, 155;
    ad hoc, 112–13, 164; proce-
    dures of, 103, 113–14, 117,
    153, 186; and tribunals of adju-
    dication, 103–4, 105, 111–113.
    *See also* Acquittals; Adjudication;
    Arbitrators; Evidence; Forty-
    niners; Hearsay testimony;
    Judicial procedure; Judicial tri-
    bunals; Juries and jurors;
    Jurisprudence; Justice;
    Justification; Lynchings; Trials,
    accusatory
Courts-martial. *See* Courts
Cowden, James S., 139(*n*20)
Cox, Mr., 73
Cox, C. C., 182*n*4
Craig, James, 214*n*16
Crane, Addison Moses, 8(*n*5), 112
    and *n*22, 194 and *nn* 7, 8, 204,
    205 and *n*37
Cranfill, Isom, 92–93(*n*7), 104(*n*6)
Crawford, Medorem, 48(*n*37)
Crime, 24, 28, 37, 56, 91, 103,
    109, 169–70; and punishment,
    26, 98–99, 105, 114; and

Californians, 30, 53; in
    Mormon country, 50–51, 54;
    organized, 53; newspaper
    reports of, 54 and *n*65; on Army
    forts, 68–71; codification of, 69,
    91, 104, 133, 150, 159,
    174–75; and criminal law, 98;
    and prosecution of, 117, 133*n*1,
    136; and criminal adjudication,
    150, 213; capital, 167, 169,
    187–89; publicity in re as deter-
    rent, 201–208. *See also*
    Antisocial behavior; Behavior,
    criminal; Deterrents; Emigrants;
    Homicide; Law; Punishment;
    Trials, accusatory
Cross, Maj. Osborne, 26(*n*5)
Curry, George L., 2(*n*5), 163(*n*10)

Daily life, overland, 22, 23
*Daily Missouri Republican*, 15*n*33
Dalton, John, 79(*n*23), 226(*n*43)
Dancing, 27
Daughters. *See* Children
Davis, Mr., 141(*n*23)
Davis, Elijah (victim), 81–82,
    182–83
Davis, Sarah, 38–39(*n*6), 69(*n*47)
Death penalty, 171, 181
Deaths, 16; accidental, 29–30, 75.
    *See also* Homicide
Decker, Peter, 2(*n*7), 9(*n*8),
    12(*n*17), 13(*n*26), 14(*n*32),
    42(*n*16), 46–47(*n*27), 53(*n*57)
Defendants, 120; rights of, 118,

disadvantages to, 128–29; exon-
eration of, 141, 147–48. *See also*
Trials, accusatory
Defense: social, 94; legal, 112
Delano, Alonzo, 2(*n*8), 17(*n*43),
63(*n*24), 71(*n*53), 101–2(*n*28),
108(*n*15), 118(*n*6), 133–37 and
*nn* 2–5, 9, 197–98(*n*18),
203(*n*33)
Delicts, 73; and delinquency, 169
and *n*40. *See also* Law
Dennison, Capt., 41 and *n*12
Dennison Company, 41 and *n*12
Deseret, 52
Deterrents, 91, 201–8 and *n*31.
*See also* Crime; Punishment:
purposes of
Deviance, social, 26
Devil's Gate (on Sweetwater River),
28, 83, 99, 100, 135–36, 227
Diaries and diarists, overland,
39–40, 133, 202–4 and *n*31;
information in, 27 and *n*7, 114,
231; lack of analysis by, 27 and
*n*7; on weapons, 75; on crime,
142, 232; on justifiable homi-
cide, 86, 142; attitudes of
average, 231–32. *See also*
Emigrants
Diarrhea, 18. *See also* Sickness
Dickinson, D. C., 19(*n*56),
30–31(*n*22), 96(*n*14), 190(*n*28)
Dinwiddie, Mr., 80(*n*27)
Discipline: enforcement of in companies, 103–4

Disease. *See* Sickness
Disputes, 19; domestic, 38–40;
employer vs. employee, 45–47;
resolution of personal, 61,
103–4; emotional causes of, 216.
*See also* Antisocial behavior:
fighting; Homicide; Quarreling
Divorce, de facto, 39
Donner Party, 220–25. *See also*
Reed, James Frazier; Snyder,
John
Dowell, Benjamin Franklin, 1 and
*n*2, 9(*n*9), 14(*n*30), 33(*n*30),
50(*n*44)
Downer, Dr. (eyewitness), 47
Downer, H. H., 2(*n*6)
Doyle, Simon, 142(*n*29), 144(*n*36)
Dragoons, 66
Drake, J[oshua?] H., 86(*n*56)
Drowning, 28, 73 and *n*1, 84
"Drumhead trials," 69, 230
Drunkenness, 73*n*1
Due process, 132, 148–50. *See also*
Law
Dunbar, Mr. (victim), 86
Duniway, Abigail Scott. *See* Scott,
Abigail Jane
Dunlap, Katherine, 1–2 and *n*4,
70(*n*49)
Dunmore, Mr. (manslayer), 86
Dunmore, Sherman (victim),
88–89, 143–44, 219–20
Dutton, Jerome, 118(*n*7)
Duty: principle of, 8, 94, 98–99,
124, 126; dereliction of, 59 and

Emigration: of 1842, 212; of 1846, 109, 216–25, 228; of 1849, 14; of 1850, 14; of 1852, 76–77, 187, 226–27; of 1860, 57

English settlers, 230 and *n*3

Epidemics. *See* Sickness

Epperson, Lucretia Lawson, 70–71(*nn* 51, 56)

Equities, 152

Evidence: probative weight of circumstantial, 96–97; importance to jurors of, 132; rules of, 117, 119, 128; insufficient, 148–150; and acquittals, 149 and *n*44; sufficient, 158. *See also* Courts; Juries and jurors; Trials, accusatory

Executioners, 133; as executors, 183–84; from messes, 190; duty of, 197

Executions. *See* Punishment

Executive Council: judicial authority of, 108–110

Expellees: problems of, 175–76, 178–79, 210, 226. *See also* Expulsion

"Express Company" of 1849, 45

Expulsion, 177, 206, 207, 219, 224; frequency of, 171, 176; agreement on, 171–73, 209; alternatives to, 173–74, 223–24; grounds for, 173–76, 216, 222, 225–26 and *n*41; vs. banishment, 175*n*13; purposes of, 175, 210–12, 216, 218–19; severity

of, 176, 178, 210, 212, 223; and survival, 177; as sanction, 209–10 and *nn* 2, 6; and retribution, 212; repeal of mandatory, 216; and social values, 223; and families, 225–27 and *n*44. *See also* Expellees

Eyewitnesses, 47, 79, 110, 143*n*32, 220*n*31; retrieval of, 71, 87, 88; availability of, 96–97; as jurors, 106, 118, 119, 137 and *n*8; as executioners, 133; to homicide, 147; to executions, 196; to floggings, 206–7. *See also* Juries and jurors; Punishment

Fair trial: overland standards for, 125, 157

Families, 25, 99, 212, 226 and *n*42, 230; influence of, 4–5, 14, 83, 223–27 and *n*40; deaths in from mountain fever, 37; abuse within, 38–40; prevalence of, 159, 170; quarreling within and expulsion, 171. *See also* Children; Women

Fatigue, 16; as defense, 215

Fear: effect of, 13–14, 22

Federal courts, 66, 69

Ferguson, P. H., 50*n*45

Ferries, 44, 77; waiting lines for, 20–22

Fiction, of American West, 35, 42

Fiduciary relationships: treatment within, 45–46; and fighting,

45–48. *See also* Companies, traveling; Emigrants
Fighting. *See* Antisocial behavior: fighting
Firearms. *See* Weapons
Fires: accidental, 40. *See also* Arson; Grass-burning
Fish, Mary C., 70(*n*51)
Fishing: as Sabbath-breaking, 8
Fitzsimmons, Samuel A. (victim), 80
Flogging: of wife, 39–40; as legal punishment, 167–69, 208. *See also* Punishment; Spousal abuse; Whipping
Food: availability of, 8, 36–37, 223; contamination of, 35
Force: and protection of property, 32–34; rule of vs. rule of law, 231. *See also* Law
Foreigners: identification of, 114
Foreman, Grant, 202(*n*28)
Forgiveness: and restoration of harmony, 213–15
Forsyth, John Robert, 124(*n*25), 183(*n*7), 197(*n*16)
Fort Boise, 37
Fort Hall, 46, 57, 58, 135, 166
Fort Kearny, 15, 16, 57, 62, 64, 66–67 and *n*37, 69, 74, 82, 142, 171–72, 203
Fort Laramie, 18, 48, 50, 57, 58, 59 and *n*9, 60 and *n*16, 61, 62–63 and *n*23, 66–70 and *nn* 37, 41, 46, 48, 80, 82–83, 94*n*10, 152, 170 and *n*41, 172–73, 204

Fort Leavenworth, 67*n*41
Forts: jurisdiction in re crime, 68–71
Fort Smith, 4
Forty-niners, 4, 8, 15, 48, 57, 58, 75–76; on social behavior, 11, 13, 16–17; and competition for lead company position, 20; on criminal behavior, 30, 68*n*44, 86, 148, 171–72; partnership of, 47; on courts-martial and executioners, 175, 197; on notoriety as deterrent, 202–3. *See also* Antisocial behavior; Courts
Foster, Rev. Isaac, 28(*n*9), 51(*n*49), 99(*n*21)
Fowler, Schuyler, 78–79
Fox, Jared, 16–17 and *n*42, 201(*n*25)
Franklin, William Riley, 12–13(*n*22)
Frasier, Mr. (victim), 142–43
Friendship: availability of, 11–12; dissolution of, 17; betrayal of, 167
Frizzell, Lodisa, 193(*n*4)
*Frontier Guardian* (Kanesville), 48(*n*5), 104(*n*3), 105(*n*8)
Frontiersmen, 232
Fur trappers, 40–41. *See also* Mountain men

Gadson, Mr. (criminal), 207
Gallows, 139*n*19, 190–91 and *n*22, 194

Gambling, 12, 27, 161

Gangs. *See* "White Indians"

Gardner, Daniel B., 30(*n*20)

Garner, James (manslayer), 79

Gee, Perry, 45(*n*25), 79(*n*23), 80–81(*n*29), 84(*n*44), 173–74(*n*10)

Geer, Elizabeth Dixon Smith, 39–40(*n*8)

*Geiger-Bryarly Journal*, 177(*n*19)

Gibbs, George, 69(*n*45)

Gila River, 93, 123, 176–77, 182–83, 194, 197, 202

Gold Rush, 3, 18, 26, 52, 53, 54, 57, 159, 176

Goldsmith, Oliver, 74(*n*4)

Goodridge, Sophia Lois, 93(*n*8)

Goose Creek Valley, 54

Gould, Charles, 59(*n*13), 91(*n*3)

Gould, Jane A., 100(*n*27), 187–88(*n*16)

Graham, Alpheus N., 78–79(*nn* 22, 23)

*Granville Company Journal*, 20(*n*59), 86(*n*59)

Grass: shortage of, 11, 18, 19, 21, 37

Grass-burning, 41, 98. *See also* Arson; Fires

Graves: headboards of, 29, 76 and *n*13, 79, 80, 201–6; emigrants on, 62, 77, 181, 194; of killers and victims, 80–81 and *n*29, 87, 88, 127, 183, 205

Gray, Charles G., 7(*n*1), 12(*n*20), 52(*n*52), 57(*n*2), 59(*n*9)

Great Basin, 98

Great Salt Lake, 54

Green, Jay, 118–19(*n*9), 121–22(*nn* 15–17), 129–31(*nn* 41, 42), 185(*n*11), 186(*n*12), 201(*n*24), 204(*n*34)

Green and Jersey County Company, 174*n*12

Green River, 50, 54, 86, 122, 135, 137, 165, 193, 203, 209

Griffith, Dr. Andrew Jackson, 34(*n*33), 77(*n*17)

Grow, D. S. I., 19(*n*55)

Grow, S. L., 19(*n*55), 34(*n*31)

Guard duty, 34–35; extra as punishment, 169–70 and *n*39, 171, 175; sleeping while on, 117, 162, 163, 170 and *n*42, 214–15

Guill, Mary Jane, 31–32(*n*27)

Guilt: evidence of, 141, 158, 161*n*5; confession of, 165

Gundlach, John H., 35(*n*38), 36(*n*41), 86(*n*59)

Guns. *See* Weapons

Hale, Israel F., 18(*n*47)

Hall, O. J., 59(*n*13), 178(*n*20)

Hamline, Mr. (victim), 174

Hams Fork of Green River, 122

Handsaker, Samuel, 53(*n*57)

Hangings. *See* Punishment

"Hangtown," 198

Hanna, Esther Belle McMillan, 77(*n*16), 194(*n*5)

Harding, Capt., 42

194–95; escapes by, 69, 76, 99; types of, 86–87; arrests of, 94, 123; trials of, 96, 97, 100, 120, 227; pursuit of, 96, 99–100 and *n*21; investigators of, 97; flight by, 99, 101–2, 135; transporting of, 101; releasing of, 117*n*4, 150*n*42; bringing to justice of, 121, 194–96; expulsions of, 209, 219; relatives of, 225–28

—within companies, 30*n*15, 45, 76 and *n*11, 84, 86, 87, 88–89, 97–98, 119, 123, 124–25, 138–41, 153–54, 162, 207–8; by partners, 84, 86, 120–22, 154, 165, 202*n*27; by hired hands, 86, 154–55, 204–5; of hired hands, 87, 94–95, 97 and *n*17, 190–91; by messmates, 101–2, 129–32, 144–46, 149, 183–84. *See also* Antisocial behavior; Crime; Disputes; Eyewitnesses; Punishment; Self-defense; Trials, accusatory; Violence

Horse thieves, 73; punishment of, 91*n*2, 168, 173, 188–89

Holt County Mining Company, 214(*n*15)

Hosstetter, Mr. (manslayer), 142–43 and *n*32

Hough, Dr. Warren, 31(*n*26)

Howell, Elijah Preston, 83(*n*39), 176(*n*15)

Hudson's Bay Company, 37, 57

Humble, W. (victim), 80

Humboldt Meadows, 45

Humboldt River, 3, 9, 11(*n*13), 35, 37–38, 42, 47–48, 54–55, 80, 85, 92, 148, 150, 188, 196, 205, 220

Hung juries, 107–8. *See also* Juries and jurors; Trials, accusatory

Hunting, 73–74

Huntley, Henry Vere, 164(*n*15)

Hutchings, James Mason, 30(*n*19), 152(*n*54)

Hypocrisy, 3

Idaho: horse-stealing in, 199–200

Illinois: emigrants from, 62; traveling companies from, 106; judges from, 121

*Illinois Journal* (Springfield), 137*n*8, 138*n*12

Illness. *See* Sickness

Independence, Missouri, 53, 233

Independence Rock, 31

Individual: role of, 15, 198–99

Ingalls, E. S., 29(*n*13), 35(*n*37)

Ingrim, Godfrey C., 86(*n*59), 95(*n*13), 99–100(*n*24), 123(*n*22), 197(*n*17), 204(*n*35)

Indians, 34, 65, 114, 200; and encounters with emigrants, 9, 25, 55–56, 62, 64, 67, 99; and property, 42, 92; danger from, 43, 52, 166, 171, 213, 225*n*40; as thieves, 50, 70, 205; and Army, 54–55, 66 and *n*37, 71; emigrant attitudes

toward, 76, 92; and homicide, 92, 138; and expulsion, 176
—tribes of: Digger, 54*n*65; Pawnees, 41–43, 52*n*52, 53, 77*n*19; Piautes, 179; Sioux, 77*n*56
Indiana, 134
Investigations. *See* Army, United States; Companies, traveling
Iowa: jurisdiction of, 140

Jenkins, Mr. (victim), 83 and *n*40
Jewett, Dr. Mendall, 1 and *n*3, 2 and *n*10
Johnson, John Lawrence, 12(*n*19), 151(*n*53)
Johnston, William H. A., 8(*n*3), 48(*n*38)
Joint-stock companies. *See* Companies, joint-stock
Jones, Carlton, 34(*n*34)
Jones, Evan O., 189(*n*20)
Judge Advocate, 68
"Judge Lynch," 139, 197, 198. *See also* Punishment: hanging as
Judges, 33, 202*n*27, 221; availability of, 25, 27, 73; appointment of, 123, 140; instructions by, 127; and attitudes toward overland justice, 194
Judicial procedure, 120–21, 232–33. *See also* Courts
Judicial tribunals: models for, 108; ad hoc, 112–13. *See also* Courts
Juries and jurors, 27, 33, 148, 202*n*27; choosing of, 104–6,

122–28, 164–65, 169, 186; duties of, 105, 140, 163, 186; and verdicts, 105, 107, 111, 119–21, 127, 141, 149; power of, 106, 108–9, 118–19, 163; foremen of, 126; motives of, 153; and penalties, 161–62, 144, 169, 185
—composition of, 118–20, 139, 201–2; from within companies, 107, 120, 223; from other companies, 95, 119–22, 227. *See also* Companies, traveling; Courts; Evidence; Eyewitnesses; Hung juries; Trials, accusatory
Jurisdictional issues, 166, 195
Jurisprudence, 91. *See also* Courts; Law
Justice, 101, 120, 157, 191, 206, 231; and members of companies, 25; informal as deterrent, 89–90; administration of, 132; miscarriage of, 136–41; summary, 181, 196–98; vigilante, 206. *See also* Courts; Vigilantes
Justifiable homicide. *See* Homicide
Justification, doctrine of: 142, 194; and antisocial actions, 146, 199–200. *See also* Courts

Kanesville [Council Bluffs, Iowa], 43–44, 138–41, 195*n*10
Kennedy, Capt., 100–101, 186–88 and *n*13
Kentuckian (manslayer), 164, 171–72

Kerns, John T., 205(*n*41)
Ketchum, Capt. William S., 67*n*41
Killings. *See* Homicide
Kimball, Mr. (rescuer), 39–40
King, Alfred D., 81(*n*31), 99(*n*21), 123–24(*n*24)
Kinkade, John Thomas, 21(*n*62)
Kirkpatrick, Charles Alexander, 13(*n*26), 229(*n*1)
Kleinsorge, Charles, 51(*n*47), 67(*n*38)
Knight, Amelia Stewart, 21(*n*63)
Knives. *See* Weapons

La Bonte River, 80
Larceny. *See* Stealing
Laird, Moses F., 77(*n*19)
Lancaster, Rev. (victim), 83
Lander's cutoff, 56
Langum, David, 113–14 and *n*28
Langworthy, Franklin, 9(*n*10), 104(*n*4)
Lassen's cutoff, 31, 53–54, 145, 167
Law, 25, 60, 65*nn*33, 34, 98, 105, 107, 137, 224; availability of, 26, 63, 73, 89–90; enforcement of, 61, 96; emigrant expectations about, 65, 91, 96, 120, 122, 231–32, 233; violation of, 73, 169 and *n*40; and law-mindedness, 90, 98 and *n*20, 198, 210, 229–33; authority of, 91, 93, 140; role of in 19th-century America, 96; Old English and common, 119–20,

132; and due process, 132, 148–50; and double jeopardy, 137; of retaliation, 206, 208. *See also* Crime; Delicts; Due process; Force; Jurisprudence; Lawyers; Legal behavior
Lawyers, 33, 99, 132, 140*n*22, 194; and escape of manslayers, 69; influence on courts by, 112, 117–18; within companies, 112, 214, 221; role of, 117, 123, 132, 135, 221; availability of, 117; on theory of notoriety, 202; on punishment, 228. *See also* Law
Lee, Byron B., (manslayer), 85, 153–54
Leeper, David Rohrer, 17(*n*45), 169(*n*39), 211(*n*8)
Legal behavior: and companies, 98; and violence, 233. *See also* Companies, traveling; Law
Legality, issue of, 194–95
Lewis, John N., 204(*n*38)
Lewis, Thomas Cotton, 47(*n*32)
Lewis County, Missouri, 101
Liquor: and crime, 69, 146–47
Little Blue River, 48, 77 and *n*19
Little Sandy River, 38–39
Littleton, Micajah, 83(*n*41)
Livestock, 70, 146–47; discarding of, 3; oxen as, 21*n*65, 47, 121–22; conversion of, 30–36; loss of, 31, 158; guarding of, 34, 215; dead, 35–36; as compensation, 127; and fighting, 217

Perkins, Elisha Douglass, 4($n$16)
Pfouts, Paris Swazey, 213($n$14)
"Philadelphia lawyers," 136
Physicians, 26–27, 28, 34, 47,
    66–67, 76, 157–58, 229; as vic-
    tims, 46
Pierce, Franklin, 236
Pigman, Walter Griffith,
    10–11($n$13)
Platte River, 13, 15, 25, 30, 82,
    97–98, 146–47; Shinn's Ferry
    on, 146–47
Poison, 18
Police, 25, 33; availability of, 73,
    119
Political norms: violation of, 157
Polk, Adam, 39–40
Popular sovereignty: rise of, 163
Powell, H. M., 124–25($nn$ 27–31),
    164($n$13), 168–69($nn$ 36–38),
    207($n$46), 230($n$3)
Pomeroy, Mr., 20
Pownall, Joseph, 85($n$53)
Prayers: at executions, 185, 186
Prejudices, 26
Prisoners: Army custody of, 65;
    transporting of, 166–67
Pritchard, James A., 75($n$7),
    173($n$9), 174($n$11)
Property, 40; loss of, 16; protection
    of, 30–33; stolen, 30–34, 60, 70,
    173; and violence, 32–33; Army
    recovery of, 60, 68; in traveling
    companies, 103; concurrently-
    owned, 103, 178–79; ownership

of, 103$n$1, 178; reclaiming of,
    152; legal claims to, 153; chat-
    tels as, 174, 212$n$9; and
    expulsion, 178–79; disposal of,
    181, 204–5. *See also* Messes;
    Stealing
Prosecution, 117–18; theories justi-
    fying, 100; influences on
    criminal, 148, 154–55
Protection: expection of, 25, 137
Provocation: and antisocial action,
    146–47, 162
Public notices: posting of, 93
Punishment, 73, 121, 147, 161;
    popular attitudes toward, 28,
    200–201; for theft, 31–34, 52,
    91$n$2, 167–68, 173, 188–89; as
    retribution, 91, 206, 210, 213,
    228; legality of, 100$n$27; methods
    of deciding, 109, 172; appropri-
    ateness of, 112, 160, 162, 209
    and $nn$ 2, 6; immediate, 121;
    variety of, 157, 164–70; impos-
    ing of, 157, 160; guard duty as,
    161, 169–70 and $n$39, 213; dis-
    cretionary, 162–64; models for,
    164, 207; and complexity in re
    property, 181; escape from, 213;
    and harmony among travelers,
    213–14, 218–19; for abandoning
    post, 214–15; diarists' attitudes
    toward, 231–32
—corporal, 160, 163, 167–69; bru-
    tality and pain of, 168, 170,
    187, 192, 207–9

Udell, John, 14(*n*31)
Utah, 51; desert, 198–99

Values: sources of, 9, 26
Van Horn, Maj. Jefferson, 177
Vengeance, 141, 157, 233. *See also* Talionic retibution
Venue: of trial and execution, 140. *See also* Trials, accusatory
Verdenal, John M., 120(*n*12), 123(*n*23), 205(*n*43)
Verdicts. *See* Trials, accusatory: verdicts
Victims, 28, 120. *See also* Homicide
Vigilantes, 196, 228, 230 and *n*4. *See also* Justice
Violence, 21, 231; and retention of property, 32–33, 46–48; and families, 38, 39; threats and causes of, 42–45, 92, 225; avoidance of, 212, 233. *See also* Antisocial behavior; Companies, traveling; Homicide; Quarreling; Spousal abuse
Virginia, 221

Wagons, 20, 25, 26, 38, 44, 123, 215, 229–30; antisocial acts to, 30, 40, 152; and executions, 37, 190–91, 197; as cause of fighting, 47, 217; weapons on, 74; and homicide, 84, 130, 154, 184; as property, 159, 178–79; and punishment, 168, 170*n*42; withdrawal of, 219–20

Wagon trains. *See* Companies, traveling
Washburn, Catherine Amanda Stansbury, 84(*n*45)
Washington, Mr., 151
Watts, John William, 46(*n*28)
Wayman, Dr. John Hudson, 48(*n*40)
Weapons: prevalence of, 21, 74; neckyokes, 30*n*15, 46; avoidance of by emigrants, 32; bows and arrows, 42; axes, 46, 63; whipstocks, 174*n*10; and self-defense, 174
—firearms, 21, 22, 44, 45, 49–50, 54, 63, 74, 134; and frontier, 42; Allen revolver, 46; handling of, 75–76 and *n*9, 78; within companies, 92–93; and homicide, 95, 130–31; and death, 142–43; and expulsion, 171–72, 223. *See also* Ammunition
—knives, 29, 44, 46, 49, 62, 101, 120–21, 151, 165, 221; butcher, 31, 144; Bowie, 68, 74, 87, 114, 174; hunting, 88, 221, 224
Weather, overland, 16; snow, 220, 225
Webster, Kimball, 18(*n*49), 37(*n*3)
West, myths of, 231
*Western Christian* (Elgin, Illinois), 26, 74(*n*4)
Whipping: as crime, 38–40; as punishment, 38–39, 68*n*44,